W9-DHG-906

Mark Twain's Mysterious Stranger

MARK TWAIN'S MYSTERIOUS STRANGER
A Study of the Manuscript Texts

Sholom J. Kahn

University of Missouri Press
Columbia & London, 1978

Library of Congress Catalog Card Number 77-10746
Printed and bound in the United States of America
University of Missouri Press, Columbia, Missouri 65201

Library of Congress Cataloging in Publication Data

Kahn, Sholom Jacob, 1918–
Mark Twain's Mysterious stranger.

Bibliography: p. 240
Includes index.
1. Clemens, Samuel Langhorne, 1835–1910. Mysterious stranger. 2. Clemens, Samuel Langhorne, 1835–1910— Manuscripts. I. Title.
PS1322.M97K3 813'.4 77-10746
ISBN 0-8262-0236-5

To John S. Tuckey

Preface

One of the temples of American scholarship has been destroyed, and it must be rebuilt. *The Mysterious Stranger* (1916) was a pillar of classic Mark Twain criticism, especially after Van Wyck Brooks's *The Ordeal of Mark Twain* (1920) made it the crux of many discussions. Essays were written about the tale, and elaborate theories about Mark Twain's literary character and entire career were constructed in which the tale played a central role.[1] But with publication of the long-awaited *Mark Twain's Mysterious Stranger Manuscripts*,[2] the general reader now can get to know what William M. Gibson has referred to as the various "Mysterious Strangers" (in the plural), which were formerly only available to research scholars. He must get used to thinking of the hitherto familiar text as "cut, cobbled-together, partially falsified" (34) and start looking at what Mark Twain actually wrote.

So many have felt the power of the "Paine-Duneka" text, as it should henceforth be properly labeled, that this will not be easy. And the newly edited manuscripts themselves, though vintage Clemens and much better than we have been led to believe, are not without difficulties. But thanks to the scholarship of John S. Tuckey, W. M. Gibson, and their associates, Mark Twain's last major fictional achievement is now open to exploration and criticism. This essay is designed, as a beginning, to show some of the delights the manuscripts offer, to facilitate understanding, and to highlight their fascinating problems.

1. See *Critics*, which includes a bibliography of "Selected Criticism" (see list of short references p. xiii).

2. A paperback edition, without the "Textual Apparatus," is titled simply: *The Mysterious Stranger* (1970). Numbers in parentheses refer to pages in this edition.

My book assumes a reader who wants to take a close look and has at hand the *Stranger Manuscripts* (the paperback edition will do). Its purpose is to lead such a reader gently through a jungle of biographical facts and into the texts themselves and also to advance a bit toward the critical goals of revealing their structure and rationale. The University of California edition does not yet seem to have been widely read, and the bad text mistitled *The Mysterious Stranger* is still available in many reprints and generally accepted as a Mark Twain classic. Thus, I have had to write an essay, not only of explication and criticism, but also of correction.

Three strategies have been adopted. First, I analyze in detail and quote copiously, especially from the newly published materials, in order to draw attention to passages I have found significant or rewarding. We know now that Samuel Clemens of Hannibal became a great virtuoso of American style and are gradually becoming aware that this mastery did not desert him in his last years.

Second, I make frequent reference to Mark Twain's other writings, early and late, in order to emphasize the fact that these writings of his last decade are far from eccentric and morbid, as was suggested by Bernard DeVoto's "symbols of despair" thesis; they are rather a ripe product of ideas long entertained and are central to an understanding of Mark Twain's entire oeuvre. Although the biographical issues are profound, they are only touched on lightly here and should be treated in depth elsewhere.

Third, in order to help clarify an exceedingly complex picture, I have placed at the end a group of appendixes and a section of supplementary notes. These materials, while important, may be of interest primarily to the advanced student; if included in the text they might prevent the general reader from seeing the forest for the trees. The presence of each supplementary note is indicated by a number in boldface type within brackets in the text; and in order to preserve the continuity of exposition, essential information from the notes is briefly repeated in the more critical and less technical body of text. Also in the notes, I shall occasionally be filling out gaps and obscurities in quotations from the manuscripts in order to facilitate exposition; all abbreviations and ampersands from the manuscripts are spelled out in full. The exact contents of most of Mark Twain's surviving manuscript fragments are painstakingly reproduced in the Mark Twain Papers editions.

I have included in Other Works Cited a fairly complete listing of the articles and reviews I have published during some dozen years spent studying various aspects of Mark Twain's final phase (the two decades following completion of *A Connecticut Yankee*); *Deo volonte,* other related books may yet follow. It is a peculiarly satisfying task now to look back and thank the many individuals and institutions who have helped make this work possible and pleasant.

When I first sent to Henry Nash Smith (then recently retired as Literary Editor of the Mark Twain Papers) my thoughts on *The Mysterious Stranger* and the problem of its ending, he encouraged me to pursue what turned out to be an exceedingly complex set of problems. His suggestions that the story of Mark Twain's sojourn in Vienna (1897–1899), an important transitional moment in his career as a writer, could best be researched in that city led me to make four happy visits there; two of these (1967, 1973) were spent, with the financial support of the American Philosophical Society (Penrose Fund), digging up documents and other materials relating to the backgrounds of "Young Satan." Like so many others, I am indebted and grateful to Professor Smith, who has stimulated so much Mark Twain scholarship and criticism in our generation.

More specifically, however, my own work could not have begun until John S. Tuckey published his pioneering monograph, *Mark Twain and Little Satan: The Writing of "The Mysterious Stranger"* (1963). This established the foundations on which all subsequent scholarship on "The Mysterious Stranger" has been built. During the years when I was working in faraway Jerusalem, Professor Tuckey's unfailing interest, sound counsel, pertinent questions, and warm humanity helped keep me going. Though I of course exonerate him from all my errors, I am proud to count myself among his "students" and happy to express my thanks by dedicating this book to him.

Intensive work in the Mark Twain Papers and on the various drafts of the manuscript was made possible by three sabbatical leaves from The Hebrew University, where I am a member of the departments of English and American Studies. These leaves were spent teaching at the San Fernando Valley

State College (Northridge, California, 1966–1967), the University of California at Davis (1973), and Simon Fraser University (Burnaby, British Columbia, 1976–1977). I am grateful to the many colleagues, librarians, students, and friends at these institutions who helped in myriad ways; once again, my experience has proved the old proposition that the best way to learn is to try and teach. I was a grateful user of facilities at the Huntington Library and the New York Public Library (the Berg Collection). And I am grateful to my home university for the leaves, support, and help with funds for typists and to Valley State College (now California State University at Northridge) and Simon Fraser University for help with the typing of manuscripts.

Mark Twain scholars are a particularly fortunate lot, not only because of the genius of S. L. Clemens, but also because of the intelligent and cooperative administration of his papers by Frederick Anderson, who has mastered the art of combining efficiency with courtesy. One despairs of remembering all the help received while in the Bancroft Library in Berkeley, but I should single out from a potentially long list Hamlin Hill and Alan Gribben. William M. Gibson (formerly at New York University) at various stages gave generously of his materials, suggestions, and criticisms. The critics of Mark Twain are legion, but I should like to place on record my special debts to the work of Van Wyck Brooks, Howard Mumford Jones, Walter Blair, Roger Asselineau, Coleman O. Parsons, Paul Baender, and Sidney Berger.

My debts to people in Vienna are recorded in annual reports of the American Philosophical Society; but to those mentioned there I must add the name of Dr. Georg Weis, a loving resident of the city, without whose help my progress would have been much slower. And I was particularly inspired during the summer of 1967 by visits to the Mark Twain House in Hartford, Connecticut, then in the gracious charge of Mrs. Serie L. Larson. Knowing the charms of that house made more vivid my realization of the "exile" brought on by Clemens's bankruptcy, the death of Susy and illness of Livy, and long years of residence abroad.

Finally, to family and friends—who began to wince after awhile whenever I mentioned "Mark Twain"—I offer apologies and gratitude for their long-suffering patience. But like

Pudd'nhead Wilson, I must reverse an old maxim: Once bit by the Mark Twain mania, never shy again. There will be more need for patience.

S.J.K.
The Hebrew University
Jerusalem, Israel
July 1977

Short References

Stranger:	"The Mysterious Stranger" as edited by Albert Bigelow Paine and Frederick A. Duneka and widely reprinted
"Young Satan":	"The Chronicle of Young Satan," labeled "Eseldorf" by DeVoto (Gibson's term, "Chronicle," seems to me less desirable—as if *Adventures* were used to designate *Adventures of Huckleberry Finn*)
"Schoolhouse":	"Schoolhouse Hill," labeled "Hannibal" by DeVoto
"No. 44":	"No. 44, The Mysterious Stranger," labeled "Print Shop" by DeVoto. This is the only true text of *The Mysterious Stranger,* but until this is universally recognized, the label "No. 44" is needed to emphasize that the Paine-Duneka text is not intended
Stranger Manuscripts: (or *Manuscripts*)	*Mark Twain's Mysterious Stranger Manuscripts,* ed. and with an introduction by W. M. Gibson (Berkeley and Los Angeles: University of California Press, 1969)
	Numbers in parentheses refer to page numbers of *Stranger Manuscripts,* unless otherwise indicated.

Other Short References

Critics:	*Mark Twain's "The Mysterious Stranger" and the Critics,* ed. John S.

	Tuckey (Belmont, Calif.: Wadsworth, 1968)
Discussions:	*Discussions of Mark Twain,* ed. Guy A. Cardwell (Boston: D. C. Heath, 1963)
Essays:	*The Complete Essays of Mark Twain,* ed. Charles Neider (Garden City, N.Y.: Doubleday, 1963)
HH&T:	*Mark Twain's Hannibal, Huck & Tom,* ed. Walter Blair (Berkeley and Los Angeles: University of California Press, 1969)
Humorous Sketches:	*The Complete Humorous Sketches and Tales of Mark Twain,* ed. Charles Neider (Garden City, N. Y.: Doubleday, 1961)
MTA:	*Mark Twain's Autobiography,* ed. Albert Bigelow Paine, 2 vols. (New York and London: Harper and Brothers, 1924)
MTB:	*Mark Twain: A Biography,* Albert Bigelow Paine, 3 vols. (New York: Harper and Brothers, 1912)
MTFM:	*Mark Twain's Fables of Man,* ed. John S. Tuckey (Berkeley, Los Angeles, London: University of California Press, 1972)
MTGF:	*Mark Twain: God's Fool,* Hamlin Hill (New York: Harper and Row, 1973)
MTHHR:	*Mark Twain's Correspondence with Henry Huttleston Rogers,* ed. Lewis Leary (Berkeley and Los Angeles: University of California Press, 1969)
MTHL:	*Mark Twain-Howells Letters,* ed. Henry Nash Smith and William M.

	Gibson (Cambridge, Mass.: Harvard University Press, Belknap Press, 1960)
MTL:	*Mark Twain's Letters,* ed. Albert Bigelow Paine (New York: Harper and Brothers, 1917)
MTN:	*Mark Twain's Notebook,* ed. Albert Bigelow Paine (New York: Harper and Brothers, 1935)
MTP:	The Mark Twain Papers, an unpublished manuscript (with page numbers from the typed copy or the manuscript, as the case may be)
MTS:	*Mark Twain's Speeches,* ed. Albert Bigelow Paine (New York: Harper and Brothers, 1923)
MTSatan:	*Mark Twain and Little Satan: The Writing of "The Mysterious Stranger,"* John S. Tuckey (West Lafayette, Ind.: Purdue University Press, 1963)
S&B:	*Mark Twain's Satires & Burlesques,* ed. Franklin R. Rogers (Berkeley and Los Angeles: University of California Press, 1967)
WIM:	*What Is Man? and Other Philosophical Writings,* ed. Paul Baender (Berkeley and Los Angeles: University of California Press, 1972)
WWD:	*Mark Twain's Which Was the Dream?,* ed. John S. Tuckey (Berkeley and Los Angeles: University of California Press, 1967)

Contents

* Page numbers refer to *Stranger Manuscripts*

Part One: Introduction

1

Toward Rehabilitation

The damage caused by the bad scholarship and partial criticism of the 1916 *Stranger* must be understood if it is to be undone. Both sets of related mistakes can be explained, though not justified, and they are not without parallels in literary history that touch some of the greatest writers. Elementary justice requires that we attempt to place ourselves in the position of Mark Twain's first literary executor, Albert Bigelow Paine, and his editor at Harper and Brothers, Frederick A. Duneka, when they were confronted with an accumulation of manuscript materials so large that it would take half a century to sort them out. But despite the importance of Paine's pioneering role as official biographer, we cannot help but agree with the editor of the *Stranger Manuscripts* that "the indictment of Paine as editor of *The Mysterious Stranger*" is a formidable one. In the words of William M. Gibson: "He secretly tried to fill Mark Twain's shoes, and he tampered with the faith of Mark Twain's readers" (3). Since Mark Twain's shoes are really unfillable by anyone else, dead or living, his faithful readers have no choice but to go back to the original texts.

Though Gibson used words as strong as *fraud* and *misrepresentational editorial work,* he also stated the case for Paine and Duneka, who represented the publishing practices and taste of their day and "thought they were acting to sustain and add to Mark Twain's reputation" (1–4). Their criteria were less scholarly than commercial, and their motives were certainly honorable—not entirely unlike those of the editors of the Shakespeare Folio. But one cannot help wishing that they had emulated instead the humility and honesty displayed later by Max Brod, who noted in the first edition of *The Castle* (1926), "Kafka never wrote the concluding chapter," and by the editors of the definitive edition of that novel (1951), in which the additional materials were clearly discriminated in the text and an appendix. By way of contrast, Paine's arrogant procedure, however sincere, muddied the waters of Mark Twain scholarship for two generations.

Unfortunately, criticism based on poorly edited texts is not a novelty; and "the sense of an ending," which has played so central a role in discussions of the *Stranger*, is properly an important element in reader response. Back of the Paine-Duneka liberties was a mistaken notion, which prevailed for about a generation, of Mark Twain as a spontaneous folk artist, relatively unsophisticated and wild, in need of the trimming and advice so generously lavished on him by his wife, by William Dean Howells, and by other "editors." Van Wyck Brooks, who was so close to that generation in time, still provides the best available formulation of the issues in *The Ordeal of Mark Twain*.[1] From the literary point of view, Brooks saw Mark Twain as a potentially great satirist who became a mere humorist because "he was prohibited, on pain of social extinction, from expressing himself directly regarding the life about him" (pp. 202–3).

The issue is sharply drawn in the chapter entitled "Let Somebody Else Begin":

> What is a satirist? A satirist, if I am not mistaken, is one who holds up to the measure of some more or less permanently admirable ideal the inadequacies and the deformities of the society in which he lives. It is Rabelais holding up to the measure of healthy-mindedness the obscurantism of the Middle Ages; it is Molière holding up to the measure of an excellent sociality everything that is eccentric, inelastic, intemperate; it is Voltaire holding up to the measure of the intelligence the forces of darkness and superstition. Satire is a criticism of the spirit of one's age, and of the facts in so far as the spirit is embodied in them, dictated by some powerful, personal and supremely conscious reaction of that spirit. If this is true, Mark Twain cannot be called a satirist. (pp. 214–15)

This seems to me an excellent formulation, but it leads to a false conclusion in the last sentence. There are two generali-

1. Van Wyck Brooks, *The Ordeal of Mark Twain*. References hereafter will be to the revised edition of 1955 and will be cited in parentheses in the text.

ties here that need specification: neither "the spirit of one's age" nor the writings of Mark Twain were adequately treated in Brooks's pioneering study. In the sequel, it becomes clear that he was attacking especially "the puritanical commercialism of the Gilded Age" and "the petty aspects of the tribal morality of America" (p. 216). But this dates, and limits, Brooks's discussion to certain intense but time-bound concerns of the early 1920s, such as the "flappers" and anti-Babbitry of the Jazz Age.

Not that Brooks was wrong, as far as he went, but he was partial and unfair, since he was using Mark Twain as a whipping boy, as an example radically distorted to serve the purposes of his rather splendid sermon. As Malcolm Cowley put it in his introduction to the 1955 edition of Brooks's work, "He is emphasizing Twain's mistakes and failures so that others can profit by them" (p. 9), while the critic's proper task should be "to see the object as in itself it really is." This was especially true of Brooks's cavalier treatment of the "multitude of discarded manuscripts" that he had learned about from Paine's *Biography* and that he had dismissed as "hit-or-miss" without ever really examining them. Again:

> "I have imagined," he [Mark Twain] said once, "a man three hundred thousand miles high picking up a ball like the earth and looking at it and holding it in his hand. It would be about like a billiard-ball to him, and he would turn it over in his hand and rub it with his thumb, and where he rubbed over the mountain ranges he might say, 'There seems to be some slight roughness here, but I can't detect it with my eye; it seems perfectly smooth to look at!' " There we have the Swiftian, the Rabelaisian note, the Rabelaisian frame for the picture that fails to emerge. The fancy exists in his mind, but he is able to do nothing with it: all he can do is to express a simple contempt, to rule human life as it were out of court. Mark Twain never completed these fancies precisely, one can only suppose, because they invariably led into this *cul-de-sac*. If life is really futile, then writing is futile also. The true satirist, however futile he may make life seem, never really believes it futile: his interest in its futility is itself a desperate registration of some instinctive belief that it might be, that it could be, full of significance, that, in fact, it is full of significance. . . . That

> sense Mark Twain had never attained: in consequence, his satirical gestures remained mere passes in the air. (p. 236)

This is another example of the same non sequitur; and the phrase "one can only suppose" gives away the fact that Brooks, like subsequent generations of critics equally ignorant of many of the primary sources, had (or should have had) a bad conscience about Mark Twain. One should not arrive at sweeping generalizations like "he is able to do nothing with it" without having examined all the evidence. But now that we have the essential facts—that is the texts—criticism can build on the stronger foundations of objective scholarship.

I

The critical issues are by no means simple, but the example of Kafka illustrates the fact that the problem of the ending should appear less central to us than it did to critics of the previous generation. Gibson has speculated "that a writer or editor who is more sympathetic to Twain's divided mind and creative dilemma in his late life" might, "in the future, produce a better version than that pieced together by Paine and Duneka" (34). But why add yet a fifth to the four distinct texts now available? Surely we have had enough synthetic concoctions by writers trying to fill Mark Twain's shoes. Of course, this is constantly being done with Mark Twain's writings and is probably one mark of his vitality as a "folk" creator: Hal Holbrook has, in fact, successfully filled his shoes as a lecturer, and Tom and Huck live on in radio and television serials and movies. But the *Stranger Manuscripts*, as Gibson says, have "their own value and interest," and any such future synthesizer will be expected to acknowledge "openly when he selects or modifies or creates or concludes."[2]

2. Something remotely like this was done by John Seelye in his remarkable tour de force, *The True Adventures of Huckleberry Finn.* He was not a synthesizer, however, but a creative "rewriter" who produced his own novel, based on Mark Twain's and in response to a generation of criticism. As he writes in the introduction entitled "De ole true Huck": "Most of the parts was good ones, and I could use them. But Mark Twain's book is for children and such, whilst this one here is for crickits [*sic*]. And now that they've got *their* book, maybe they'll leave the other one alone" (p. xii).

The history of literature would be much poorer without its long list of uncompleted masterpieces: *The Faerie Queene*; Bryon's *Don Juan*, *Kubla Khan*, and *Christabel*; and the like. These do tease the imagination and have occasionally tempted readers to write continuations, but for the most part readers and critics have been content to leave well enough alone. And an entire aesthetic has emerged since the twenties—along with Dada and other vagaries of "modernism"—as a result of which we are less concerned about whether Rodin smoothed over the rough edges of his sculptures or whether Mark Twain revised and wrote *Finis* after some of his later writings.[3] Twain wrote often of speaking from the grave, and he has done so, and is still doing so, through posthumous publications; he must have known that he would have things of importance to say in the year 2000 and beyond. He mildly regretted, however, that some of his manuscripts—all of which were carefully preserved and many of which were typewritten—had to be left in a rough state because he had grown "tired of the pen."

Like Emily Dickinson, this posthumous Mark Twain has proved to be one of the liveliest and most modern of contemporary writers. Three editions of the *Autobiography* have aroused interest and controversy; and the release in 1962 of Bernard DeVoto's collection, *Letters from the Earth*, which included "The Great Dark," provoked a warm response. It seems clear to me that Clemens knew very well what he was doing, and like Emily Dickinson was keenly aware of how far ahead he was of the prevalent taste of his times. But that he was writing "not for publication" in his own lifetime does not mean that he was not being serious. Or, to simplify that triple negative, by writing "not for publication" he seems to have released energies that enabled him to reach new, profound, rich levels of literary achievement. Dull spots and loose ends remain, but these minor faults—which would probably have been lessened by a final revision—are overshadowed by the enormous sweep of Mark Twain's imagination. For this reader, at least, the total effect is one of mature mastery and control.

3. See Richard Ellmann and Charles Feidelson, Jr., eds., *The Modern Tradition: Backgrounds of Modern Literature*, which ends with a selection on "The State of Doubt"; and the section on "Non-Finito" in *Proceedings of the Fifth International Congress of Aesthetics: Amsterdam 1964*, pp. 219–62.

Occasional incompleteness and lack of revision are less important than the central critical question: How good is the "Stranger"? More precisely: What are the literary values of the *Stranger Manuscripts* that distinguish them from the Paine-Duneka *Stranger*? And the first, perhaps also the last, related question that troubles the critic is this: What is the nature and degree of the unity that the manuscripts do, or do not, display? This was the problem that, in the first instance, caused Paine to seek and, mistakenly, find a conclusion for "Young Satan" in the notorious "dream" chapter that has been the cause of so much discussion and debate.

The proportions of the problem are immediately evident in the new book: the manuscripts total 371 pages; the familiar *Stranger* text used approximately 100 of the first 137 pages and then leaped to a conclusion taken from the last 3 pages! Yet the remaining 268 pages are an important part of Mark Twain's creation. The gaps between what he actually wrote and the texts the critics have been discussing are in fact enormous. They are so great, in fact, that criticism really must begin all over again to grapple with these late works of Mark Twain. However, in the next chapter, when we begin to examine the ways in which the various "Stranger" texts are related to each other, it should become evident that even when we examine the manuscripts as a whole the problem of the ending has not disappeared; instead it has shifted from the familiar *Stranger* text to "No. 44," the text for which the ending was expressly written. I believe that my analysis of the 185 pages of "No. 44"—which by no means pretends to exhaust all its nuances—will demonstrate that it does indeed have a well-designed structure. A central thread of mystery, concerning the true identity of the protagonist so peculiarly named, makes this the only text which properly should bear as title *The Mysterious Stranger*. (The figure who bears the two names of *Satan* and *Philip Traum* in "Young Satan" is not, in this elementary sense, mysterious.) And despite the genetic links, it is quite different in plot, purpose, narrative techniques, period, atmosphere, and style from its incomplete predecessor, "The Chronicle of Young Satan."

Given its own special character, "No. 44" is not only consistent and coherent—needing perhaps only some minor editing before it is given, without apologies, to the general reader in a popular edition—but it is also in fact complete. No one who takes the trouble to read it attentively, I think, will want to deny its fascination; but only continued criticism will succeed in clarifying all of its meanings and values and its proper place in the Mark Twain canon. For many readers it will take a long time to realize that our great American "innocent," after writing his *Ulysses* in *Huckleberry Finn,* so to speak, went on to produce a sort of wild *Finnegans Wake* before he died. I think "No. 44" is superior to "Young Satan" and pretty much in a class with *A Connecticut Yankee,* although it is certainly very different from that other historical fantasy and possibly superior to the *Yankee* because of its maturity.

The "all is a dream" section (chapter 34) is far from simple or nihilistic, but it does seem in "No. 44"—as it did not in the Paine-Duneka *Stranger*—to be a conclusion both appropriate and right. The failure of the 1916 editors to see this demonstrates that they misunderstood both "Young Satan" and "No. 44"; and the fact that so many critics discussed the "dream" section seriously in relation to the earlier text indicates a like blindness, excusable by the fact that the vast majority had never even seen the version to which the ending properly belonged. But aside from ignorance, there is also the issue of critical values, involving interpretations and evaluations of both texts as they now appear: "Young Satan" and its possible endings and "No. 44" and its actual ending. This issue is curiously paralleled by the neoclassical critics' attack on the ending of *King Lear*. The quarto and folio texts are different in many details, so that any edition of *Lear* represents a set of compromises; but neither of the texts has the "happy ending" that Nahum Tate introduced in his "improved" edition. As Hazelton Spenser wrote:

> In seeking to motivate Cordelia's failure to speak out, Tate recognizes the structural weakness of Shakespeare's play from a realistic point of view, which, of course, is precisely the point of view it is fatal to adopt. Nor does his happy ending bring aught but outrage to King Lear, whose bitter cup seemed less significant to the adapter than the billing and cooing of Cordelia and Edgar. . . . Worst of all is the so-called happy ending. In

> Tate's alteration the principle of poetic justice receives the most pitiable sacrifice in all the English drama.[4]

There is a rough analogy between Tate's "ethical purpose" and Harper and Brothers's desire to turn Mark Twain's satire of "Young Satan" into a boy's book, with a fairy-tale ending, appropriate for the Christmas trade.

Of course, we share Charles Lamb's indignation, which he expressed in the well-known essay "On the Tragedies of Shakespeare," at Tate's having dared to "put his hook in the nostrils of this Leviathan"; on the other hand, so excellent a critic as A. C. Bradley has testified that he shares the Restoration sentiments:

> If I read *King Lear* simply as a drama, I find that my feelings call for this "happy ending." I do not mean the human, the philanthropic, feelings, but the dramatic sense. . . . Surely, it says, the tragic emotions have been sufficiently stirred already. . . . this catastrophe, . . . does not seem at all inevitable. It is not even satisfactorily motivated.[5]

As Bradley put it, an awareness of the necessity for the deaths of both Cordelia and Lear requires a point of view "wider" than both drama and tragedy. He finds in Shakespeare's masterpiece a mythical, titanic conflict between "the powers of good and evil in the world" (p. 211), as a result of which "we feel at last, not depression and much less despair, but a consciousness of greatness in pain, and of solemnity in the mystery we cannot fathom" (p. 223).

Somewhat similarly, the "dream" conclusion seemed inadequately motivated in the *Stranger* and was so shocking to "the genteel tradition" that it provoked unsuccessful attempts to explain it away. These attempts were usually biographical, citing the aging Clemens's pessimism or cynicism and discussing the "dream" chapter, not as the end of a story, but as Mark Twain's personal testament of despair. A major result of our present, better understanding of "No. 44" will be insight into the implications of the stranger's farewell speeches and into their many links with the rest of Mark Twain's text.

4. Hazelton Spenser, *Shakespeare Improved: The Restoration Versions in Quarto and On the Stage*, pp. 242, 252.

5. A. C. Bradley, *Shakespearean Tragedy*, p. 204.

II

As we have seen in the quotations from Brooks, it used to be fashionable to think of Mark Twain in the company of Swift and Rabelais; and if the style of any of his works can be thought of as fully Rabelaisian, it is that of "No. 44." Some sentences from Samuel Putnam's introduction to *The Portable Rabelais* demonstrate this association:

> Too big for his contemporaries to grasp in all his elusive many-sidedness, he was commonly regarded by them as an erudite buffoon; and this reputation, unfortunately, has clung to him down the centuries. . . . Voltaire could still allude to him as a "drunken philosopher who wrote only when he was intoxicated," and could describe the *Gargantua and Pantagruel* as "an extravagant and unintelligible book . . . prodigal of erudition, ordures, and boredom"—a judgment which reminds one of certain present day criticism of James Joyce![6]

We are less apt to think of Samuel Clemens as erudite, because, even more than Melville, he was so largely self-educated; and if he was a sort of philosopher, his inebriation was certainly not that of an alcoholic, but rather that of a divine amateur.

I bring in these great names not to make any invidious comparisons or false equations but to prepare the reader for a complex aesthetic experience. The "modes and moods" of the manuscripts—to adopt a phrase from Tuckey—are "variable," and some few parts are guilty of the primal literary sin: they may induce boredom. But as is true throughout his extensive canon, the percentage of gold in Mark Twain's literary ore is surprisingly high. Most of the time I find him at his mature best in "No. 44," in full control of his incomparable language, a master of the art of satiric fiction. For a relatively unrevised text—though actually the *Stranger Manuscripts* include about 44 pages (558–603) of "Alterations in the Manuscript"!—it is in fact remarkably well integrated. But it must be approached with an open mind and without the expectation that America's great humorist will now "do it again" in the vein of *Huckleberry Finn*, the *Yankee*, or whatever. Like any original work of art, "No. 44" is sui generis.

6. François Rabelais, *The Portable Rabelais*, ed. Samuel Putnam, pp. 2–3.

Finally, J. S. Tuckey once asked: "But does the Paine-Duneka edition, under the existing circumstances, deserve to perish, to endure, or to prevail?"[7] In view of the conclusions just summarized, I should say:

To prevail? Certainly not. "No. 44" should prevail, as Mark Twain's final creation and as the only complete version.

To endure? Certainly as a literary curiosity illustrative of the special taste and editorial practices prevalent in the second decade of the twentieth-century United States; it has entered so largely into literary history and critical discussion that it should remain available for reference, like the Nahum Tate *Lear*. It should perhaps also remain available as a concession to some readers' taste: it is certainly easier reading than "No. 44" and superficially more "complete," though less coherent, than "Young Satan," if those are the criteria being applied.

To perish? Probably from the general reader's library, after the other versions have grown familiar; certainly from the purview of the serious student of Mark Twain's art. It would be scandalous to continue teaching the Paine-Duneka version to advanced students; or to have undergraduates read it without an appropriate textual note setting forth the elementary facts of how it came into existence.[8]

7. *Critics*, p. 90 (see list of short references p. xiii).

8. In order to set the record straight—and despite the copyrights and the previous publications that will be affected—I suggest that future publications be required to bear such labels as the following:

1) *The Chronicle of Young Satan* (Mark Twain's text).

2) *Young Satan: Abridged and "Concluded"* (The Paine-Duneka version of "The Mysterious Stranger").

3) *The Mysterious Stranger* ("No. 44") (Mark Twain's text).

Until something like this is done and widely accepted, Clemens will continue to sleep restlessly in his grave, indignant at the persistent violation of his clear intentions.

2

Genesis: The Two "Strangers"

A fortnight before leaving Vienna, on 12 May 1899, Clemens began a long letter to William Dean Howells, his old friend and literary confidant. This was to prove a memorable weekend, and the customary frankness of this communication reflects Clemens's complex state at the time. Commenting on yet another blunder by one of his publishers—Frank Bliss of the American Publishing Company—he exploded: "Damn these human beings, if I had invented them I would go hide my head in a bag." He had taken Friday off to answer "a part of the accumulation of letters" and vented his partly feigned irritation at the children (Clara and Jean, who "*never* seem to have time to answer anybody's letters but their own") by writing: "What they are in the world for I don't know, for they are of no practical value as far as I can see. If I could beget a typewriter [a typist]—but no, our fertile days are over. However, I mustn't stop to play now," he continued; and this last was a healthy sign for Clemens, who loved play and captivated the world when he projected himself imaginatively and playfully into the books of Mark Twain.

This letter—vivid with details about Vienna and with other critical observations, ironies, and sarcasms—was continued Saturday morning, reporting a happy fact: "Twenty-four young people have gone out to the Semmering to-day (and tomorrow), and Mrs. Clemens and an English lady and old Leschetizky and his wife have gone to chaperon them." Reveling in the complete privacy for work that this yielded, Mark Twain wrote at 6:00 P.M. that same day:

> For several years I have been intending to stop writing for print as soon as I could afford it. At last I can afford it, and have put the pot-boiler pen away. What I have been wanting

was a chance to write a book without reserves—a book which should take account of no one's hopes, illusions, delusions; a book which should say my say, right out of my heart, in the plainest language and without a limitation of any sort. I judged that that would be an unimaginable luxury, heaven on earth. There was no condition but one under which the writing of such a book could be possible; only one—the consciousness that it would not see print.

It is under way, now, and it *is* a luxury! an intellectual drunk. Twice I didn't start it right; and got pretty far in, both times, before I found it out. But I am sure it is started right this time. It is in tale-form. I believe I can make it tell what I think of Man, and how he is constructed, and what a shabby poor ridiculous thing he is, and how mistaken he is in his estimate of his character and powers and qualities and his place among the animals.

So far, I think I am succeeding. I let the madam into the secret day before yesterday, and locked the doors and read to her the opening chapters. She said—

"It is perfectly horrible—and perfectly beautiful!"

"Within the due limits of modesty, that is what *I* think."

I hope it will take me a year or two to write it, and that it will turn out to be the right vessel to contain all the ordure I am planning to dump into it. (*MTHL*, pp. 698–99)

This statement, when fully understood, will provide most of the basic clues necessary for understanding "The Chronicle of Young Satan." The first paragraph is a declaration of independence by a writer whose literary career, as so many careful scholars and critics have shown, was not so much cramped as shaped by his sensitive awareness of the expectations of his reading public and of the "civilized" Eastern society he had joined when he made his home in the Nook Farm area of Hartford, Connecticut.[1] The previous summer in Vienna, he had experienced a creative rebirth that yielded, along with much else, the fragmentary manuscript published as "The Great Dark" and a powerful fable, "The Man That Corrupted Hadleyburg"; around the same time he began writing the "wicked gospel" that was eventually published, after Olivia Clemens's

1. See Kenneth R. Andrews, *Nook Farm: Mark Twain's Hartford Circle.*

death, as *What Is Man?*.[2] His beloved Livy was probably among those whose feelings and "hopes, illusions, delusions" he wished now to ignore; nevertheless, the fact that she had recently given her somewhat shocked approval to the opening chapters of this new work seems to have added to his sense of imaginative release and freedom.

This "intellectual drunk"—begun at some point during the previous weeks, continued that weekend, and carried on that summer in Sanna, Sweden—resulted in the first half of "Young Satan," roughly through the first part of chapter 6. As Mark Twain indicated to Howells, the gestation process had not been an easy one. The two false starts were probably, first, the section (chapters 1 and 2, the opening of chapter 3, and part of chapter 10; this incorporated the "St. Petersburg Fragment") he had completed in its first version soon after his arrival in Vienna, in the early winter of 1897–1898; and second, the abortive attempt to bring an angel into the Hannibal of Tom and Huck, in the "Schoolhouse Hill" fragment written in the early winter of 1898–1899. What distinguished his third attempt was the fact that, through its "tale-form" Mark Twain believed he could, as he specified in the letter, "make it tell what I think of Man." His desire to show humanity in a "shabby poor ridiculous" light, with a scent of "ordure" in the treatment, indicates that he had now resumed work on a didactic satire that he intended to write in the vein of Swift and Rabelais.

Most of the themes and ideas, and many of the literary devices, in these chapters had long been present in Mark Twain's writings; but now they were beginning to flower, to paraphrase Livy, in horribly beautiful ways. One cannot emphasize too often, in view of the widespread publication of the Paine-Duneka text called *The Mysterious Stranger*, that the "Young Satan" texts were all fragmentary and that none were revised for publication. Even as such, they are of the greatest interest to lovers of Mark Twain and include some of his most memorable passages. In the next chapter, we shall begin to look at these various texts in the order in which they were written.

The Two "Strangers"

One must first, however, get rid of the accepted notion that all the texts in the *Mysterious Stranger Manuscripts* are vari-

2. See *WIM*, vol. 19 (see list of short references p. xiii).

ant versions of a single story. This false idea was a natural consequence of the forced grafting of the "Conclusion of the book" fragment—the notorious all-is-a-dream ending intended for "No. 44"—onto the never-completed "Young Satan." And obviously, as Gibson wrote, "A case can be made for Paine" (3). James M. Cox, in fact, has argued that case most profoundly but, I think, unsuccessfully.[3] That two generations of critical readers were bemused by the Paine-Duneka sleight of hand would seem to prove that there was some basis for their editorial decisions and procedures.[4] Indeed, in a remarkably perceptive essay by so fine a critic as Edwin S. Fussell, this yielded a most paradoxical result: he argued that the false conclusion provided the best basis for "meaningful analysis"! To quote a key sentence: "The final chapter of *The Mysterious Stranger* outlines a general theory of solipsism, and if this is accepted as the ultimate framework of the story, meaningful analysis becomes possible."[5] This is simply one of the clearest, most thorough examples of the confusion created by the *Stranger* text, a confusion that was almost universal. But the case for the Paine-Duneka text can only be historical-biographical, in the sense that it reflects primarily the taste and mistakes of a bygone era; such criticism cannot be concerned with the literary values of what Mark Twain actually wrote.

Basic Situation

In fact, there are two distinct works of major importance in the *Manuscripts* volume, quite different in character, though not unrelated.[6] Before taking up the final products in detail,

3. *Critics*, pp. 195–220.

4. But I can testify that, well over a decade ago before I had seen any of the *Manuscripts*, as a reader and teacher, I almost instinctively felt that the concluding chapter was not organically related to what had gone before. Whenever I taught the *Stranger* in the late fifties, I would begin by telling my students to ignore the concluding chapter; from all the scattered facts I could then gather, and from the internal evidence of the text itself, I had concluded that the two parts did not belong together—despite the valiant, but misguided, efforts of critics to reconcile the discrepancies.

5. *Critics*, p. 76.

6. As Tuckey has put it, in his most recent statement of the problem: "The three versions"—he thinks of "Schoolhouse" as a third version, whereas I shall treat it as an abortive digression in the writing of "Young Satan"—"are not so much different drafts of one story as three different stories" (*Critics*, p. 86).

we must see both what unites and what separates them. They do share a "basic situation" (Henry Nash Smith's phrase): a protagonist in Austria tells his story in the first person and is involved with a supernatural stranger. But there are radical differences too; and few of the elements making up this situation are found exclusively in these texts. Mark Twain wrote other European tales, notably *The Prince and the Pauper*, the *Yankee*, and *Joan of Arc*, in two of which (the *Yankee* and *Joan*) he used first-person narrators; and of course his masterpiece, *Huckleberry Finn*, owes much of its charm and power to the inimitable voice of the boy who recounts his adventures. As to the supernatural: in the *Yankee*, which marks the transition to his final phase, Mark Twain had a sort of grown-up Huck—the very name "Hank" is an echo—tell about even more fantastic adventures involving drastic dislocations in space and time. The transportation of a Connecticut mechanic to King Arthur's court was a daring conception, and it placed strains on Mark Twain's imagination and style analogous to those evident in the *Stranger Manuscripts*.[7]

Similarly, the character of the stranger should be placed in the larger context of Mark Twain's "transcendent figures," as Paul E. Baender called them.[8] Other examples would be not only Hank Morgan, but also the stranger in "The Man That Corrupted Hadleyburg" and, with certain qualifications, Joan of Arc. Henry Nash Smith summarized their traits, which become "more fully developed with the passage of time," as follows: "They are isolated by their intellectual superiority to the community; they are contemptuous of mankind in general; and they have more than ordinary power. Satan, the culmination of the series, is omnipotent."[9] Or, as Smith put it elsewhere: "In *The Mysterious Stranger* the principal novelty in basic situation is that the stranger is explicitly supernatural."[10]

7. Henry Nash Smith has analyzed and criticized, too severely for my taste, the confusions in the role of the Yankee; see *Mark Twain's Fable of Progress: Political and Economic Ideas in "A Connecticut Yankee."* James M. Cox has related these confusions to Hank Morgan's style in a chapter headed "Yankee Slang" in *Mark Twain: The Fate of Humor.*

8. Paul E. Baender, "Mark Twain's Transcendent Figures" (Ph.D. diss.).

9. Henry Nash Smith, *Mark Twain: The Development of a Writer*, p. 136.

10. Henry Nash Smith, "Mark Twain's Images of Hannibal," p. 100.

But while the general drift of these statements is true, *omnipotence* is not quite the right word for the powers of an angel; and the category of the "supernatural" is too loose to describe these Mark Twain creations with precision. As we shall see, "Satan"[11] is quite different from Forty-four, possibly in his ultimate nature, but certainly in Twain's treatment of him; the two strangers are by no means to be equated. Gibson's composite sketch of this complex character is admirable in its way, but naturally enough he stressed the continuities he found rather than the differences. So: "Satan, alias 'No. 44,' is the primary character *in all three manuscripts* and the most complex in his acts, his satirical bent, the 'fatal music of his voice,' his Socratic way of speaking, and his origins" (14, my italics). Building on pioneering essays by Coleman O. Parsons, Gibson analyzed various aspects of his presumably unitary character and traced some of the attitudes Clemens expressed toward Satan in earlier writings. These and later examples (16–19) all illustrate an attitude of ambivalence: the early figure, in Gibson's words, is "diabolic or angelic"; and the emergence of "full, imaginative portraits" is dated from "the autumn of 1899 on" (18)—as we have seen, a more accurate date might be spring, when Mark Twain dropped work on "Schoolhouse" and returned to work on "Young Satan." Though he does not follow through on this point, Gibson's use of the plural *portraits,* like his concluding section headed "The 'Mysterious Strangers' " (33–34), implies a recognition of some of the differences we shall be emphasizing.

One of the basic tensions in Mark Twain's later writings is indeed between the natural and the supernatural; but there are others: between waking experiences and dreams, realities and appearances, realism and fantasy, human frailty and power, humor and satire, and the like. Further, within the limited realm of the supernatural, Twain experimented with many variations and tried many treatments: throughout his work we find angels and "miracles" of various kinds, "mental telegraphy" and spiritualistic mediums, burlesque satire and mock-heroic descriptions, and passages that approach the true sublime, though these last are usually undercut by humor. Given this broad spectrum of "effects," as our literary showman liked to

11. I write the name of the angel in "Young Satan" in quotation marks in order to distinguish him from his uncle, Satan, the traditional Devil.

call them, all sorts of thematic and stylistic links can be made among the various manuscripts and with earlier works (such as the *Yankee, The American Claimant,* and *Joan of Arc*) and other posthumously published manuscripts (especially *Which Was the Dream?*). Thus, to link "Young Satan" and "No. 44" merely on the basis of the angels in both is somewhat arbitrary.

Another aspect of the basic situation is, of course, that both tales are set in the Austrian town of Eseldorf (Assville or Donkeytown); but this too has its complexities. Smith has written, in an honorable scholarly tradition, of The Matter of Hannibal; we may similarly speak of The Matter of the River, The Matter of the West, and The Matter of Europe, among others.[12] Though certain elements of The Matter of Hannibal are being used (the village community, and the gang of boys, in "Young Satan"; and Clemens's experience as a printer's "devil" apprentice,[13] in "No. 44"), they are radically transformed, and the settings and problems are basically European, not American. In our genetic account of "Young Satan," we shall see how Mark Twain vacillated between Hannibal (the "St. Petersburg Fragment" and "Schoolhouse Hill") and Europe in his unsuccessful attempts to bring that tale into focus.

Time and the Writer

Angels suggest not time, but eternity. And no doubt chronology can be overstressed in dealing with Mark Twain's creative processes: the more he changed, we might say, the more he remained the same. But he himself was deeply, almost obsessively, concerned with the facts and vagaries of memory and habit, of change and recurrence—time phenomena all—and never more so than during the decade that produced the "Strangers." I want now to consider a number of related time factors relevant to our problem.

COMPOSITION. Except for the historic accident of the creation of the *Stranger* text, "Young Satan" and "No. 44" might never have been yoked together. The author's work on them was spread over the better part of a decade: he "completed"

12. Among attempts made to summarize the last is Arthur L. Scott, "Mark Twain as a Critic of Europe" (Ph.D. diss.). And various aspects of the subject are adumbrated in Roger B. Salomon, *Mark Twain and the Image of History.*

13. See Appendix E: "Mark Twain and Printers."

"Young Satan" (and "Schoolhouse") by August 1900; and he wrote "No. 44" between 1902 and 1905, with a final addition in 1908.[14] Furthermore, the "Young Satan" fragments were written entirely in Europe, while "No. 44" was begun and finished in the States, with the substantial middle part penned in Florence.

Without falling into a forced periodicity, we may yet feel that each of Mark Twain's three mature decades had a sort of unity, and variety, of its own: his forties (1875–1885) were framed by the Matters of Hannibal and the River, with Europe in the middle; whereas his fifties were strongly oriented to Europe, with sporadic returns to Hannibal or America. And his sixties produced a variety of new works and tendencies, along with a continuation of earlier matters. Though "No. 44" is a culmination of various experiments, early and late, it is an independent work and can stand by itself; and so can some of the other striking and surprising products of Mark Twain's exciting last decade.

HISTORICAL PERIOD. The elementary task of establishing the time frame for a historical fiction was botched by Paine and Duneka. Their choice of 1590 for the *Stranger,* while not without some slight textual justification (510), resulted in an obvious anachronism when, in chapter 2, "the oldest servingman in the castle" is described as giving the boys coffee to drink—with the explanation that this delicacy was captured from the Turks "at the siege of Vienna." There was such a siege by the Turks in 1529, but the one that brought coffee to Vienna was in 1683—as any reader of Austrian history, or tourist guidebooks, would know. This fact goes well, however, with the date Mark Twain actually intended for "Young Satan": 1702 (422, 510); it is altogether a much more "modern" story than the date of 1590 would imply.

Contrariwise, there is no coffee mentioned at the beginning of "No. 44," which is dated 1490; but in chapter 22, Forty-four explains some of his anachronistic language ("Corn-pone! Arkansas! Alabama! Prairie! Coffee! Saccharin!") to the nar-

14. By way of comparison, we note that the two previous decades had brought forth *Tom Sawyer, A Tramp Abroad, The Prince and the Pauper, Life on the Mississippi,* and *Huckleberry Finn* (1877–1885); and the *Yankee, The American Claimant, Pudd'nhead Wilson,* and *Joan of Arc* (1889–1896).

rator and says, "Coffee: they have it in the Orient, they will have it here in Austria two centuries from now" (330)—that is, in 1690!

Clemens was an old hand at reporting, and at writing historical fictions, and he was rarely careless about such details.[15] He was merely made to seem careless by Paine's irresponsible editing.

AGE. Both stories are presented as autobiographical narratives, and they illustrate a problem central to the very nature of autobiography: the relationship between the age of the narrator as he speaks or writes and his age at the time of the incidents in the action. This often is integral with the author's point of view and purpose in writing: there is a vast difference, for instance, between a man in middle age looking back to his childhood or adolescence or his early maturity and an old man remembering those same years or the riper achievements of middle age.

The contrast between the two points of view is marked and may have something to do with the incompletion of "Young Satan" and the relative failure of *Joan*. The latter begins with a foreword by the Sieur Louis de Conte addressed "to his great-great-grand nephews and nieces": "This is the year 1492. I am eighty-two years of age. The things I am going to tell you are things which I saw myself as a child and as a youth." The gap between generations under such circumstances may be too great to be adequately bridged by narration.

By way of contrast, when Mark Twain wrote *Old Times on the Mississippi* in 1874, at the age of forty, he was looking back a mere decade and a half with a nostalgia intensified by the intervention of the Civil War and physical separation from the valley; and this gave him the integrated point of view that sets chapters 4–20 off so beautifully from the rest of *Life on the Mississippi*.

In "Young Satan," as in *Joan*, the narrator is supposed to be an old man remembering his boyhood; but this aspect of Theodor Fischer's character has not been worked out consistently. In the initial situation, a small gang of three boys encounters a somewhat older youth; clearly, though "we were not over-

15. Salomon quotes a letter (never sent) about a detail in *Joan*: "I am cautious in matters of history." *Mark Twain and the Image of History*, p. 183.

much pestered with schooling" (36), they are all still schoolchildren. Is the point of view primarily that of a boy like Tom Sawyer or Huck Finn, or is it that of an old man?[16] In the episode of the Hussite woman in chapter 1, for example, Theodor speaks with a sort of Huck Finnian irony, as if he still accepted Father Adolf's "orthodox" view of repentance and of reward and punishment. But later, as when confronted with some of the consequences of the angel's interventions in the life plans of various villagers (chapters 6–7), he may speak from the perspective of an experienced adult. Thus: "Many a time, since then, I have heard people pray to God to spare the life of sick persons, but I have never done it" (129). And: "He didn't seem to know any way to do a person a favor except by killing him or making a lunatic out of him. . . . privately I did not think much of his processes. *At that time*" (164, my italics). Presumably, Theodor has subsequently changed his mind. These changes in point of view may be accounted for in terms of the stages by which the writing of "Young Satan" proceeded, as we shall see.

The situation in "No. 44" is much closer to that in *Huckleberry Finn,* a fact that helps account for its superior integration. August Feldner tells his tale as a young man of sixteen—by chapter 23, "barely seventeen"—and the action takes place in two or three months during the winter of 1490–1491. He is clearly older than Theodor and has been out of the village "as much as a year" (229).[17] Further, at the outset August is not one of a gang of boys but an apprentice in a small working community, and Forty-four is described as "apparently sixteen or seventeen years old" (235); they develop a private relationship, an adolescent comradeship, involving no other young men in the print shop.

Paradoxically, then, though "Young Satan" is supposedly

16. This problem is analyzed at length by Thomas Blues, *Mark Twain and the Community,* chap. 3: "The Yankee as Old Man." See especially pp. 59–65.

17. The age difference between August and Theodor may be thought of as paralleling that between Huck Finn and Tom Sawyer, which is left vague, though this reader at least has always thought of Huck as older than Tom. I should place Huck close to August at about 15 or 16, whereas Tom and Theodor both strike me as aged about 13 or 14. Compare the love attitudes of Tom to Becky and Huck to Mary Jane, in their respective novels.

narrated by an old man, it has more of the naivety of boyhood; and though "No. 44" is told by a seventeen year old, it is altogether the more mature creation of the two.

Finally, in both the "Stranger" tales (as in related fictions such as the *Yankee, Joan,* and "Hadleyburg") there is much experimentation with aspects of the time dimension, including prediction of the future. This is involved, in complicated ways, with Mark Twain's ideas about the universe, history, life, and man, with his world picture. In "Young Satan," we are told: "It was wonderful, the mastery Satan had over time and distance" (150). In "No. 44," some of the same motifs are repeated, but they differ, in the concluding chapters especially, in that they are apocalyptic: time is made to run backward, and an awful darkness is created for an "Assembly of the Dead." The sense of completion in the later work, then, is not just a result of the fact that a complex pattern of themes and relationships has been worked out to a conclusion; it is also a result of the central vision that infuses the whole and is different from the central vision in "Young Satan."

Angels: Ambiguous and Mysterious

At the heart of the fascination, and the difficulty, of the "Stranger" materials, of course, are the transcendent figures of the angels who flit in and out of the stories and notes with constantly changing functions and names. As already suggested, it has been too readily assumed that "Satan, alias 'No. 44,'" is really one character assuming various shapes. Luckily, we now have a wealth of material relating to this problem and can almost feel on our intellectual pulse the progress of Mark Twain's gropings and vacillations as he created "Satan" and Forty-four.

In the background is the long history of Clemens's involvement with biblical and religious themes in general and with the figure of Satan in particular.[18] In 1891 he wrote a memoir of his mother in which she is described "saying a soft word for the devil himself . . . who prays for Satan?"[19] And in "Is

18. The spadework on this subject was done by Coleman O. Parsons in two essays: "The Devil and Samuel Clemens" and "The Background of *The Mysterious Stranger,*" in *Critics,* pp. 155–68 and 109–26. See also W. C. S. Pellowe, *Mark Twain Pilgrim from Hannibal,* and Allison Ensor, *Mark Twain and the Bible.*

19. *MTA,* 1:117.

Shakespeare Dead?" (1909) he wrote a "fabulous" account, as Parsons called it—but it may have had some basis in fact—of his having written, at the tender age of seven, a "biography" of Satan![20] At a more mature age, in 1858, he wrote a letter repeating the common romantic admiration for Milton's Satan: "What is the grandest thing in Paradise Lost?—the Arch-Fiend's terrible energy!" In Parson's summary: "The Clemens theology was trinitarian. It involved contempt for the Old Testament God, championship of the insulted and injured Satan, and immense respect for the universal Creator." Finally, in "Concerning the Jews," written in the summer of 1898, when "Young Satan" was still at an early stage, he said: "Of course Satan has some kind of a case, it goes without saying. . . . As soon as I can get at the facts I will undertake his rehabilitation myself, if I can find an unpolitic publisher."[21]

The full story of "The Devil and Samuel Clemens" would require a separate book. Concentrating on our two "Stranger" versions, we find that the bases of the characterization and the treatments are quite distinct, in some ways, at opposite poles. The central idea of "Young Satan" is strongly emphasized from the start, in the title and the opening chapters: we are dealing not with Satan himself, but with a member of his angelic family, creating an interesting ambiguity, to be sure, but not a mystery. Hence the Paine-Duneka title was an obvious misnomer. The Devil's existence and doings are strongly emphasized in chapter 1, especially in connection with the evil Father Adolf, who "had absolutely no fear of the Devil"—a fact that evokes a sort of Huck Finnian respect from Theodor: "For after all is said and done Satan is a sacred character, being mentioned in the Bible, and it cannot be proper to utter lightly the sacred names, lest heaven itself should resent it" (41).

Chapter 2 begins with talk of ghosts and angels, however, and there is no mistaking the simple directness with which the youthful stranger tells the boys he is "an angel." To be sure, this is followed by the name *Satan* (italicized by Mark Twain); but we are told very quickly that "he [the Devil] is my uncle,"[22] and that our "Young Satan" is of "good family": "He [the

20. *Essays*, pp. 413–15.

21. *Critics*, pp. 159, 160–61, 162.

22. There is a notebook entry along this line, dated 8 December 1895: "What uncle Satan said" (17).

traditional Devil] is the only member of it that has ever sinned" (47–48). Our "Satan" is an unfallen angel, and he is curious about the human race; that is the main point, and the reader has no doubts about it whatsoever, since he shares the secret with the boys. Some of the other characters may sense a mystery: when Wilhelm says, "I think he is the Devil," Marget responds, "Or an angel" (94). But this is Theodor's narrative, and for him and his readers the true identity of Philip Traum is crystal clear. In "No. 44," by way of sharp contrast, no direct connection is made between Satan and the stranger.[23] And the mystery of the stranger's identity is one of the chief cruxes of the plot in "No. 44," the only text that should properly be titled *The Mysterious Stranger.*

Various other differences, and the equally rich continuities of theme and treatment, between "Young Satan" and "No. 44" will emerge more fully from detailed analyses of the texts. My purpose in this chapter has been merely to establish, in a preliminary way, their distinctness, to complete a necessary divorce of the forced and incompatible marriage perpetrated by Paine and Duneka in their 1916 text. Only then can serious reading and criticism be expected to begin.

23. Tuckey put into parentheses a point that I think cannot be emphasized too strongly: "The 'mysterious stranger' of 'Print Shop' is just that: whereas the '44' of 'Hannibal' [Gibson's "Schoolhouse"] reveals that he is Satan, Jr., this one guards the secret of his identity" (*Critics*, p. 152).

Part Two: False Starts

3

"Young Satan" Emerges

We are ready now to explore the five stages by which, during a period of more than three years, Mark Twain developed his first "Stranger" idea: (1) the first Eseldorf chapters, which incorporate (2) the "St. Petersburg Fragment" (1897–1898); (3) "Schoolhouse Hill" (December 1898); (4) the beginning of the "intellectual drunk" reported in the letter to Howells (spring and summer 1899); and (5) the last treatment of "Young Satan," written before the return to the States in 1900. And, since Mark Twain never brought "Young Satan" to a conclusion, we will need to consider, along with the manuscripts, some of the various related working notes that survive. In any study of uncompleted writings and projects by an author of proven mastery, certain questions naturally arise:

What were the imaginative ideas or purposes, however incomplete, that were seeking expression? Often the failures of a great writer are more interesting than the "successes" of a mediocre one.

Why were partial successes not carried through to completion? Our answers to this question can only be speculative; but when considering "Young Satan," we do have a later, not unrelated, work that was successfully completed—or so I shall attempt to demonstrate.

We are interested in the "Young Satan" fragments, therefore, not only as products of Mark Twain's imagination, but also as they foreshadow and throw light on "No. 44." Besides the general problem of exploring the imaginative worlds Mark Twain was striving to construct, we will be concerned most particularly with his changing conceptions of his protagonists-narrators and of the angel figures that impinge on their lives.

St. Petersburg (1897)

Mark Twain's original inspiration—his Ur-stranger idea, so to speak, which persisted for well over a year, until he gave up working on "Schoolhouse Hill"—was to bring a figure called *Satan* into the Hannibal world of Tom and Huck. Tuckey began reconstructing the circumstances that preceded the writing of what he labeled the "Pre-Eseldorf" pages [1] (and Gibson, the "St. Petersburg Fragment"), and he drew attention to a notebook entry of June 1897: "Satan's boyhood—going around with other boys and surprising them with devilish miracles." The "St. Petersburg Fragment," written very soon after Mark Twain's arrival in Vienna in late September 1897, seems to have later become so inextricably woven into the texture of "Young Satan" that Gibson decided it was not worth reconstructing separately [**1**].

Of special interest is the fact, to which we shall have to return, that the good priest, later called Father Peter, was originally named Mr. Black.[2] In view of the role that the Negro was playing for Clemens during those months (George Griffin, who had been the Clemenses' beloved butler in Hartford, died around June; the Clemenses heard the Jubilee Singers in Switzerland during August 1897; and Twain was recalling childhood memories for his autobiography) and of the fact that the Duplicate of Forty-four in "No. 44" will later be called Emil Schwarz (*black* in German), this is a significant detail and may help explain why Mark Twain dropped, or suppressed, the idea of a Satan-in-Hannibal tale at the time.

A more central explanation can be found in Tuckey's summary of the state of affairs in January 1898, when Mark Twain had completed the first major spurt of writing on the tale that was eventually to become "Young Satan": "He was writing well. And it is noteworthy that Hannibal seems not to have been the imaginative base of much of this writing. He had found significant new material"—as a result of his first encounter with Austrian politics and Viennese anti-Semitism, which is summarized in Tuckey's chapter 2—"and an appropriate way of treating it."[3]

In this and the next chapter, I shall be discussing the parts of "Young Satan" as they appear in *Stranger Manuscripts* and examining them according to the stages of their compo-

1. *MTSatan*, pp. 25–36, chap. 3, passim (see list of short references p. xiii).
2. Not "Mr. Block," as Tuckey read the manuscript (*MTSatan*, p. 23).
3. *MTSatan*, p. 38.

sition. Since what Mark Twain wrote is different in some essentials and in very many details from the Paine-Duneka *Stranger*, the reader familiar with the latter text is urged now to put it out of his mind, to the extent that such a thing is possible, in order to give Mark Twain's text a fresh reading. At some later stage, should he want to examine the Paine-Duneka revisions in detail, he may consult the detailed annotations of that text and the succinct summary of its problems ("*The Mysterious Stranger*: Mark Twain's Texts and the Paine-Duneka Edition") provided by John S. Tuckey.[4] My purpose being different, I do not intend to repeat the full analysis supplied by Tuckey. However, I shall refer to some of the familiar revisions from time to time in order to formulate critical points through comparison and contrast.

Eseldorf (1897–1898)

At the same time that he shifted the setting of the "Stranger" from St. Petersburg to Eseldorf, Twain made a decision to experiment with the ambiguities implied in the paradoxical idea of an unfallen angel named *Satan* [2]. The difficult problem remained of how to handle the figure of the real Satan who lurked in the background and who would certainly be more familiar to the general reader.

In preparing the ground for "Satan's" emergence, Mark Twain's method was to work through contrasts. Chapter 1 of "Young Satan" presents a world of sharp satire not unlike the stronger parts of the *Yankee* [3]. We quickly perceive that Twain's target is not going to be political: the "prince *with a difficult name*" (my italics) is far in the background and will not reappear; the name of his principality is unimportant. Mark Twain's criticisms here are religious and are directed most particularly at the Catholic Church, its bishops, and its priests—with the worst elements of the latter concentrated in the figure of Father Adolf, a wicked priest with "no fear of the Devil."

The fullness of Father Adolf's evil is exposed in a five-page passage (36–41), cut by Paine and Duneka, about "Gretel Marx the dairyman's widow," who was influenced by a "Hussite woman named Adler" [4]. With his "fishy eyes" and his

4. *Critics*, pp. 1–74, 85–90.

"purple fat face," the wicked father is one of Mark Twain's more vivid creations—closer to Huck's Pap, on the whole, than to the comic Merlin of the *Yankee,* though the latter was probably in the minds of Paine and Duneka when they transformed Adolf into a relatively mild astrologer.

The significances of the Gretel Marx episode are conveyed by cutting sarcasms: the "ignorant and foolish" people who respond to Frau Adler are "those few who could read," and their worst crime is reading the Bible and hymnbooks; when Frau Marx is caught in the act, Father Adolf "knocked the book out of her hand" (37). As punishment, the Holy Virgin causes (according to the father) the deaths of both Frau Marx's horses. But when Frau Marx heeds the father's advice and as part of her "real repentance" buys "a lottery ticket bearing the number of the date" of her horses' deaths, she is rewarded by a draw of "fifteen hundred ducats!" (38). We are told that this "was the best lesson and the wholesomest our village ever had." The satiric ironies are, if anything, too obvious.

As already noted, Theodor's point of view, particularly in relation to Father Adolf, is like that of Huck Finn when he talks, for example, of the Widow Douglas and Miss Watson. In both cases there is the same sort of double vision: the surface respect of an immature mind reflecting conventional ideas taught him by adults contrasts with the real critical attack implicit in the actual facts and the absurdities of what the narrator is telling and occasionally implicit in the tone of his narration or comments. (Mark Twain's mature views are in ultimate control, of course. One paradigm, among many, of the resulting irony can be taken from chapter 42 of *Huckleberry Finn*: "Then they all agreed that Jim had acted very well, and was deserving to have some notice took of it, and reward. So every one of them promised, right out and hearty, that they wouldn't cuss him no more.") Thus, the opening paragraphs of Theodor's story tell us of the pleasure he has in "the Age of Faith" but proceed to show that the "paradise" of his boyhood—in Donkeytown!—was based on ignorance. "It was discontentment that came so near to being the ruin"—or the salvation?—"of Gretel Marx" (36).

The wicked father specialized in suicides and funerals, conducting the latter best (like the Duke in *Huckleberry Finn*) when "he hadn't too much of a load on, but only about enough to make him properly appreciate the sacredness of his office" (39)! But the full depth of Father Adolf's involvement with Satan is emphasized by his being "always on hand at the bridge-head on the 9th of December, at the Assuaging of the Devil," about which we are told in a well-written episode (39–41) that I shall label "Cheating the Devil."

There are many traditional elements in this episode, and in fact a medieval source for it has been found.[5] The seven-hundred-year-old bridge would have been built around the year 1000; and the idea of the Devil working for the "wages" of Christian souls he hopes will be consigned to hell is very old, though the particular form of it we associate with the figure of Faust was not given literary form until the sixteenth century. In any case, there is something vaguely Faustian about the written "bond" that makes this particular tradition, in Theodor's eyes, "history." The initial situation is an anticlerical satire: when the Devil insisted on his bond, it was to prevent his being cheated by the priests. "Always before, when he built a bridge, he was to have for his pay the first passenger that crossed it—everybody knowing he meant a Christian, of course. But no matter, he didn't *say* it, so they always sent a jackass or a chicken or some other undamnable passenger first, and so got the best of him" (39).

Poor Devil! This time too he is outwitted and cheated of his expected prey. When Satan (not our "Young Satan") angrily demanded his bond, he was told he had it, in the shape of a dead Christian, that is, he had the body but not the soul. "Then the prior and all the monks went through with a great lot of mock ceremonies, pretending it was to assuage the Devil and reconcile him, but really it was only to make fun of him and stir up his bile more than ever." This "mock Assuaging is repeated every 9th of December, to this day," and the significance of Father Adolf's having "no fear of the Devil" is further emphasized by an obvious and expected allusion to the famous inkstand thrown at Satan by Luther (whose name was eliminated by Paine and Duneka): "The same was claimed for Luther, but no one believed, for he was a heretic and liar.

5. Originally, William M. Gibson commented in an explanatory note: "This seems to be the kind of legend that Mark Twain invented freely in *A Tramp Abroad*; I have found no source for it" (469). This lack is now supplied: see Appendix A, "Sources for 'Cheating the Devil.'"

This was so, for the Pope himself said that Luther had lied about it" (41).

It is hard to say who comes out worst in this elaborate series of rather heavy-handed ironies. Though the attitudes are Huck Finnian, the style lacks Huck's subtlety and lightness [5].

Ambiguous Angel

The atmosphere of the opening chapter, then, is created by oppressive ironies, ignorance, superstition, and a villainous priest; but there are some rays of light in the gloom. The good priest, Peter, had been heretically "talking around in conversation that God was all goodness and would find a way to save *all* his poor human children"—which brings forth what are perhaps the most profoundly Huck Finnian of Theodor's comments: "It was a horrible thing to say . . . and it was out of character for him to say it, too, for he was always good and gentle and truthful, and a good Catholic" (42). And Father Peter's daughter, Marget, "had the best head in the village, and the most in it."

The general effect in chapter 2 is in sharp contrast to the earlier dark mood. Theodor's narrative regains the paradisiacal atmosphere of the opening pages, this time without benefit of references to the clergy and the sleep of the Middle Ages. The boys have "the run of the castle park," and thanks to the "oldest serving-man"—a sort of Uncle Remus in whiteface—they learn to smoke and drink coffee and they enjoy ghost and angel stories. The effortless transition here—"one May night"—is a miracle of literary tact: "Soon there came a youth strolling towards us through the trees, and he sat down and began to talk in a friendly way, just as if he knew us." This is followed by a perfectly controlled exhibition of the angel's powers: he reads minds, makes fire to light Theodor's pipe, and above all "won us over," both through his actions and his words. This sequence of "Young Satan's" first appearance is for many readers the most memorable part of the story. It has a subtly modulated rhythm, alternating between external "tricks," suitable perhaps for an ordinary magician, and more symbolic actions aimed at the intellect and soul. "There was never anything so wonderful and so interesting." Some of the strange things done by "Satan" satisfy the boys' appetites ("you have only to wish and find") and others amuse them; the latter culminate when the youth makes birds of clay that "flew away singing" while he is telling them he is an angel. But he immediately reassures them that "there was no occasion for us to be afraid of an angel, and he liked us anyway."

The aesthetic principle governing chapter 2 might be characterized as "sugaring the bitter pill," because the real purpose of this first encounter, aside from showing "Satan" winning the boys' friendship, is to make a devastating attack on the boys' conventional religious notions. The angel softened the blow each time, as he administered a series of severe shocks.[6] While making toy people, he tells the boys his name is "Satan"; he laughs at their surprise and then casually saves a toy woman from falling. Explaining that his is "a good family" and that the Devil is "the only member of it that has ever sinned," he makes them feel "that it is just a fearful joy to be alive." The weave is intricate, but the figure in the carpet emerges clearly.

An angelic year is a human millennium, and "Satan" is sixteen angelic years old. As "a little child a thousand [human] years old," he had been a favorite of the uncle for whom he had been named. When he was nine, seven thousand human years before, "the Fall" happened but "did not affect me nor the rest of the relationship. . . . We others are still ignorant of sin. . . . We cannot do wrong; neither have we any disposition to do it, for we do not know what it is" (49). But this is said while "Satan" commits "wanton murder"—from the point of view of Theodor—against two quarreling toy workmen who annoy him in the same way that a person might be annoyed by a buzzing mosquito. And when the miniature funeral that ensues becomes noisy, he "mashed all those people into the earth just as if they had been flies, and went on talking just the same."

Our general problem as readers is clear enough: this is indeed a new sort of double vision, more radical than that of Huck and intended as a total condemnation of human vanity. We are inevitably troubled by the ambiguities involved, which do not end with the angel's unfortunate name. (Of course, Mark Twain was careless here. The Hebrew name *Satan* translates as *adversary* and could hardly have been given to a

6. See below, the section headed "The Sense of Humor" (Chapter 5).

sinless angel, that is, to the Devil before he fell.) Thus: "He had seen everything, he had been everywhere, he knew everything, and he forgot nothing," or so, at least, it seems to Theodor. But "Satan" spoke of "the daily life in heaven, he had seen the damned writhing in the red waves of hell" (50); and does not this very language imply that "Satan" is aware of distinctions between good and evil, innocence and sin? More generally, does not knowing "everything" include knowing about sin? The only way to keep these and similar statements from being flat logical contradictions is to distinguish between kinds of knowledge and to specify which kinds are actually beyond the angel's ken. And in fact this aspect of the angel's ambiguous character is worked out later in "Young Satan."

While "Satan" keeps "talking right along" and working his "enchantments" upon the boys, they—and we—are at once repelled and attracted by what he says and reveals. The damned in hell are made to seem "so many imitation rats in an artificial fire." And "truth is good manners; manners are a fiction" (51). Evidently the angel is "wholly without feeling, and could not understand" (52). On this level, too, there is ambiguity—for does not "Satan" tell the boys "he liked us anyway?"

The ambiguities inherent in the angel as a fictitious character are expressed, then, with respect to both the reader's knowledge and the reader's feeling, as well as with respect to the angel's troubling name; and Theodor's emerging double vision finds an objective correlative in the conspiracy of silence "Satan" imposes on the boys. Henceforth, the youth they know as an angel will appear in the village as Philip Traum, and he will make it impossible for them to reveal his secret; the village and "Satan" plots can thus continue to develop along parallel lines, interacting all the while. Now, "Satan" announces that he must go away on an errand, which he does not explain, but which we will come to understand better from later evidence.

Before he vanishes, however, thinning away like a soap bubble, he completes his initial attack on the boys' religious ideas and human vanities by invoking a version of the chain of being (to which we shall return) unlike the traditional one in which man has been placed midway between the angels and the animals. In "Satan's" version, emphasis is placed on the great differences of scale: "One cannot compare things which by their nature and by the interval between them are not comparable," Theodor says in response to "Satan's" Socratic questioning. And the angel proceeds:

> Man is made of dirt—I *saw* him made. I am not made of dirt. Man is a museum of disgusting diseases, a home of impurities; he comes to-day and is gone to-morrow, he begins as dirt and departs as a stench; I am of the aristocracy of the Imperishables. And man has the *Moral Sense*. You understand? he has the *Moral Sense*. That would seem to be difference enough between us, all by itself. (55)

In chapter 3, the two plots begin to blend; and "Satan's" enigmatic statement about the Moral Sense prompts the boys to ask Father Peter about its value. When the wicked father says the Moral Sense is "the one thing that lifts man above the beasts that perish," they "went away with that kind of indefinite sense you have often had of being filled but not fatted" (60). And so forth: we shall not go on analyzing each succeeding section in the same detail, since the basic pattern of "Young Satan" has been established by the first two chapters; in what follows, this same juxtaposition of human and angelic values is elaborated into an overwhelming, cosmic irony.

Tuckey[7] and Gibson are in substantial agreement that the first Eseldorf section of "Young Satan" presents, as Gibson says, "a unified tale of Father Peter's discovery of the gold, the accusation against him, his trial, vindication, and final 'happiness'—the madness that Philip Traum bestows on him" (487–88). This last, of course, dramatizes the most shocking of the truths that the angel teaches the boys.

Actually, this view of madness is of ancient vintage, it is good orthodox Christian doctrine and was used by Swift. It combines two related ideas: "Man was born to trouble, as the sparks fly upward" (Job 5:7), so that perfect happiness is impossible in this vale of tears; and a fool, or madman, may be possessed of a kind of superior wisdom or insight.[8] In Mark Twain's version: "No sane man can be happy, for to him life is real, and he sees what a fearful thing it is. Only the mad can be happy. . . . The few that imagine themselves kings or gods"

7. *MTSatan*, pp. 38–39.
8. See, for example, Walter Kaiser, *Praisers of Folly: Erasmus, Rabelais, Shakespeare*.

(164). Theodor comments: "He ["Satan"] didn't seem to know any way to do a person a favor except by killing him or making a lunatic out of him . . . privately I did not think much of his processes. At that time." There is a deep pathos in the old man's ravings and in his promising Marget and Wilhelm the throne: "There, little lady, have I done well? You can smile now—isn't it so?" We are inevitably reminded, mutatis mutandis, of Lear and Cordelia.

Looking back over this swiftly written first version of "Young Satan," one does indeed find it to be a powerful and unified tale, especially if the pages about "happy insanity" are included. It is not well proportioned perhaps, and some of its ideas (like the statement about the Moral Sense) are only mentioned and not developed; it moves, however, with a kind of inevitability to a conclusion that, though paradoxical, is consistent with the double vision that led up to it. Gibson, speculating about how "Young Satan" might end, wrote: "One very real possibility might be to conclude with the vindication of Father Peter and his going happily insane. The virtue of this choice is that Twain at one time thought of this as his proper conclusion; the difficulty is that the very fitting ending in madness does not provide a proper exit for Satan."[9] And though the village plot has been brought to a conclusion, the education of Theodor and the other boys has not been carried far enough. (But what education is ever complete?)

Theodor's final irony—"At that time"—reminds us that he is an old man remembering and narrating an experience of his boyhood. One might indeed end there. But Mark Twain was obviously not satisfied and went on to create two more considerable batches of manuscript. At the time he wrote this first version, he had not yet ventured very far into the deep waters of experimental writing; and though the conception and evocation of the angel are magnificent and new, the plot repeats patterns he had used before, time and time again. As Daniel McKeithan has shown in *Court Trials in Mark Twain* (1958), ending a story with a trial was an old standby, recently used to good effect in *The Tragedy of Pudd'nhead Wilson, Tom Sawyer, Detective,* and *Joan of Arc*; the lawyer Wilhelm Meidling, in fact, is a sort of Austrian variation on David

9. William M. Gibson, "Mark Twain's Mysterious Stranger Manuscripts: Some Questions for Textual Critics," p. 190.

Wilson. In other words, though Mark Twain had made a strong assertion by creating his ambiguous angel, he had not yet done enough with his inspiration. Probably a desire to try his wings even further in this vein of satiric fantasy is yet another reason[10] he returned in the years ahead so lovingly, but with sporadic and fading enthusiasm, to the figure of "Young Satan."

Vienna Interlude (1898)

During the period of approximately ten months[11] between the time Mark Twain finished the first version of "Young Satan" and the time of his next attempt, the writer was far from idle. We should at least glance at those contemporary preoccupations that are related directly to the themes of "Young Satan."

The year 1898 was a major turning point in Mark Twain's career.[12] His conquest of the journalistic, liberal, and aristocratic Viennese society was almost total; indeed it was so exceptional, even in a city notorious for its love of celebrities, as to have become legendary. During the winter months, he withdrew from the limelight somewhat because of the death of brother Orion in December and the illnesses of his wife, Livy, and his daughter Jean; he was in touch with dramatic circles, however, especially with the world-renowned "Burgtheater," and he was considering becoming a sort of impresario-mediator between the Austrian stage and American and British theaters. A lecture-reading he gave early in February was enormously successful. His dramatic activities that winter included writing a play (*Is He Dead?*) and a number of translations from German, none of which were ever produced. But his strong sense of the importance of a national theater, and especially of the tradition of tragedy (exemplified by the Burgtheater production of Adolf Wilbrandt's *Der Meister von Palmyra*), found eloquent expression in an essay "About Play-Acting."

Mark Twain's characteristic interest in "transcendent figures" burgeoned with the Vienna spring. One such figure was

10. See also the excellent suggestions by Gibson (6–7) and Tuckey (*MTSatan*, pp. 39, 44–45).

11. January–October 1898.

12. For a general discussion of this problem see my essay, "Mark Twain's Final Phase."

the "Austrian Edison," inventor Jan Szczepanik, who, in March, made Twain "feel like Colonel Sellers" again; another was the Norwegian explorer Fridtjof Nansen, whom Twain met in May; yet another was the musician Theodor Leschetizky, who was teaching Twain's daughter Clara and introduced her to the young Russian-Jewish pianist Ossip Gabrilowitsch, who was to become Clemens's son-in-law in 1909.

Mark Twain's reactions to his encounters with the virulent Austrian anti-Semitism were embodied in "Concerning the Jews," where Satan and the French are brought together in a significant way:

> I can stand any society. All that I care to know, is that a man is a human being—that is enough for me; he can't be any worse. I have no special regard for Satan; but I can at least claim that I have no prejudice against him. It may even be that I lean a little his way, on account of his not having a fair show. All religions issue bibles against him, and say the most injurious things about him, but we never hear *his* side. We have none but the evidence for the prosecution, and yet we have rendered the verdict. To my mind, this is irregular. It is un-English; it is un-American; it is French. Without this precedent Dreyfus could not have been condemned. Of course Satan has some kind of a case, it goes without saying. . . . We may not pay him reverence, for that would be indiscreet, but we can at least respect his talents. A person who has for untold centuries maintained the imposing position of spiritual head of four-fifths of the human race, and political head of the whole of it, must be granted the possession of executive abilities of the loftiest order. (*Essays*, pp. 236–37)

Mark Twain traced hatred of Jews to envy of their superiority and of their being "favorites of Heaven," and he compared this hatred to that resentment of the "Yankee" for his "formidable cleverness" that had prevailed in the Mississippi Valley of his boyhood. And "even the angels dislike a foreigner. I am using this word foreigner in the German sense—stranger."

Other facets of his concern with social problems involved more overt forms of violence than anti-Semitism. Baroness Bertha von Suttner engaged his interest in a movement for world peace. In the newspapers, however, he daily encountered such realities as America's war with Spain, the Dreyfus affair, and the assassination of Austria's lovely empress at Geneva in September. The tangled web of love and hate was thus not only pervasive, but some of its political manifestations could be literally explosive and symbolically apocalyptic.

Insight into Clemens's state of mind can be gained from a notebook entry dated 7 January 1898,[13] which is just about the time that he was "completing" his first Eseldorf text. It begins: "Last Sunday I struck upon a new 'solution' of a haunting mystery"—that of the seeming duality of personality that R. L. Stevenson had recently treated in *Dr. Jekyll and Mr. Hyde* (1886). Rejecting his own earlier attempt in "The Facts Concerning the Recent Carnival of Crime in Connecticut" (1876) to explain this mystery in terms of conscience, he cited evidence found by French psychologists of the school of Charcot that an individual's "other person is in command during the somnambulic sleep"—Sam Clemens had been a sleepwalker as a boy —"that it has a memory of its own and can recall its acts when hypnotized . . . , but that *you* have no memory of its act. . . . To this arrangement I wish to add this detail—that we have a spiritualized self which can detach itself and go wandering off upon affairs of its own—for recreation, perhaps" (*MTN*, pp. 348–49). This last "dream self" has obvious affinities to the angelic "Satan" he had just been creating; furthermore, the dream self "flies to the ends of the earth in a millionth of a second. Seems to—and I believe, *does*" (350).

Clemens spent that summer of 1898 hard at work in Kaltenleutgeben, a lovely health resort near Vienna; and various mixtures of psychological understanding and fictional experimentation produced three remarkable manuscripts in the following order: "My Platonic Sweetheart"; the work Bernard DeVoto titled "The Great Dark"; and "The Man That Corrupted Hadleyburg," the only one of the three to be published during Clemens's lifetime. The links among these works and the "Stranger" texts are so many that they warrant separate study; and the major symbolic motif of dream versus reality, familiar to readers of "The Great Dark," has already been explored in rich detail by John S. Tuckey in *Mark Twain's Which Was the Dream?* (1967). At this point, I want to mention only two relevant links: the diabolic-satiric role, which hardly needs to

13. Mistakenly labeled "London, Jan. 7, '97" by Albert Bigelow Paine in *MTN*, p. 348.

be elaborated, played by the "stranger" who hoaxes the self-righteous community of Hadleyburg; and the further development of Clemens's views of the self in "Sweetheart."

There is an engaging frankness about Mark Twain's report and analysis of his recurring love dreams in "My Platonic Sweetheart" that implies, I think, a rare maturity of self-knowledge. In our present context, I want merely to draw attention to a long passage—cut by Clemens himself from a text prepared for publication but later withdrawn entirely[14]—that continued the line of speculation begun in the notebook entry of 7 January. This passage also begins with a reference to the "Carnival of Crime" article; but this time William James's *Psychology* (1890) is mentioned and the analysis is made a bit more precise by the addition of a third self, "the dream-*artist*" (my italics): This third person must be "in us," for "we *share* his memories with him." In 1898, he wrote that "of late years" he had come to distinguish "the dull *me*" (the "waking self") and his "somnambulist partner" (also "commonplace") from "my dream self" who is "another and spiritualized self who nightly or daily, at home or church or wherever the chance offers, takes a holiday for a couple of seconds." This third, artist self

> has adventures, sees wonderful things, makes love, falls over precipices, gets lost in mazes, is pursued by shrouded corpses and other horrors and cannot make headway for fright, gets mixed up in quarrels while doing his best to avoid them, enlists for the war and retreats from the field in front of the first volley, gets run away with by scared horses, tries to deliver lectures without any subject, appears in crowded drawing rooms with nothing on but a shirt; in a word, does a thousand rash and foolish things which nothing could ever persuade my workaday "me" to do.

He "then comes back home and remembers it all, with a memory for form, color and detail compared to which mine is as blank paper to a printed book." His "company" are "dream-creatures"—"that is to say, *real* creatures and immortal, not imitations like us, and perishable. . . . It seems reasonably likely

14. The cut text was published after Twain's death by Paine in 1912 and appropriately included in the volume that contained *The Mysterious Stranger* (New York: Harper and Brothers, 1916).

that dream-selves are permanent." And the dull "somnambulic sleep can be reproduced by hypnotism" (*MTP*, pp. 36A–38, 39–40). All this is a further stage in the development of our ambiguous angel and is very close to Twain's conception of the Duplicates in "No. 44."[15]

A significant detail is that the "platonic" sweetheart in this piece, unlike a "negro wench" described with vivid detail in the notebook entry of 7 January (*MTN*, pp. 351–52), is "a good girl," so that "in all the forty-six years of our acquaintanceship I have never known her to shame herself with an impropriety of conduct or utter a speech which I should not be willing that all the world might hear." It is clear, I think, that Mark Twain had not really dropped his initial inspiration but was exploring some of its implications in a variety of modes and settings.

15. The complex anatomy of the self in "No. 44" and its changing relationships to the stranger and the Duplicates are at the heart of our story. See Chapter 9.

4

"Schoolhouse Hill"

When Mark Twain took up his pen in November 1898 to start working again on the "Stranger" idea, he had recently finished "The Man That Corrupted Hadleyburg." Olivia Clemens wrote in a letter on 7 October: "I have not known Mr. Clemens for years to write with so much pleasure and energy as he has done during this last summer" (*MTP*). The "Hadleyburg" story is a masterpiece of construction and concentration: it moves swiftly, straight to the mark, without a wasted word. And it brought Mark Twain's mind back to his native soil and people. It was natural, therefore, that his next efforts to dramatize his concept of an ambiguous angel should similarly return to his very first idea, that of bringing Satan to Hannibal (the fictional St. Petersburg).

Comfortably, even luxuriously, established at the new Hotel Krantz in Vienna, and with his friend Henry H. Rogers investing Clemens's financial nest egg in Federal Steel (on 2 November, Clemens wrote him: "I would rather have that stock than be free from sin"! [*MTHHR*, p. 371]), Mark Twain began a sketch for a story in one of his notebooks:

> Story of little Satan, jr, who came to Petersburg (Hannibal) went to school, was popular and greatly liked by Huck and Tom who knew his secret. The others were jealous, and the girls didn't like him because he smelt of brimstone. *This* is the Admirable Crichton. He was always doing miracles—his pals knew they were miracles, the others thought them mysteries. He is a good little devil; but swears, and breaks the Sabbath. (428)

Not only are we back in Hannibal with Huck and Tom, but the angel is now a son of the Devil, rather than his nephew. He resembles "Young Satan" in most respects, but a radically new element is introduced by the sentence, "*This* is the Admirable Crichton" [6], which was inserted later.

In section D-2 of Clemens's working notes we find: "Meidling is the wonder of the region—the Admirable Crichton" (428). This is a variation of the "transcendent figure" idea, one that tends to take us away from the supernatural, since James Crichton was an actual child prodigy of Scottish origin (1560?–1582). Hence, there is a certain appropriateness in the sympathy and understanding Forty-four gets from "Archibald Ferguson, the old Scotch schoolmaster" (177). The Admirable Crichton "displayed considerable classical knowledge, was a good linguist, . . . and above all . . . possessed an astounding memory."[1] When Mark Twain was toying with ideas for reworking Father Peter's trial by having Father Adolf actually summon the Devil and having "Satan" act against them both, he still thought of Meidling as an "Admirable Crichton." The idea at that time seems to have been to have "Satan's" angelic powers defeat Meidling's natural, human gifts, however superior the latter were to those of the other people in "the region." Now, however, in the "little Satan" sketch, the italics in "*this* is the Admirable Crichton" indicate that Twain had realized he might blend the figure of the ambiguous angel with that of the famous prodigy of learning. This was certainly an appropriate direction to take if he was going to shift his setting to Schoolhouse Hill. In Eseldorf, the supernatural angel could demonstrate an infinite superiority to the "gifted," but merely human, young Europeans. In Hannibal, a miraculously superior being, acting like Crichton, could be used to humorously suggest the provincial backwardness of American schoolchildren.

The sentence that follows "*this* is the Admirable Crichton," with its distinction between "miracles" and "mysteries," is equally significant. In the first stage of "Young Satan," Twain was already using this difference as an important element for distinguishing the parallel plots: the boys know the angel's secret, so that the miracles "Satan" performs in the village are not mysterious to them. In "Schoolhouse," Forty-four seems to be performing miracles, but when asked: "How do you manage these things?" he replies: "I have no method—meaning I have no mystery. I see what is on the page—that is

1. *Encyclopaedia Britannica*, 14th ed., 6:690.

all" (181–82). As we shall find, a similar sort of "natural supernaturalism" is one of the keynotes throughout "Schoolhouse."

Thus, the general idea behind the "little Satan" sketch was to use both the Devil and his perhaps unfallen relative, a procedure that would make possible a certain amount of obvious fireworks of the brimstone variety and at the same time suit the naturalistic, skeptical side of Mark Twain's mind. One major feature of little Satan's ambiguity involves the problem of "his future sovereignty." A son of the Devil, indeed, might be expected some day to inherit his father's throne; and Forty-four in the "Schoolhouse" notes will be referred to as a "prince." But how could so many princes all reign in hell? And is not the Devil immortal anyway? Perhaps new hells will be created, in which these princes will some day be sovereign; and little Satan's errand on earth may be part of his preparation for rule, for his "business," as a full-fledged devil. If this was Mark Twain's intention, then perhaps study of the human race—which includes learning about sex from mortal women! —is necessary for the education of a "good" devil. The idea certainly has intriguing satiric possibilities.

By and large, Mark Twain seems to have been thinking at this time along lines parallel to those that produced his exquisite *Captain Stormfield's Visit to Heaven*, extracts from which were first published in 1909, though the idea went back to 1868. If he had ever written the story adumbrated in the "little Satan" sketch,[2]—"doing" hell this time, instead of heaven—it might have been a fit companion piece to that extravagant and touching fantasy [7].

Quarante-Quatre

"Schoolhouse," poorly integrated and unevenly written, is altogether the least satisfactory of the "Stranger" manuscripts. But it has some strong moments and clearly was a necessary digression by means of which Mark Twain could formulate certain aspects of the problems he was then exploring. When he tried to place those problems back in Hannibal, it seems, they became tangled with the complex web of associations rep-

2. See also our discussion of "The Devil's Sunday-School" (Appendix B).

resented by Tom and Huck and the rest of Clemens's childhood world; these had earlier yielded some of his best writing, but more recently the vein had finally petered out.[3] More accurately, instead of Mark Twain's working that vein for more fiction, the man Clemens was now returning to those rich memories—remarkably accurate, as both Dixon Wecter and Walter Blair discovered—for purposes of autobiography. For imaginative creation, the distancing provided by the Austrian setting would be needed.

Meanwhile, however, distracted by renewed social and political connections in Vienna, Mark Twain could indulge himself by falling back into the accustomed fictional world of St. Petersburg, by dropping first-person narration and writing as omniscient author (thus moving from the more complex mode of *Huckleberry Finn* back to that of *Tom Sawyer*), and by playing with such relatively superficial phenomena as spiritualistic séances.

A chief function of "Schoolhouse" was to help Mark Twain define more fully his newly conceived character. As in the "little Satan" sketch, he appears as a son, rather than as a nephew, of the Devil; and in the working notes (430–49) as well as in the text we can follow the vacillations of a writer in search of an appropriate name for his character. That this problem—related no doubt, however vaguely, to the traditions of the ineffable name of God and of the complex angelic hierarchies—did concern him profoundly is clear from the last speech of the angel, after he has provided the Hotchkiss family with a little devil for a servant: "Give him a name—he has one already, and so have I, but you would not be able to pronounce either of them. Goodbye" (218). A similar inability to pronounce the stranger's name will become crucial in "No. 44." In Clemens's notes we find two sets of evidence relating to this very peculiar name: one suggesting merely that a euphonious number was intended and another supporting H. N. Smith's suggestion that the number *forty-four* is a multiple of the name of the Jewish twins ("the Lev'n boys") Clemens knew in Hannibal.[4]

3. It ended with "Tom Sawyer's Conspiracy" (1897), *HH&T*, pp. 152–242 (see list of short references p. xiii). But, as we shall see at the end of this chapter, there were "More Images of Hannibal."

4. See Appendix C: "Some Possible Meanings of the Name 'No. 44.'"

We know precisely why the angel begins speaking in French. These details do not appear in the text, but the working notes make clear Mark Twain's intention: "No one knows where he eats and sleeps but Huck and Tom—it is in Paris. Papa has his chief agency there" (435). And further: "Has been 2 days in Paris and knows French" (433). This is yet another expression of Clemens's long-standing Francophobia, which was being exacerbated those days by the Dreyfus affair.

In this opening chapter we encounter, in contrast to the May setting of Eseldorf, "a frosty morning" when the children of "Petersburg village" are struggling "up the naked long slant of Schoolhouse Hill . . . against the fierce wind" (175). The basic situation is an old standby, used in the opening chapters of *Tom Sawyer,* in which a "new boy" has to be initiated into the community: "A new boy in the village was a rarer sight than a new comet in the sky" (176). A contrast is made between this stranger, "handsome beyond imagination," and last year's newcomer, Henry Bascom, "whose papa was a 'nigger' trader" and who is mean, proud, and "this year's school-bully." Immediately, the former begins behaving in a fashion compatible with his appearance, which has suggested to "some of the boys" descriptions from "books about fairy-tale princes and that sort." Beginning in French, which old Archibald Ferguson can also speak, Forty-four rapidly displays his superior intelligence, his fantastic memory (so perfect as to suggest a phonograph), and his gift for languages. Forty-four's mimicry of the Scotch schoolmaster is delightfully humorous; the entire chapter may be some sort of satire on current methods of instruction in foreign languages.

So far the strange boy has displayed chiefly a remarkable memory, but Ferguson at least is aware that "this *intellectual* conflagration" (my italics) may be something more than natural: "Truly it is a day of miracles." When asked why the Hotchkiss family took him in the previous night, Forty-four replies with biblical simplicity: "It was cold, and I was a stranger." And when Ferguson's question "Whence did you come—and how?" evokes only a silent bow, the schoolmaster realizes he has committed an "indiscretion" and humbly apologizes for leaving the room ahead of one he now clearly accepts as his superior; Mark Twain leaves open the question of whether he has recognized that the wonderful boy is a supernatural being. This is the last we shall see of "Old Ferg," whom I find to be a peculiarly vivid and satisfying fictional creation.

Bewitchments

We need to recall the detail of "Mr. Black" in the original "St. Petersburg" materials because, in the chapters that follow, Negro characters will be used to develop the idea of miracles qua witchcraft. But first the power of Forty-four is coolly displayed to defeat and humiliate the school bully, as well as his "nigger-trader" father, "an unloved man, but respected for his muscle and temper" (189)—the point being that our gentle stranger is no "Miss Nancy." The only emotion the angel shows in this episode is "despair," when he tries to understand Tom Sawyer's American slang: "It was but a poor dictionary—that French-English—and over-rich in omissions" (186–87).

The next chapter brings us to the house of Oliver and Hannah Hotchkiss, yet another of the domestic pairs remarkable for their differences of temperament that Mark Twain delighted to create. Somewhat like Clemens's brother Orion, Mr. Hotchkiss "changed his principles with the moon, his politics with the weather, and his religion with his shirt"; and "his good Presbyterian wife was as steady as an anvil. She was not a creature of change." Since "the latest thing in religions was the Fox-girl Rochester rappings," Mr. Hotchkiss "was a Spiritualist for the present." A varied group of neighbors have dropped in "to get sight of the miraculous boy."

We soon perceive that this self-righteous community has affinities with Hadleyburg, though Petersburg is more permeated with a spirit of genial humor. The most obvious link is in its worship of money, as Mr. Hotchkiss's account of his lodger's remarkable behavior makes clear:

> "He paid four weeks' board in advance—cash down! Petersburg can believe the rest, but you'll never catch it taking that statement at par."
>
> The joke had immense success; the laugh was hearty all around. Then Hotchkiss issued another fortifying laugh, and added—
>
> "And there's another wonder on top of that; I tell you a

> little at a time, so as not to overstrain you. He didn't pay in wildcat at twenty-five discount, but in a currency you've forgotten the look of—minted gold! Four yellow eagle-birds—and here they are, if you don't believe me."
>
> This was too grand and fine to be humorous; it was impressive, almost awe-inspiring. The gold pieces were passed from hand to hand and contemplated in mute reverence. (192–93)

This leads later to a satiric episode in which "a flood of gold and silver coins" pours out of Forty-four's pockets; and like Mrs. Richards in "Hadleyburg," the religious husband confesses that "I shan't sleep very well with that pile of money in the house" (198–99).

Most vivid at this point are the observations and insights provided by the elderly slave woman, Aunt Rachel, who notices such significant details as the fact that the miraculously provided new candle is of wax; as Forty-four's frequent changes of clothing; and as the transformation of the house-cat ("old Sanctified Sal"), ordinarily suspicious of strangers, into a friend of this unusual newcomer: "By Jimminy dey's bewitchment here som'ers." She also notices that not only is his pocket a cornucopia of food for the cat, but Forty-four can also speak "cat-talk" and "mouse-talk." Why had not Rachel and her husband, Jeff, told about these "bewitchments" before?

> "You reckon you'd a b'lieved Jeff? *We* b'lieves in bewitchments, caze we knows dey's so; but you-all only jist laughs at 'em. Does you reckon you'd a b'lieved me, Miss Hannah?—does you?"
>
> "Well—no."
>
> "Den you'd a laughed at me. Does a po' nigger want to git laughed at any mo' d'n white folks? No, Miss Hannah, dey don't. We's got our feelin's, same as *you*-all, alldough we's ign'ant en black." (196)

A further form of "witchcraft" briefly displayed at this point involves love: Annie Fleming, niece of the Hotchkisses, "had lost her tender little inexperienced heart to the new boy without suspecting it"; "she was just turned eighteen" and worships Forty-four "as the fire-worshipers worship the sun" (196–97). The comedy of love, to be elaborated at great length in "No. 44," is not developed at all in "Schoolhouse," but Mark Twain's early intention is formulated in a working note:

> Has never seen a human girl or woman until now. *Except in heaven*
> Hellfire Hotchkiss./*Annie Fleming*. He feels a strange and charming interest in her. By the books he gathers that this is "love"—the kind that sex arouses. There is no such thing among his brothers and sisters. He studies it in the books. It seems very beautiful in the books. Presently the passion for Hellfire grows—becomes absorbing—is mutual. Papa uneasy—he is the only person who knows 44's secret. 44 sees that the happiness of hell—which is purely intellectual—*is tame compared to this love.* [emphasis added in pencil] He has found more in this random visit to earth than he bargained for.
> In time he is obliged to tell his secret to Hellfire—horror! Heartbreaking scene. He has done *wrong*? Denies it. (438)

There are many problems here. The link with "Hellfire Hotchkiss" is complicated by the fact that, in the manuscript devoted to her (completed over a year earlier, in Switzerland), she had been a tomboy, "the only genuwyne male man in this town" (*S&B*, p. 187).

Further, we may be somewhat puzzled by the "purely intellectual" happiness of hell, which elsewhere in the notes is described in its more familiar role as a place of torment; but we recall that in the "little Satan" sketch there was a "pleasure Lake" in hell. At this stage, as we shall see, the ambiguity of our angel figure includes his having been raised "partly in hell" (109) and the fact that the only emotion he had thus far displayed was indeed an intellectual despair at his inability to understand Tom's language. Finally, here the Devil is "the only person who knows Forty-four's secret"; but in "little Satan," Huck and Tom also know his true identity.

No doubt these and related uncertainties—about attitudes toward hell, sex, love and about other emotions—contributed to Mark Twain's decision to abandon the "Schoolhouse" version at this time. Half a decade later, however, after shifting the character Forty-four to Austria, he would feel freer to explore playfully these and other touchy areas.

Wavering Points of View

The deeper Mark Twain got into his "Schoolhouse" version, the more miscellaneous his episodes became. By the end of chapter 3 he had effectively established the presence of Forty-four in Petersburg as an "extraordinary person," first in the school, and then in the eyes of the neighbors forgathered in the Hotchkiss house. Where could he go from there? With a few exceptions, the episodes that follow are poorly contrived, for the most part repeating stale ideas from previous writings. For example, a dialogue between Hotchkiss and the marvelous boy makes rather banal use of whiskey and tobacco but then supplies some fresh details about the "foreigner." He was raised "partly in heaven, partly in hell"; his father is Satan; and his "servants" are "little devils" who appear in the room:

> Trim and shapely little fellows they were; velvety little red fellows, with short horns on their heads and spiked tails at the other end; and those that stood, stood in metal plates, and those that sat—on chairs, in a row upon settees, and on top of the bookcase with their legs dangling—had metal plates under them—"to keep from scorching the furniture," the boy quietly explained, "these have come but this moment, and of course are hot, yet." (211)

Various elements are blending in this sequence. "Satan's" act of bringing a newly published book from the British Museum in the interval "while you were stooping for your pipe and glass" (210) illustrates the idea stated in the 7 January note that the "unhampered spiritualized body flies to the ends of the earth in the millionth of a second"; a conception that there refers to dreams is now transferred to the angel. The devil servants, called "slaves" later by Mr. Hotchkiss (219), understand "only French."

The ambiguities we noted earlier involving the angel in "Young Satan" are even more evident now, and Mark Twain tries to clarify some of them by toying with the idea of a hierarchy of devils corresponding to some of the traditional hierarchies of angels. Thus, these "servants" are not "relatives" of Forty-four, but "sons of my father's *subordinates*" (my italics); and Forty-four himself is "not a devil" (212–13). Mark Twain's problem here is clarified somewhat by one of the working notes: "His associates have always been his devil brothers and sisters—a vast multitude, not named, but numbered. *They* have no wives nor children—there is no third generation" (437). This notion was probably related, in some way, to the one of having Forty-four learn about love and sex from a human woman: there must be a degree of novelty for him in the earthly experience.

It may be difficult at first to see how Forty-four could have brothers who were devils and not be a devil himself. The solution lies in the fact that his brothers and sisters are "all in heaven except the few thousands born in hell in the past 7 days" (444). In other words, his double relationship to heaven and hell enables him to be both "an actual angel and son of a devil" (217). Whatever logical sense this might make, such a basic ambiguity could prove a fatal obstacle to a storyteller, who needs a reasonably firm conception of his main character and a correspondingly firm point of view. The ambiguity persists in "Young Satan," but it has been smoothed over there by making the angel the Devil's nephew.

Errors and Errands

In any case, the plot of "Schoolhouse"—what there is of it—has more or less petered out when Forty-four reveals his identity to Hotchkiss. There is some further play with the "genuine little devil" servant, a "red stranger" Hotchkiss named "Edward Nicholson Hotchkiss—after a brother that was dead" (218)—a detail difficult to disassociate from the fact that Samuel Clemens's own brother Orion had died just a year earlier. Mr. Hotchkiss persuades Aunt Rachel and Uncle Jeff that "there was no harm in this devil, but a great deal of good. . . . We have been misinformed about devils" (219). For one thing, "he can run errands—any errand you want, Rachel"—within limits, it seems, because at the end we see him "trying to tame the cat and not succeeding." That is the end of the action in this manuscript.

What does remain to be noted, however, is an important dialogue in chapter 5 between Hotchkiss and his lodger in which Mark Twain's conception of his angel figure was partially reformulated. Explaining that he is fifteen "years" old, Forty-four somewhat confusingly tries to clarify the ratio between human and angelic time: "A day, with us, is as a thousand years with you."[5] Hotchkiss says, "It is astronomy to me"; and the angel adds, "Measurements of time and eternity are merely conveniences; they are not of much importance."

Forty-four's retelling of the story of the Fall, which happened "a week ago,"[6] is for the most part traditional:

> "I was in heaven; I had always lived in heaven, of course; until a week ago, my father had always lived there. But I saw this little world created. I was interested; we were all interested." . . .
>
> "Is hell so new?"
>
> "It was not needed before. No Adam in any of the millions of other planets had ever disobeyed and eaten of the forbidden fruit."
>
> "It is strange."
>
> "No—for the others were not tempted."
>
> "How was that?"
>
> "There was no tempter until my father ate of the fruit himself and became one. Then he tempted other angels and they ate of it also; then Adam and the woman." (214–15)

That Satan ate the forbidden fruit first is the traditional story he himself tells in Milton's *Paradise Lost* (book 9, lines 575–601).

What seems most original in Mark Twain's version is his statement, however hesitant, that an error underlay Satan's original act:

> "Now why he was moved to taste it himself is not clear; I shall never know until he tells me. But his error was . . . in supposing that a knowledge of the difference between good and evil was *all* that the fruit could confer."
>
> "Did it confer more than that?"
>
> "Consider the passage which says *man is prone to evil as the sparks to fly upward.* Is that true? Is that really the nature

5. But the details that follow were not carefully worked out: "A *minute* of our time is 41⅔ years of yours" should obviously read: "An *hour* of our time" (my italics); see the correct calculation in a working note (443).

6. Compare "That Day in Eden (Passage from Satan's Diary)," in which the Fall occurs after one hundred years (*Essays*, pp. 668–72).

> of man?—I mean your man—the man of this planet?"
> "Indeed it is—nothing could be truer." (216)

This somber version of man is quoted from the Book of Job (5:7).

> "It is not true of the men of any other planet. It explains the mystery. My father's error stands revealed in all its nakedness. The fruit's office was not confined to conferring the mere knowledge of good and evil, it conferred also the passionate and eager and hungry *disposition to DO evil. . . .*[7] Ah, my father's error brought a colossal disaster upon the men of this planet. It *poisoned* the men of this planet—poisoned them in mind and body. I see it, plainly."
> "It brought death, too."
> "Yes—whatever that may be. I do not quite understand it. It seems to be a sleep. You do not seem to mind sleep. By my reading I gather that you are not conscious of either death *or* sleep; that nevertheless you fear the one and do not fear the other. It is very stupid. Illogical." (216)

One may be surprised, especially given Mark Twain's interests, not to find Hotchkiss drawing attention here to a consciousness of dreams in sleep, the fear of which in death gave Hamlet pause.

The distinction between miracle and mystery established earler is sustained: in "Schoolhouse," as in "Young Satan," there is no mystery about the identity of the stranger. The "mystery" referred to here concerns the origin of sin and evil in the great fallen archangel, and it is traced to an error of the intellect. (We are not told the motivation behind the first act of disobedience: "I shall never know.")

Of central importance for our understanding of Mark Twain's conception of his angel is the statement that follows:

> "The fundamental change wrought in man's nature by my father's conduct must remain—it is permanent; but a part of its burden of evil consequences can be lifted from your race, and I will undertake it. Will you help? . . . I cannot map out a

7. Writing about a year earlier, Mark Twain had "Satan" tell the boys in Eseldorf: "We cannot do wrong; neither have we any *disposition* to do it; for we do not *know* what it is" (49, my italics).

> definite plan yet; *I must first study this race.* Its poisoned condition and prominent disposition to do evil differentiate it radically from any men whom I have known before, therefore it is a new race to me and must be exhaustively studied before I shall know where and how to begin. Indefinitely speaking, our plan will be confined to *ameliorating the condition* of the race in some ways in *this*[8] life; we are not called upon to concern ourselves with its future fate; that is in abler hands than ours."
>
> "I hope you will begin your studies right away."
>
> "I shall. Go to bed, and take your rest. During the rest of the night and to-morrow *I will travel about the globe* and personally examine some of the nationalities, and learn languages and read the world's books in the several tongues, and to-morrow night we will talk together here." (217)

This reunion never does take place in the fragmentary "Schoolhouse," of course; but three points made in this dialogue were soon to be incorporated in "Young Satan":

First, there are various attempts to improve the human condition, to ameliorate "a part" of the "burden of evil consequences" of the Fall "in this life."

Second, the project of "studying" the human race in its various nationalities and languages provides the basis of some of the excursions made by "Satan" with Theodor. Study and amelioration are the two chief burdens of the angel's "purpose in coming to the earth" (213).

A third point later used in "Young Satan" relates to the ambiguities of knowledge and feeling we found in the angel. The Devil's error was in not perceiving—until he had the actual experience of eating the apple—the difference between mere theoretical or intellectual "knowledge of good and evil" and the active or willful "disposition to *DO* evil" [8].

More Images of Hannibal

Such was the angel's situation at the end of the "Schoolhouse" text itself; but we have in addition a fairly large body of working notes from that period (436–49) that provide clues to Mark Twain's further intentions. As might be expected, they are all oriented to the Hannibal-Petersburg setting and to

8. Mark Twain's italics; all the other emphases in this passage are mine.

the conception mixing the Admirable Crichton and the son of the Devil. In general terms, the idea permeating all these materials is the romantic one of genius (Nietzsche's Overman) as satanic or "demoniac" (Dionysian). Mark Twain was toying with an idea he had shared over two decades earlier with his brother Orion for "doing" hell; and he was also embodying some of his paradoxical ideas about good, evil, and the Moral Sense in the project of a "Devil's Sunday-School." If he had really let himself go on this theme, he might have achieved something approaching Blake's *Marriage of Heaven and Hell*; but, in actuality, the closest thing to this in his later writings is the powerfully ironic effect of the accumulated maxims in "Pudd'nhead Wilson's Calendar."

One need not probe very far to understand why Mark Twain dropped work on "Schoolhouse" at this time. He had been drifting along, with little sense of direction, and most of the writing was uninspired; by way of contrast, the beginning he had made with "Young Satan" had turned out very well—"horribly beautiful." He had now settled in his mind various issues about the angel's character and functions that had been troubling him. He was probably still anxious not to hurt Livy, any more than he might have to, by publishing his "wicked gospel"; it was more comfortable, therefore, to express those unconventional ideas in a European, rather than an American, setting.

Spring had come again to Vienna, and after some relatively quiet and unproductive months early in 1899 Clemens's thoughts were directed toward leaving Austria and going home to the States—though two full summers were yet to pass before he actually left Europe. It was probably in April that he began working again on his "bible," which would eventually appear as *What Is Man?*. And the following month he resumed writing, with renewed enthusiasm, on "The Chronicle of Young Satan."

But though both "Young Satan" and "No. 44" were Austrian tales, Mark Twain had not given up The Matter of Hannibal in writing them. In his pioneering essay, "Mark Twain's Images of Hannibal,"[9] Henry Nash Smith describes the print-shop story as the last phase in a developing image: "For Eseldorf

9. *Discussions*, pp. 92–103.

is Hannibal. In writing this story Mark Twain is destroying the image which had served him for thirty years as a metaphor for all human society" (p. 102). Actually the Matters of Hannibal and Europe were later interwoven in complicated ways; and Smith's notion of an image completely "destroyed" is therefore oversimplified [9]. In that final decade, Hannibal did not so much disappear as become transformed in radical ways. Mark Twain never abandoned Huck Finn and Nigger Jim: they were pushed underground but kept popping up with a remarkable persistency.

5

"The Chronicle of Young Satan"

After Mark Twain had gone back to his Eseldorf story, he wrote Howells: "Twice I didn't start it right; and got pretty far in, both times, before I found it out. But I am sure it is started right this time." This statement is a natural source of confusion. I have interpreted the two false starts—because of the phrase, "got pretty far in"—to be the first Eseldorf section (1897–1898) and "Schoolhouse" (1898), since both are substantial bodies of manuscript. But if one emphasizes the idea of not "starting right," the two wrong attempts might be the "St. Petersburg Fragment" (1897) and "Schoolhouse"; that is, the two fragments with American settings.

In any case, the fact remains that, in May 1899, Mark Twain did not start over again; nor did he make extensive new alterations in the Eseldorf manuscript (520–28). I imagine he simply reread what he had written of "Young Satan," and, finding it good enough on the whole, picked up the thread where he had left it in January 1898.

He was putting aside for the moment the character Forty-four and going back to writing about the Devil's nephew, rather than about his possible son. He had clarified, in his mind and in his notes, some of the problems of time ratios, heaven and hell, love and sex, witchcraft, and the like. Above all, he had an awareness that Satan's error had arisen from a failure to distinguish between a purely intellectual "knowledge" of good and evil and a felt-and-experienced knowledge[1] of evil that includes the disposition to act evilly.

Concretely, he was launched now into a part of his tale concerned not so much with Satan's error as with man's mistaken estimate of his own "character and powers and qualities

1. This is actually closer to the usage of the Hebrew Bible, where "knowing" a woman means to love her in the sexual sense.

and *his place among the animals*" (my italics). And despite some extremely powerful episodes and passages, the material would become increasingly miscellaneous, tending at times toward incoherence.

To summarize: Mark Twain now realized that he had already started his Austrian tale right and could go on well from the point where he had left off—with Father Peter in prison, Marget friendless, and Ursula learning to tell "a new kind of lie." Ursula does in fact take the center of the stage for a while, as "Satan" continues the education of this representative "Austrian" (Bohemian) peasant woman. Her faith is a radical and sturdy one: "The rich don't care for anybody but themselves; it's only the poor that have feeling for the poor, and help them. The poor and God. God will provide for this kitten" (65). But when Ursula adds, "Not a sparrow falls to the ground without His seeing it," she has no answer to the angel's pointed question, "But it falls, just the same. What good is seeing it fall?" This is the problem of evil in little, and Ursula is horrified and helpless when it is presented baldly to her peasant mind.

Along with his Socratic questioning, "Satan" supplies demonstrations of his teachings. His very presence is invigorating: "The old woman jumped to her feet . . . as briskly as a young girl. . . . That was Satan's influence; he was a fresh breeze to the weak and the sick, wherever he came." In fact, then, it *is* God—or rather his ambiguous angel—who gives strength to the weak kitten, which then provides "Satan" with a device for supplying the needs of Father Peter's family. He calls it a "Lucky Cat" and, overcoming Ursula's superstitious fears by appealing to her cupidity, puts money in her pocket:

> In her heart she probably believed it was a witch-cat and an agent of the devil; but no matter, it was all the more certain to be able to keep its contract and furnish a daily good living for the family, for in matters of finance even the piousest of our peasants would have more confidence in an arrangement with the devil than with an archangel. (67)

And when "Satan" later, in his role as Philip Traum, reassures her about the cat, "Don't be troubled—it will provide," she responds with a fervor conveyed by one of Mark Twain's most effective sentences: "That sponged the slate of Ursula's feelings clean of its anxieties, and a deep financial joy shone in her eyes" (70). She has been completely "converted" by the angel.

Noteworthy at this point is a change in emphasis that subordinates the other boys and brings Theodor and his family strongly to the fore. The narrative shift is from a predominance of "we boys" to the first-person singular: "I was in trouble . . . I was walking along the path, feeling very downhearted" (64). In the Paine-Duneka text, Theodor is closely involved for a period with the affairs of Father Peter and Marget, as spectator and friend, but that side of the relationship does not seem well motivated or developed. When Father Adolf accuses the good father of theft and the boys are the latter's only witnesses, we are told:

> Our parents were harder on us than any one else. Our fathers said we were disgracing our families, and they commanded us to purge ourselves of our lie, and there was no limit to their anger when we continued to say we had spoken true. Our mothers cried over us and begged us to give back our bribe and get back our honest names and save our families from shame, and come out and honorably confess. (62)

In the Paine-Duneka *Stranger* (as in "Young Satan") the following accusation appears in the singular: Marget's being "in need of friends . . . was my parents' fault, not mine, and I couldn't help it" (64).

In the abridged *Stranger*, Theodor's parents fall into the background, reappearing only after the "witchcraft" party given by Marget; then the families of all three boys gather in Theodor's home, and Theodor's father takes the lead in the discussion about the threat of "The Interdict!" (chapter 7). Throughout most of the 1899 additions, however, the *three* families—Marget's and Thodor's and "Satan's"—are very much present, along with the entire village community. By merely wishing (67), Theodor brings himself and "Satan" into Marget's parlor, though "Marget wondered how we got in without her hearing us." The angel "seemed only interested in being friendly and telling lies," but this "was no harm in him, for he was only an angel and did not know any better" (71). Was he really lying, however, as Theodor thought?

There is a well-sustained tone of humorous irony and double entendre throughout this episode, of the kind we have been calling Huck Finnian, as Philip Traum tells Marget about his uncle "in business down in the tropics," and so forth. From one of the passages cut by Paine and Duneka, we learn that "Satan's" uncle had "business everywhere," traded in "souls," and lived in "a colony" of mixed nationality "but mainly French" (68–69). Our angel flatters Ursula, and says,

> he hoped some day to bring her and his uncle together. Very soon Ursula was mincing and simpering around in a ridiculous girly way, and smoothing out her gown and prinking at herself like a foolish old hen, and all the time pretending she was not hearing what Satan was saying. I was ashamed, for it showed us to be what Satan considered us, a silly race and trivial. Satan said it was time his uncle was married, for he entertained a great deal, and always had company staying with him, and to have a clever woman presiding over the festivities would double the attractions of the place . . .
>
> Marget thought he must be a most lovable gentleman and much sought after. Satan said he was; and a great help to the clergy—but for him they would have to go out of business. (71)

(This last, anticlerical paragraph was also cut by Paine and Duneka.) At this stage, clearly, Mark Twain's imagination was still playing with ideas adumbrated in the "little Satan" sketch—notably those relating to visiting hell and having its prince come to earth and establish a Sunday school.

In general, these pages have introduced the stranger, Philip Traum, into the community, by way of Marget's household, and have explained his family connections in greater detail. After humorous episodes in which their encounters with "Satan" are skillfully modulated by the angel to the levels of understanding and intelligence appropriate to mistress and servant, both Marget and Ursula have succumbed to his spell, become invigorated, and accepted the bounty provided by "Satan."

Animals and Witchcraft

But Mark Twain had not forgotten one main drift of his plan at this point: to examine man's place among the animals. After the angel has shown Theodor the jail and the factory as his two main illustrations of man's inhumanity to man, he derides the human race: "They think themselves better than dogs" (74). The Clemens family, especially Jean, were active proponents of movements for the prevention of cruelty to animals (antivivisection, and the like), and here the loyal dog is given his special innings; whereas in "No. 44" the cat will take pride of place, as we shall see. The episode that follows tells of "Hans Oppert, the village loafer," who was "always clubbing his dog, which is a good dog, and is his only friend." The dog exhibits the Christian virtue of forgiveness to his beloved master: "What do you think of your race? Is heaven reserved for *it*, and this dog ruled out, as your teachers tell you? Can your race add anything to this dog's stock of morals and magnanimities?" (76). A final touch of anticlerical irony is supplied, this time by Seppi, who says, "the dog had forgiven the man that had wronged him so, and maybe God would accept that absolution *in place of the priest's*" (my italics).

The satiric point of Mark Twain's inverted chain of being was to criticize man's perverse and cruel uses of the Moral Sense; and no use was more striking, or more appropriate to the Eseldorf setting, than that justifying a belief in witchcraft and justifying the persecutions resulting from that belief. In the section that follows (77–89), a rhythmic pattern reappears that was earlier established by having the angel leave from time to time on "errands." In the first part, he is absent: "There was a very dull week, now, for Satan did not come" (opening of chapter 4). Later he returns, crashes Marget's party—"It's the young stranger we hear so much about and can't get sight of, he is away so much" (85)—and saves Marget from the imputation of witchcraft.

Whatever particular sources in literature and life may be found for the excursus into witchcraft that follows, the time periods chosen for both "Stranger" tales were notably rich in such developments, as Clemens was well aware. A manuscript fragment that came to light after the *Stranger Manuscripts* was published describes "The Great Witchcraft Madness" as appearing in America for "a historical moment—that is to say, a year or thereabouts"—a reference to the Salem trials in 1692. Therefore, its "domestic interest for us" is relatively minor; whereas in Europe "the business of pitilessly and persistently and systematically" persecuting witches "dates back only four centuries and lasted in full vigor only two of the four" (DV

129 (4)—*MTP*). That is, going back from about 1890, the two centuries in question would extend from 1490 to 1690; and "No. 44" and "Young Satan" could thus be seen as historical fictions dealing with the inception and termination of vigorous and systematic witch-hunting in Europe.

We eventually move back to Father Peter's household and the community: Father Adolf rightly suspects that "there was witchcraft at the bottom" of Marget's affluence (81) and decides to bring this "outrage" into the open when she announces a party for forty guests. With "Satan" away, the forces of evil seem capable of defeating those of good. The majority of the villagers are following their all-too-human instincts of self-interest and fear; and even the boys fail to warn Marget of her danger: "We found we were not manly enough nor brave enough to do a generous action when there was a chance that it could get us into trouble" (82). The evil father is puzzled at this "new kind of witchcraft": "No apparitions, no incantations, no thunder," and "Satan" "the discoverer of it!" He feels himself on the verge of a double triumph and soon invades Marget's party, where he "began to eat, with a grand appetite," in his gross way. One might expect him to avoid religiously the delicacies provided by witchcraft; but this hypocrite has "no fear of the Devil," as we recall.

Literary success is all in the style and the managing, and my imagination is engaged here by the gradualness with which the angel makes his presence felt, a process that culminates when, as "a transparent film," "Satan" melts into the priest's body and makes him go wild before the eyes of the bewildered community. There is a fine poetic justice displayed—since Adolf's character is really that of a sanctimonious devil—when "Satan" turns the priest's own weapons against him; the scenes in which the possessed father, inspired by the angel, goes gracefully berserk (85–87) are subtly humorous. And the following scene, in which the boys' fathers interpret and react to the events at the party, is also effective. This time, they note, the hated father's crucifix has not protected him from "this awful visitation of witches and devils"; and they are torn between the threat of an interdict and their lingering fear of Adolf and his malicious ways.

The village plot, in sum, has been successfully deepened and thickened in these pages, insofar as it relates to the conflict between the good priest and the evil priest; at the same time, we are provided with further illustrations of humanity degraded in the name of religion and of the Moral Sense.

Lovers and the Angel

But intermediate between the public theme of witchcraft and the private story of Theodor's relations with "Satan" is the private-public realm (as it were) of love and sex. In this area, because of his relative immaturity, Theodor can only be an adolescent spectator, though Mark Twain involves him intimately by having part of the story revolve around his sister, Lilly. This is one of the points at which the gap between the narrator's present age and his age at the time of the story is stressed: Theodor speaks of "not knowing much about women then—nor now, probably" (109). A pair of young lovers may feel themselves alone on an island of bliss, but of course their families, and ultimately the entire community, are also concerned.

This aspect of "Young Satan" was greatly lessened and confused by a long cut (90–111) made by Paine and Duneka; the cut section culminated in the following summary paragraph:

> I went to my bed with heavy thoughts. What a lot of dismal haps had befallen the village, and certainly Satan seemed to be the father of the whole of them: Father Peter in prison, on account of the money laid in his way by Satan, which furnished Father Adolf the handy pretext he needed; Marget's household shunned and under perilous suspicion on account of that cat's work—cat furnished by Satan; Father Adolf acquiring a frightful and odious reputation, and likely to be burnt at the stake presently—Satan responsible for it; *my parents worried, perplexed, distressed about their daughter's new love-freak and the doubtfulness of its outlook; Joseph crushed and shamed;* Wilhelm's heart broken and dissipation laying its blight upon his character, his ambition and his fair repute; *Marget gone silly, and our Lilly following after;* the whole village prodded and pestered into a pathetic delirium about non-existent witches and quaking in its shoes: the whole wide wreck and desolation

> of hearts and hopes and industries the work of Satan's enthusiastic diligence and morbid passion for business. And he, the author of all the trouble, was the only person concerned that got any rapture out of it. By his spirits one would think he was grateful to be alive and improving things. (111)

I have italicized here the parts referring to situations and characters that were eliminated in the *Stranger* text.

The twenty-odd pages cut by Paine and Duneka help lighten and humanize the story and increase its relevance to the life of Samuel Clemens [**10**]. The figure of Wilhelm is much less perfunctory in "Young Satan" than in the *Stranger*: this young lawyer (shades of "Pudd'nhead" David Wilson) also writes poetry that Marget thinks "beautiful" and is the "champion at chess in all that region" (91); so that when he is completely outdone at both these skills by Philip Traum, the contrast is all the more emphatic. And with chapter 5, which follows, allusions to the Clemens family begin to multiply. Theodor goes for "five days' holiday . . . on my uncle's farm in the country," which reminds us of Uncle John Quarles's farm, where young Sam used to spend his summers and which was a "heavenly place for a boy" (*MTA,* 1:96). The father and mother of Theodor are given not only names (Rupert and Marie) but also definite characters; and Mark Twain makes an interesting Freudian slip here—to which attention is drawn by Gibson[2] —when he makes Theodor's father the judge (95, 100—shades of Judge Clemens), rather than Nikolaus's father as was stated earlier (43, 88). And so much attention is generally paid by biographers to Twain's brothers, Orion and Henry, that we usually forget that Sam Clemens had two sisters, Pamela and Margaret. Pamela, the one who married Samuel Moffett, may have entered into the characterization of Lilly [**11**].

Including Lilly in the story enabled Mark Twain to give fuller development to the love plot. Contrasted to Marget's Wilhelm is "Joseph Fuchs the brewer's son and heir" (100), who is in love with Lilly and who has few talents other than the inherited wealth of his nouveau-riche father but has plenty of vanity and is "a good enough young fellow": "he was honest and clean and true, and had warm affections and deep feelings" (101). Theodor feels sorry for his sister:

2. See textual note 95.36 (511).

> For this was a man, and could meet her on her own human level, and make her brief breath of life happy, and share with her the peace and oblivion of the grave afterward; whereas in her innocence and ignorance she was *fixing her heart of flesh upon a spirit*, a wanderer of the skies, an object as unattainable as a comet and not more competent to meet the requirements of a this-world fellowship. (101, my italics)

Joseph calls the angel a "magician" and strikes home with a penetrating question: "We all know Father Adolf is possessed of a devil; that being the case, what is the matter with Philip Traum?" (103).

But, as Theodor later comments (chapter 6), from his vantage point of adult experience: "I ought to have known that when a woman gets her head set, particularly in a love matter, she hasn't any sense" (109); and Lilly remains enchanted by "Satan" and jealous of Marget. The two couples are counterpointed; and "when Wilhelm Meidling came walking in . . . he seemed like an angel of deliverance, specially commissioned by Providence" (104)—though this "angel" is under the influence of liquor!

Kinds of Knowledge

Along with the traditionally comic business of love rivalry, these pages dig a bit deeper into the problem of angelic versus human kinds of knowledge and experience. Since a priest could not marry, the question of whether "Satan" is "studying for the ministry," as he told Theodor's father (96), or is going to aim at the "higher" profession of authorship, with a plan "to write the history of the Roman jurisprudence and codify the Roman laws" (99), as he told Lilly, is important—not only for Lilly's sake, but for the sanity of the reader, who probably thinks that an understanding of jurisprudence requires some conception of justice and value! Our angel's ambiguity—at least, to readers with merely human perceptions—remains unresolved, since he persists in using the language of ordinary evaluation (if not necessarily of "morality"), as when he says later, "we do not know good fortune from bad, and are always mistaking the one for the other" (129).

The only possible way of coping with these ambiguities, as we have said, is to make distinctions among the kinds of knowledge; and some of these are briefly explored with reference to poetry, music, and chess. "Satan," when he performs fantastic feats of memory and prediction in playing chess, as well as in performing poetry and music, reminds us of Forty-four in "Schoolhouse."

Lilly's jealous lover, Joseph Fuchs, expresses the ordinary man's view of Philip Traum: he is doing "things which the people can't understand" (101), is probably "possessed of a devil" or is a "magician," and "they'll burn him, soon" (103). Lilly's own feelings are aroused and indirectly defined when Wilhelm comes and reports Marget's strange behavior: "I worship him!" Marget has said, in reference to "Satan"; and though Wilhelm's own jealousy is inflamed with drink, he does not blame her, since "it is a madness, you see; it is enchantment" (106–7). But the true nature of Lilly's "silliness" comes out in the dialogue with her brother: "What do you know about Philip Traum? Nothing. . . . Do we know what the laws are which govern him?" Theodor's reaction is: "Of course I knew" —by which he means that he knew the secret of Traum's angelic identity—"but it was not my privilege to let out that fact" (110).

The problem may have been one of fictional "fact," on a very elementary level; but it was probably a desire to go beyond—to play (however absurdly, grotesquely, satirically) with further complications inherent in the "mystery"—that was to lead Mark Twain, in the years ahead, to make another try, to write "No. 44." Here, he merely gave Lilly a pathetically brief speech:

> Through my sympathies, my perceptions and my love I know him; know him as no one else knows him; know him as no one else can ever know him. And you shall not take my golden hope from me—no one shall! He will love me yet, and only me.

This sentimental touch—as well as Theodor's response: "There was a glory in her eyes that made her beautiful. I had not the heart to spoil it"—operates too melodramatically, too crudely, to convey what one senses, from other parts of the "Young Satan" fragments, Mark Twain was striving to express. To fully formulate his ideas, he would need one more spell of work on "Young Satan," all of his work on "No. 44," as well as other occasions on which various kinds of knowledge, and self-knowledge, could be explored.

London Interlude (1899–1900)

Between October 1899, when he probably put aside the "Young Satan" manuscript, and June 1900, when he took it up again, Clemens was living in London so that Jean could have the "six or nine months" of additional Kellgren treatments thought necessary for her cure. On 17 May, he wrote to Rogers that Jean had "passed the main crisis and turned a corner"; and the following month a rejuvenated Mark Twain resumed work on "Young Satan."

As was usual for most of his best work, Mark Twain had found a rural setting for the summer; early in July 1900 he moved to Dollis Hill in Kilburn, half an hour from the heart of the city. On 31 July, he wrote to Rogers: "There are 6 acres of hay and sheep, the lawn is spacious and there are plenty of old forest trees for shade." "We could not be more secluded nor more thoroughly in the country, if we were fifty miles from London. . . . I like it here; I haven't been to town for three weeks." He speaks of "the tale I am writing" as one he would like to go on with after his return to the States in the fall. He had only three full months of relaxed creation, however, before he reached the end of his resources for "The Chronicle of Young Satan."

The second half of "Young Satan" (111–74), written for the most part in London and in the peace and quiet of Dollis Hill, represents the final fruit of Mark Twain's residences in Vienna, Sanna, and London. Though these pages are subject to the same criticism as the Sanna pages—they are similarly fragmentary and poorly integrated—there is a noteworthy improvement in the quality of most of the writing [**12**].

Issues of determinism versus freedom, and the radical gap between the human and the angelic, still remain central. But the problem of scale—as expressed by the statement retained in chapter 7: "You people do not suspect that all of your acts are of one size and importance, but it is true; to snatch at *an appointed fly* is as big with fate for you as is any other appointed act" (my italics)—is given more elaborate, and more satiric, treatment. That little fly bulks much larger, as do animals in general [**13**].

Determinism, Freedom, and Life Plans

The main emphasis in the midde section had been on man's satirically conceived inferiority to the "higher animals," as it is displayed preeminently in his capacity for witch-hunting. Now Mark Twain was going back to the double purpose Forty-four had formulated at the end of "Schoolhouse": to study, and ameliorate the condition of, the damned human race. Central to the earliest pages (written probably during the first days in London) are ironic reverberations in the phrase that concludes the summary paragraph we have quoted, describing "Satan's" pleasure "to be alive and *improving things*" (111, my italics). What does *improve* mean here? Is it the same as *ameliorate*? And what about salvation in the life to come? We recall that in "Schoolhouse" Forty-four says, about the conditions of the human race: "We are not called upon to concern ourselves with its future fate; that is in abler hands than ours" (219).

In any case, there is no doubting the seriousness of the sections that follow (111–33): along with the opening chapters written in 1897–1898, they are the chief basis for finding qualities of literary greatness in "Young Satan." (Paine and Duneka retained all these pages, making only minor revisions.) The sequence is well organized and beautifully sustained in style and tone, on the whole; the flaws are minor and remarkably few for an unrevised manuscript.

The uncertainties at the beginning are obvious. Mark Twain was launching on new seas, with the courage of a true discoverer. Having wound his village plot up into a bundle of knots, he was happy to put these aside for a while and let his story travel—"for change of scene shifts the mind's burdens to the other shoulder and banishes old shop-worn weariness from mind and body both" (112). Why to China? Gibson informs us that Clemens, angered at the time by the role of the European powers in the Boxer Rebellion, and by the role of the British in the Boer War, had "Satan" refer sardonically to both situations in chapters 6 and 8 (7). But with the freedom of a creator, Mark Twain quickly brushed these contemporary references aside—"I will go into that by and by . . . it would interrupt my tale to do it now"—and sat Theodor and "Satan" down on a mountaintop for a Socratic dialogue [**14**].

The germ idea for this dialogue seems to have come from

the "little Satan" sketch, where the Devil was to be converted to Methodism and change his ways. So here: "We talked together, and I had the idea of trying to reform Satan and persuade him to lead a better life. I . . . begged him to be more considerate and stop making people unhappy." The ironies are obvious, relating back to earlier ideas about the Moral Sense and to some of the ambiguities that lurked in Mark Twain's use of such terms as *amelioration, improvement,* and, here, *a better life.* Now he was ready to tackle this problem head-on and relate it further to the fact of determinism. To Theodor's untutored understanding, the angel's behavior seems "impulsive and random," but "Satan" soon makes clear that he always knows precisely what he is doing and what all of the consequences will be. The gap between crudely human views of causality and the angel's infinitely rich knowledge (for all practical purposes, omniscience) creates a series of ironies that Mark Twain develops with consummate skill.

The sequence has two parts, theoretical and practical-illustrative: first the angel tries to explain his view of human destiny, and then the truth of that view is demonstrated in chapter 7. As to the theories: the view of man as a combined "suffering-machine" and "happiness-machine," with a tendency toward a predominance of "suffering"; the contrast between real intellect of the angelic sort and man's "foolish little vanities" and "Moral Sense"; and so forth—all this we have encountered before and will encounter again in *What is Man?.* The relatively new insistence here on scale is related, no doubt, to Mark Twain's imaginative play with the ratios between human time and angelic time, which we have already expounded. Again, the chain of being is involved; having already challenged tradition by inverting the human and animal positions in that chain, he was now proceeding to question the cosier implications of that orderly view of the universe. Not only was man's position less exalted than sometimes conceived, but his actual size and duration, in the astronomic spaces and light-years, was minuscule. To bring this difference home to our human sense of proportion, Mark Twain used at this point a contrast between a spider and an elephant (113–14).

But this was chiefly an analogy for the more important contrast between man and the angels with respect to what "Satan" calls "intellect." The angel says: "My mind *creates*! . . .

Creates without materials"—ex nihilo—"out of the airy nothing which is called Thought." And this point appears to be an explanation of some of the earlier incidents involving chess, poetry, music, and love. A distinction is made between liking and loving. "His love is for his own kind—for his equals. An angel's love is sublime, adorable, divine, beyond the imagination of man—infinitely beyond it! But it is limited to his own august order. If it fell upon one of your race for only an instant it would consume its object to ashes" (114).

Mark Twain seems here to have abandoned his notion of having the angel learn about love from a mortal woman; when Theodor thinks of "poor Marget and poor Lilly" (a reference cut by Paine and Duneka), "Satan" assures him "they are safe." But "I like"—whatever that could mean for an angel, in view of what has just been said: can an elephant *like* a spider?—"you and the boys. I like Father Peter, and for your sakes I am doing all these things for the villagers" (115). Nor are the ambiguities in the angel's conceptions of good and evil resolved by the following formulation: "Your race never know good fortune from ill. They are always mistaking the one for the other" (115). What could an *angel* mean by such a statement?

"It is because they cannot see into the future," the angel proceeds. "What I am doing for the villagers will bear good fruit some day; in some cases to themselves, in others to unborn generations of men." Only from a point of view, then, that includes *whole lifetimes* "from cradle to grave" can one truly judge; as Aristotle wrote in the *Nicomachean Ethics*, "happiness is a divine gift," and a happy man is "one whose activity accords with perfect virtue and who is adequately furnished with external goods, not for a casual period of time but for *a complete or perfect lifetime*" (my italics). Though the angel here uses language of "moral" evaluation—"good fortune" and "good fruit"—he remains for the most part aloof and indifferent as he toys with the "careers" of the villagers; it is Theodor and Seppi who react with human emotion and snap judgments to the various, alternative "life-plans."

The problem of freedom is not solved—it never has been—but is stated as follows by "Satan": God does not "order the career," in the sense that there is complete predestination, "no. The man's circumstances and environment order it. His first act determines the second and all that follow after." Any change in any of the linked events, however, will change the entire chain: "Suppose it had been appointed that on a certain day, at a certain hour and minute and second and fraction of a second he should snatch at a fly, and he *didn't* snatch at the fly. That man's career would change utterly, from that moment" (115). (Because Paine and Duneka were cutting almost all the passages that refer to flies, they changed "snatch at a fly" to "go to the well.") Columbus might have "become a priest and died obscure in an Italian village," instead of discovering America.

Is the chain of causality then inexorable, since man "of himself . . . cannot get away from the consequences of his first childish act"? No, says the angel, "I can free him." In truth, Mark Twain's views are expounded by "Satan," man's good or ill fortune comes to him from outside, from his initial heredity or "make," to begin with, and then from all the circumstances that shape his life; but since angels act mysteriously—"No one will ever know that I was the cause"—this leaves to man an illusion of freedom.[3]

The notion of hosts of angels liking (or disliking) man and governing men's lives can be seen as a variation on traditional ideas of providence and grace and is rather appealing. Less palatable, because it undercuts our usual hierarchies of values, is the idea that "all of your acts are of one size and importance" (116). But Mark Twain took it seriously and made it the keystone of his imaginative arch in this sequence. Because Nikolaus will close his window during the night, he will rise in the morning two minutes later, and "thenceforth nothing will ever happen to him in accordance with the details of the old chain. . . . There will be consequences" (117): both he and Lisa Brandt will drown, and later Frau Brandt will be burned at the stake—or as "Satan" says, "advantaged" (130). The crux of Mark Twain's allegory of freedom here lies in the alternatives that emerge from seeming trivia. Nicky had "a billion possible careers, but not one of them was worth living" (118), in "Satan's" all-too-human opinion; now he will have the speedy release of death. As to Lisa, she will be saved "from ten years of pain and slow recovery from an accident, and then from nineteen

3. And see below, "The Problem of Freedom" (Chapter 10).

years of pollution, shame, depravity, crime, ending with death at the hands of the executioner. Twelve days hence she will die; her mother would save her life if she could. Am I not kinder than her mother?" (118–19).

Mark Twain's exempla may seem crude, in the extremity of the contrasts they set up, but they make their points all the more effectively as a result, and their power is enhanced by a pervasive tone of irony. Father Peter's case is summed up by: "His good name will be restored, and the rest of his life will be happy"; not till much later do we learn that he will end up as "the one utterly happy person in the Empire" (163) only as a result of insanity. "Satan" has "such strange notions of kindness. But angels are made so, and do not know any better" (119).

Father Adolf is now "on the cold side" of the moon: "He has a long and cruel and odious life before him, but I will change that, for I have no feeling against him and am quite willing to do him a kindness. I think I will get him burnt." The ironies, then, cut many ways, across our conventional notions of both good and evil. The sharpness of "Satan's" tone in speaking, with a "chuckle," of the evil father made little sense when we found it mentioned only in reference to the mild astrologer in the *Stranger* text. In "Young Satan," it seems most appropriate.

Thus, in over forty rather miscellaneous pages, various kinds of knowledge, human and angelic, have been discriminated for the reader and their virtues and limitations described or dramatized. To our human sense, the angel's aloof intellectuality is chastening, but it is also limited and not an adequate substitute for simple warmth of feeling.

The satiric effect is suitably climaxed by a mob scene on the day of Frau Brandt's execution. The point of all the previous examples is hammered home when "Satan" obeys the boys' thoughtless request—"Oh, stop them, Satan!"—and thereby changes the mob's "whole afterlives." Henceforth, "We did not wish to know. We fully believed in Satan's desire to do us kindnesses, but we were losing confidence in his judgment" (132). The conclusion is perfect:

> We saw her chained to the stake, and saw the first thin film of blue smoke rise on the still air. Then her hard face softened,

> and she looked upon the packed crowd in front of her and said with gentleness—
>
> "We played together once, in long-gone days when we were innocent little creatures. For the sake of that, I forgive you."
>
> We went away then, and did not see the fires consume her, but we heard the shrieks, although we put our fingers in our ears. When they ceased we knew she was in heaven notwithstanding the excommunication; and we were glad of her death and not sorry that we had brought it about. (133)

This entire sequence is an excellent illustration of the paradox of art. We have moved quite a distance from the lighthearted statement about the angel's "improving things": pathos has been piled on pathos, but the effect is certainly not tragic. In a curious way, this pathos is exhilarating; we recall particularly the double vision of chapter 2 and find ourselves similarly entranced. Humanity shines through the satire and irony with a power and grace worthy of Swift; the sharp attack and tender sensitivity to human suffering somehow complement and strengthen each other. As Howard M. Jones wrote, "In Twain the spirits of Voltaire and Rousseau fought for control,"[4] and nowhere more obviously then here. Seppi said, about Nicky: "We always prized him, but never so much as now, when we are going to lose him"; and one result of the knowledge granted by "Satan" is that Nicky, after the first day his friends spend with him in the shadow of his death, "was radiant and said he had never had such a happy day" (123). And Frau Brandt's soul has indeed gone to heaven.

Theater of Civilization

In sum: while exploring ways of "ameliorating" the human condition, Mark Twain dramatized a critique of the enlightenment philosophy that was based on the pursuit of happiness and rational progress and was so strong in the United States.

4. Howard Mumford Jones, *Belief and Disbelief in American Literature*, p. 96. In a chapter entitled "The Pessimism of Mark Twain" (pp. 94–115), Jones reminds us that Clemens "perpetually contradicts himself" (p. 101); but generally I find him coherent in his thinking. The original gift of his genius was his ability to formulate ancient principles in ways peculiar to his own temperament and experience of life and to write fictions to illustrate truths in which he believed. He was not a formal philosopher.

In his imaginative satire, an ambiguous angel dramatically inverts that philosophy by praising death and insanity. Now, Mark Twain still had the love intrigues and the shocking denouement of Father Peter's trial in reserve, but he was adrift as to how to go on with the other part of "Satan's" errand, the study of the human race. The problem of future events, with which he had been playing, broadened out therefore into a more general concern with dimensions of time and distance. Possibilities now, in a sense, had become infinite—and indefinite.

The result is that the last chapters of "Young Satan" are increasingly miscellaneous, ending up in the middle of nowhere. As if weary of ultimate issues, the boys in chapter 8 want merely "to be entertained"; and the angel puts on a "show" in which, after the Garden of Eden is briefly mentioned, a series of murders, wars, and other catastrophes is used to illustrate the "progress" of "civilization"; the biblical chronicle does not lack similar events, of course. "Satan's" "theater" is Christian-European history; and after reaching the "present" of 1702, "Satan" moves on to describe the future of nineteenth-century "progress," which is exemplified by the weapons of destruction and works up to a climax in the Boxer Rebellion, Boer War, and other developments close to the period when Twain was writing. This is all rather obvious, and it is carelessly written.

There are repetitions that show Mark Twain was unsuccessfully trying to feel his way toward new materials: we are told, once again, that "Seppi and I had tried in a humble and diffident way to convert" the angel—but this time they are discouraged in their missionary work when he bursts into laughter. These pages retain their force, in both versions; and much of that force derives from the peculiar qualities of "Satan's" laughter, described as "unfeeling" and "unkind" and finally as an "evil chuckle" (138). Again, our responses are troubled: "evil," in an unfallen angel? The problem is not unlike that of the divine laughter in the Bible and in Milton and calls for a similar solution, for a solution distinguishing, within the complex phenomenon that is humor, between the intellectual and the emotional (sometimes sadistic) elements. But it is hard not to feel that "Satan," for all the basic ambiguities we have been noting, is speaking out of character here—too much like his uncle, the Devil, or like Mark Twain. What has happened to his "intellectual" aloofness?

"Satan" soon changes his manner, however, and says gently: "No, we will drink each other's health, and let civilization go." The heavenly wine they drink brings "a strange and witching ecstasy" and thoughts of immortality. The *Stranger* text ends here with a question about the "radiant" goblets that go up into the sky: "Should I ever see mine again?" A paragraph cut from *Stranger* follows in "Young Satan" and supplies a kind of choral commentary:

> Until this day I do not know. I never asked, and Seppi never asked. It is best not to inquire too far, in some matters, if you want to be comfortable. I had doubts about Seppi's ever seeing his goblet again, and I know he had doubts in my case, for some reason or other. These doubts restrained us and we did not pry into each other's fate further than concerned the present life. (139)

The doubts have to do not so much with the problem of knowledge as with the possibilities of heaven versus hell, of course; the latter may be subtly suggested, for example, by Twain's use of the phrase "witching ecstasy," despite the qualifying phrase, "as of heaven."

Since in other contexts the angel has read the thoughts of Theodor and answered his unspoken questions, "Satan's" silence here is meant to be disturbing to Theodor's, and the reader's, complacency. The counterpointing of the angelic laughter with that lovely "triplet of radiant sundogs" is strangely effective.

The Angel and the Fly

The eleven pages of cut material (139–50) that follow are somewhat repetitious of ideas already stated or hinted at, but they are not without their own force and novelty. They begin with a lovely picture—derived from the descriptions of Jesus' boyhood in the *Apocryphal New Testament*—of "Satan" socializing with "a lot of vagrant animals," which he considers "better" than human company. The angel finds no smell unpleasant, "but we"—that is, the boys—"drew the line at the polecat." The revised chain of being is illustrated again: "They were fond of each other because in a manner they were kin, through their mutual property in the absence of the Moral Sense." The tone is more quaint than satiric here: "The wild creatures trooped in from everywhere, and climbed all over Satan" (140).

The episode that grows out of this scene, however, is anything but idyllic. "Satan" assumes the guise of "a rough and ragged poacher," and "he got a broken-legged rabbit out of a trap, healed it with a touch and let it go—and there were the keepers in ambush; and they swarmed out and surrounded him, catching him in the act." What follows is a dramatization of human villainy and hypocrisy, picking up the theme from chapter 3 concerning lying. When "Satan" speaks of "honor," as a "stranger," he is told by the chief keeper: "I do not waste my time and my master's in bartering arguments with your kind of vermin." Underlying their conversation is the problem of knowledge, again, and "Satan" says, significantly, "*I know* the four[5] of you" (my italics) and proceeds to expose their secret guilts.

This will be followed by other episodes in which the arrogance of arbitrary and petty power is rebuked, as happens most thoroughly in the episode set in India (168–72). While still in Eseldorf, however, "Satan" turns the guilty Bart into a stone statue and also, taking the shape of Father Adolf, sets "the persecuted village wild once more" (143). There are two twists here, grotesquely humorous, that reflect Mark Twain's experiences and moods in Vienna, where he was entranced by the lively art world of theater, music, painting, and sculpture. Bart's family is naturally grief stricken: "They flung their arms around the statue, and kissed it and cried over it, and could not be comforted."

But then we find a parody of realism in art: the crowd is "full of wonder" at the statue's "minute fidelities to fact," which culminate in "a fly . . . on the left cheek; it was like the frozen flies you find on the panes, winter mornings, white-shrouded in glinting frost." Siebold, the drunken artist, praises

5. There are actually three, though Mark Twain clearly intended four. Curiously, Conrad Bart, the chief keeper, gets split into two people, "Conrad" and "Bart" (142). I think this was probably the result of carelessness, but it is just possible Mark Twain was playing with ideas of dual (or triple) personalities here.

the "modeling and tone." A sort of frozen reality, then, has come to be valued as the highest art; and "when the season of first-mourning had expired," the mourners' grief finds pecuniary compensation, since the statue is placed on public exhibition:

> The family quickly grew rich, and in the next generation obtained nobility in Germany at the usual rates. After many, many years it was sold, and passed from hand to hand and country to country, and now for a long time it has been in the Pitti palace in Florence, earning its living as a Roman antique. (146)

A sardonic version of art history.

The other grotesque twist also involves that little fly, which was barely mentioned in the cut *Stranger*! There is a coroner's inquest to look into the circumstances of Bart's "petrification" (an old chestnut of Mark Twain's humor, of course, as in "The Petrified Man" perpetrated in Virginia City in 1862), which gets bogged down in problems of values derived from the chain of being:

> Then the jury rendered a verdict that deceased had come to his death by the visitation of God. Also the fly.
>
> The coroner was not willing to accept the verdict, because it included the fly.
>
> The jury insisted that they could not exclude the fly without irreverence, since God in His inscrutable wisdom had seen fit to honor the humble animal with an equal share in His visitation.
>
> The coroner said it was manifest to any thoughtful mind that the overtaking of the fly by the visitation was an accident, and not intentional. (144)

In a world of perfect providence, there are no accidents: " 'Not even a sparrow falls,' and so forth and so forth; and neither does a fly" (145).

Though writing humorously, Mark Twain is deadly serious here, as is evidenced by the last words of the foreman of the jury, which echo Martin Luther: "Such is the verdict, and by it we stand or fall. *Wir können nicht anders.*" The coroner, however, standing on the dignity of the law, ends with "no verdict" and rules that the "deceased must therefore remain unburied—that is, in consecrated ground. He may be a suicide" (146). Incidentally, the coroner's decision indirectly lays the foundations of the family's fortune—a final ironic touch.

This thematic summary of the Conrad Bart episode does not do justice to its qualities. Like the "Cheating the Devil" passage, it stands by itself and is hardly related to the rest of "Young Satan"; having the angel turn himself into Father Adolf (143), through no inner necessity whatsoever, was probably a result of Mark Twain's awareness that he was making digressions having little obvious justification. But Bart is a real villain, and the uses of the word *stone*—the man petrified into a statue and the stoning of "Satan," who reacts "like a person . . . refreshing himself with a shower-bath"—are symbolically interesting. The mock coroner's inquest at the end is tightly organized and well written, reminding us in these respects of the town-hall scene in "Hadleyburg." And just as a deterministic system has to make some provision for freedom and change, as we have seen, so a flattened or inverted hierarchy of values must make provision for flies and microbes [15].

Both sets of issues are real and important, however irreverent and (I suppose) superficial Mark Twain's treatment. The mock-heroic speech of the foreman of the jury, for example, includes a successful parody of the Declaration of Independence:

> Sir, this jury cannot concede, without the most awful irreverence, that an all-compassionate Providence would lift its hand against even so humble a creature as a fly without just and righteous cause. We cannot and will not concede that this fly fell by accident. This fly was guilty of an offence which is hidden from us and which we are not privileged to pry into. What it did is a secret between itself and its Creator (and perhaps the coroner!) but it *was* guilty, and that guilt is witnessed and forever established by its fate. Let it be a lesson to us all.
>
> *The Coroner.* Then you stand to your verdict.
>
> *The Foreman, impressively.* God helping us, we do; and to the issue we do solemnly commit our lives, our fortunes and our sacred honor. (*Voices.* Amen!) (145)

The effective style, I submit, is an indication of Mark Twain's essential seriousness here.

Time and Distance

At the beginning of chapter 9, Mark Twain made an effort to pick up again the thread of the earlier story he had all but abandoned in the Conrad Bart digression. Having just taken up the idea of "no accidents" in a different context, he went back briefly to the problem of life plans and reformulated an idea implicit in the earlier sequence, namely, that "any change might happen to be for the worse," that it might be skipping "one kind of unhappiness to land in one of a different breed, and not any easier to bear." Now, however, Theodor accepts also the human need for "surprises"; to paraphrase Matthew: sufficient unto the day is the evil—and the joy—thereof. But the notion of having a future chronicle of his friend Seppi "beautifully printed in many large volumes" is quaint, almost sentimental: "I have lost a grandchild to-day. I have his [Seppi's] good letter of pity and condolence in my book" (148). This is one of the few glimpses we get of Theodor as an old man.

Mature wisdom, then, has taught Theodor not to seek to read ahead in life's book, not to probe the future's secrets. "But I am wandering too far from my boyhood," he says, and then goes back again in memory to the old days when the angel was around. With Nicky gone, only he and Seppi have the friendship of "Satan," and they skillfully use the power of prediction this gives them to gull the other boys by placing bets on "sure things." The use of future time here reminds us of the *Yankee*—a clever sort of fooling! As we are told at one point, "This was by art" (149).

But despite the light humor, Mark Twain's chief target was still religion and the exaggerated doctrines of providence and predestination as he understood (or misunderstood) them. Nor was our friend, the fly, forgotten. After one of the betting episodes: "We were not sorry, for it was wrong for them to bet on Sunday. It seemed to me that it was a plain judgment on them. And not an accident, but intentional. Seppi said it was as manifest as the fly's case. Seppi knew about judgments, for his uncle was in the ministry" (150). This parody of "Satan's" studying for the ministry may suggest that Mark Twain, groping for a new direction, was still toying with the old idea of the "Devil's Sunday-School."

Another *Yankee* touch is the suggestion that an ability to

predict the future can be applied to journalism, by providing "scoops." Characteristically, the "man who wrote the daily news-letter in the cathedral town ten miles up the river" is in danger of being jailed as a "wizard," since literacy has a touch of magic in it. When confronted with a choice of possible careers, this eighteenth-century Austrian newsman "elected to be hanged" at the end of fifteen years—a sardonic comment on the life of a newspaperman.

Unfinished Book

At about this point, the reader is naturally wondering in what direction all these scattered episodes are heading and where "The Chronicle of Young Satan" could possibly end. He is happy to be brought back, in chapter 10, to the familiar village of Eseldorf, the love story of Marget and Wilhelm, and Father Peter's trial. This is ground already covered in our consideration of the body of manuscript completed in 1897–1898, and it culminates in the union of the lovers and in the good father's "happy insanity." Where could Mark Twain go from here? I see little point in trying to complete his story for him but can make two suggestions.

First, Theodor, the narrator, is presented as an old man looking back to his boyhood, and some way of bridging this gap between youth and age—a gap Twain was also exploring in a nonfictional way around the same time in the dialogues of *What Is Man?*—may have been intended. "I have lost a grandchild today" (148), he tells us. That such a statement would imply a fairly large amount yet to be written is self-evident.

Second, "Satan's" mastery over "time and distance" may provide a central clue. We have seen that some play with time followed immediately after the statement in chapter 9 about the grandchild; and after disposing of Father Peter's trial in chapter 10 and philosophizing about the sense of humor and "papal infallibility," our narrator goes on with more of the same. But, beginning with the trip to India, there is a shift of emphasis to the space dimension; and there might well have been plans for more geographical excursions, like the earlier ones to France in the west and China in the east. In 1702, there would have been plenty of room for satiric explorations of all the continents, including even Australia and South Africa, which were among the regions Clemens had recently visited during the world tour he wrote of in *Following the Equator*. And he might well have wanted to play with historical views of the Western Hemisphere, of North and possibly even South America, of those early years. We recall Forty-four's plan in "Schoolhouse" to "travel about the globe and personally examine some of the nationalities, and learn languages and read the world's books in the several tongues." Consider what Mark Twain's "Satan" might have done with Salem, Massachusetts, in 1702!

With the intimate village plot unraveled, I imagine, the general direction would have been outward, toward exploring the great world—a movement that would have reflected the American "revolt from the village."[6] Presumably, the ideas about determinism versus freedom, man and the angels, the sense of humor, and the other ideas with which the manuscript abounds are the chief lessons that had been learned by Theodor long ago and were subsequently illustrated when they could be documented by a lifetime of observation and experience. In this way, as he had written to Howells, Mark Twain would have told "what I think of Man, and how he is constructed." Time, space, the chain of being: these are some of the key ideas governing the actual, and perhaps the potential, structure of the plot—what there is of it.

As he enlarged his geographical canvas, our satirist's targets would probably have become increasingly political. He had an easy—perhaps too easy—device for moving at will from scene to scene, which prefigures in an uncanny way what we accomplish daily when we tune in on television newscasts: "We often went to the most distant parts of the globe with him, and stayed weeks and months, and yet were gone only a fraction of a second, as a rule" (150) **[16]**.

6. A basic cause of Mark Twain's failure to complete "Young Satan" was probably the centrifugal tendency that came with the abandonment of the village plot. As he once wrote in 1882 in a notebook: "Human nature cannot be studied in cities except at a disadvantage—a village is the place. There you can know your man inside and out—in a city you but know his crust; and his crust is usually a lie" (*S&B*, p. 11). See also above, "Theater of Civilization"; and the comments on the superior integration of "No. 44" in "Time and the Writer" (Chapter 2).

The Sense of Humor

But these flittings from scene to scene lead nowhere, and what the reader remembers most vividly at the end of "Young Satan" are the angel's (Mark Twain's) extended observations on the sense of humor. The "evil chuckle" first appeared in chapter 8, and laughter recurs in the following chapter more elaborately, and more meaningfully, dramatized. Again, the episode involves man's inhumanity to man, here "a born lady who was known to have the habit of curing people by devilish arts, such as bathing them, washing them and nourishing them" (151) is hung as a witch. She was stoned: "All were throwing stones and each was watching his neighbor" (152). "Satan" laughs "to see three cowards stoning a dying lady when they were so near to death themselves" and goes on to accurately predict the death of one in five minutes. "Satan" himself casts no stone.

The point of the episode, the cowardice of mobs, is one made repeatedly by Mark Twain; its most familiar expression is in the Colonel Sherburn episode in *Huckleberry Finn* (chapter 22). In both these cases, I think, his real target was the lynch mob: not long after, in 1901, he wrote "The United States of Lyncherdom," and at one time he projected a book to attack the practice of lynching in the States. "Satan" tells Theodor, "there were sixty-eight people there, and sixty-two of them had no more desire to throw a stone than you had" (154), and then launches into a diatribe: "I know your race. It is made up of sheep. It is governed by minorities, seldom or never by majorities"—and so forth. The Salem witchcraft trials do indeed come into the picture now, but not satirically:

> Some day a handful will rise up on the other side and make the most noise—perhaps even a single daring man with a big voice and a determined front will do it—and in a week all the sheep will wheel and follow him, and witch-hunting will come to a sudden end. In fact this happened within these ten years, in a little country called New England. (154–55)

"Satan's" next bit of "humor" has to do with men at war: "what mutton you are, and how ridiculous." (This theme was taken up at greater length, in 1905, when Mark Twain dictated "The War Prayer," a masterpiece of sardonic irony and rhetoric.[7] "Satan's" explanation of the "grotesque self-deception" patriotic citizens practice in wartime, included by Paine and Duneka, is more specific and meaningful in "Young Satan," where it is illustrated by "the little shameful war" of the British against the Boers: "To please a dozen rich adventurers her statesmen will pick a quarrel with a couple of wee little Christian farmer-communities" (156). "Satan's" act of pulling "down the corner of his eye with his finger," as Gibson notes, is an Italian gesture that conveys "polite but profound skepticism" (470).

After the discussion of "happy insanity," Theodor reports a debate with "Satan" as to whether or not the human race possesses the sense of humor. Paine and Duneka gutted the angel's statement of its chief applications by deleting his explanation of the "high-grade comicalities" that most men with "dull vision" do not perceive are chiefly political (for example, "hereditary royalties and aristocracies") and religious. Tuckey and Gibson (7) inform us about the immediate historical contexts that made Mark Twain see as humorous the doctrine of papal infallibility—"which even God on His throne is obliged to submit to" (165). This leads into an oft-quoted generalization that "nothing can stand" an assault by the powers of laughter.

The two omitted pages that follow refer to Robert Burns ("a peasant" who "will break the back of the Presbyterian Church" and "set Scotland free"); and they then present the story of a clash between an "infallible" papal decree and an assassinated king's widow, concluding:

> "Meantime the prayer had been received in heaven from fifty-one sources—and recorded. The record will be meekly expunged—by order from below. Is that funny—or isn't it? I think it is; in fact I know it is; but none of your race will find it out. Why don't you laugh?"
>
> *I said I was too much hurt to laugh.* I said our religion was our stay, our solace and our hope; it was the most precious thing we had, and I could not bear to hear its sacred servants derided.
>
> I think it touched him; for he became gentle and kind at once,

7. Janet Smith, ed., *Mark Twain on the Damned Human Race*, pp. 64–67.

> and set about banishing my trouble from my mind. It did not take him long—it never did. He flashed me around the globe, stopping an hour or a week, at intervals, in one or another strange country, and doing the whole journey in a few minutes by the clock, and I was in a condition of contentment before we had covered the first stage. Satan was always good and considerate, that way. *He liked to rough a person up, but he liked to smooth him down again just as well.* (167–68, my italics)

These last sentences make explicit the rhythmic pattern we detected in chapter 2.

The sense of humor provides the right note on which to conclude our consideration of "The Chronicle of Young Satan." Now that we can trace accurately its various stages (five in all)—and can pinpoint the various places in which this fragmentary narrative was drafted, never to be finally revised—we understand better some of its confusions and incoherencies. But its keynote, remarkably well sustained under these circumstances, is the grand cosmological and moral irony created by the juxtaposition of angelic and human situations and values. The angel's ambiguity, created by the name he bears and by Mark Twain's vacillations about his relationships with the Devil, also results in a kind of satanic comedy. Like most profound satire, and despite incompleteness, this work belongs in that rare company, it exists in a no-man's-land between the territories occupied by "pure" tragedy and "pure" comedy.

All the virtues of the Paine-Duneka *Stranger* are in "Young Satan"—and more. The latter does drift off into the middle of nowhere, ending with a mediocre Indian scene; and some of the parts eliminated in 1916 are relatively trivial and lacking in intensity. But the "intellectual drunk" Clemens experienced in 1899 was a real, if sporadic, inspiration. Some other parts now restored are excellent, on a par with the best passages in a text that includes some writing equal to Mark Twain at his best.

The *Stranger,* along with its moments of power, puzzled us. In "Young Satan," a text about one-third longer, the latter moments may have become somewhat weakened and dissipated; but we see more clearly what Mark Twain was trying to do and the means he was using to accomplish his ends. All of the superfluous mystery has been cleared up, and on the whole the magic of a great satirist and literary artist remains.

"The Chronicle of Young Satan" should retain a high position in the classic Mark Twain canon; it is in some ways poorer and in some ways richer than the *Stranger*, but it is most certainly, and splendidly, Twain's own.

Part Three: The Mysterious Stranger ("No. 44")

6

The Writing of "No. 44"

Two full years went by between the time Mark Twain abandoned "Young Satan" and the time he began "No. 44" in late October and early November of 1902. He returned to the States a conquering hero who had emerged from his bankruptcy ordeal more popular and loved than ever. His *Complete Works* were in print; his fame was secure and had been endorsed by leading critics and universities, endorsements that culminated in a doctor of letters degree from Oxford in 1907. He was much sought after as a speaker on important occasions and occasionally gave readings and made appearances for charitable causes. Some of his more vitriolic opinions, though committed to manuscript, remained unpublished during his lifetime; but he frequently attacked venal politicians, barbaric cruelties, obscurantisms and superstitions, hypocrisies, and the scourge of war; and he defended the weak and helpless (men and animals), the rights of authors (copyright legislation), rationality, good writing, and civilized values generally.

Mark Twain continued to write short pieces, as the spirit moved him, for such periodicals as *Harper's Magazine, Harper's Bazaar, North American Review*; and he published occasional books, all but the privately circulated *What Is Man?* under the imprint of Harper and Brothers. In October 1901, after a year at 14 West Tenth Street in New York City, the Clemens family moved to a quieter home at Riverdale-on-the-Hudson; and it was there that Mark Twain began to tinker with the old opening chapter of "Young Satan" and to write chapter 2 of "No. 44," with typing assistance from Jean and from Isabel V. Lyon, who went to work as his secretary about mid-November 1902.

Mark Twain's last decade is the most heavily documented,

but least understood, period of his life. Most recently, Hamlin Hill has opened up some of its problems in *Mark Twain: God's Fool* (1973), which tells the story of Olivia Clemens's last years, of the illnesses of Jean and Clara, and of the complex role played by Isabel Lyon, who lived with and "managed" for Clemens until a rupture in 1909. Clemens wrote his version of the relationship in the "Ashcroft-Lyon Manuscript," which Hill characterizes as "one of the most remarkable manuscripts of his entire career" (*MTGF*, p. 228). Since my purpose is not primarily biographical, I will discuss here chiefly those aspects of Twain's last decade that relate to "No. 44."

The three largest bodies of material relevant to *The Mysterious Stranger* are autobiographical and biographical. Autobiographical material has appeared in three partial editions (by A. B. Paine, Bernard DeVoto, and Charles Neider), but we still lack a definitive text; most relevant for our purposes is DeVoto's *Mark Twain in Eruption* (1940), though like Paine, DeVoto took many editorial liberties. Alongside this inchoate "autobiography," the curious reader has available two antithetical versions by biographers. Best known is the last volume (chapters 212–96) of Paine's *Biography*, in which "the traditional Mark Twain" is "preserved" (Paine's words) and Miss Lyon is barely mentioned; as Hill has put it, Paine "was a willing participant in the suppression of the unpleasant facts" (*MTGF*, p. 268). At the other extreme, Hill has painstakingly collected and used many hitherto suppressed manuscripts in order to tell a truer story and to correct Paine's radical distortions; but all the evidence will become available only when the complete correspondence, notebooks, and autobiography have been published. Meanwhile, we have also the sketchy concluding chapter ("Whited Sepulchre") of Justin Kaplan's "Freudian" biography, *Mr. Clemens and Mark Twain* (1966).

Thus, no one has yet put into writing an account of those years that is both full and balanced. For all his heavy documentation and despite a sincere desire to be fair, Hill has given us "*Hamlet* without the Prince": he pays relatively little attention to Mark Twain's literary creativity during those years, dismissing most of the surviving manuscripts as uncompleted and incoherent. A basic purpose of my entire book is to begin correcting this imbalance.

Beginning

"No. 44" was written in three main stages. During most of the winter of 1902–1903 the illnesses of Livy and Jean, as well as other distractions, prevented serious work; but in April 1903, probably, Mark Twain again resumed work on the "Stranger." In June, Sam and Livy revived their old custom of going to Quarry Farm in Elmira for the summer, where they were joined by the children in August. By that time, Mark Twain had finished 110 pages of manuscript, to the end of chapter 7, and had probably written as well some "Eddypus" satires, aimed partly at the founder of Christian Science.

Since Livy was still very weak, the doctors recommended a change of climate; and on 24 October, the family sailed for Italy, settling for the winter at the Villa di Quarto in Florence. With few distractions, Mark Twain went back to his pen for occupation and solace, writing "The $30,000 Bequest" and other short pieces, including some autobiography. In January 1904, when Clemens wrote to his minister friend Joseph Twichell that he was working "on a couple of long books (half-completed ones)," he was probably referring to "Which Was It?" [**17**] and "No. 44" [**18**]. He thus wrote the middle chapters of the latter (8–25), as well as the concluding chapter (34), somehow, during the last months in the life of his beloved Livy, who died on 5 June 1904 [**19**].

In brief, the stages in the writing of "No. 44" correspond closely to its main parts, which can be labeled roughly the beginning (chapters 1–7), middle (8–25), and end (26–34); exceptions to this scheme are chapter 34, which was written in 1904 as the planned ending, and chapter 33, which was supplied in 1908 as the final link to this ending. We shall see that each of these parts is well organized, with its own internal logic.

The fact that most of "No. 44" was written in the shadow of illness and death is no doubt relevant to our understanding of its central theme, which is an exploration of the confrontation between a fifteenth-century world of practical work in a print shop and the various forms of mystery and miracle associated with the stranger. Problems of health, doctors, and especially various forms of "mind cure" had long been of intense personal and intellectual interest to Clemens, as to his entire family; it was certainly no accident that Clara eventually became an ardent believer in Christian Science [20].

One hypothesis that emerges from the circumstances surrounding work on "No. 44" is that Mark Twain turned to that manuscript as an escape from the severities of illness in his family. The Austrian setting may have reminded him of happier days in Vienna. But through the veil of fiction he was also reliving some of the most intimate and poignant aspects of his adolescence and of his later courtship of Livy, as we shall see.

Middle

Despite some unpleasant complications with the Italian landlady, the first months in Florence were not lacking in hope and happiness. As Mark Twain wrote to Twichell on 7 January 1904: "This secluded and silent solitude, this clean, soft air, and this enchanting view of Florence, the great valley and snow-mountains that frame it, are the right conditions for work. They are a persistent inspiration."[1] The literary results were certainly rather fine.

Writing for love and not for money, and with no intention of having the work published in his lifetime, Mark Twain was reaching down to his deepest levels of concern and conviction in "No. 44." The freedom from censorship need not have resulted in a superior work of literature, but it remains an important biographical fact. The soul of an artist at such periods of loss and grief should perhaps be granted privacy, be left free from the prying biographer's analysis; but it is hard to do this when the artist was creating a work of psychological fiction at around the same time.

The biographical issues are of the greatest complexity, and we should therefore consider with caution, although we cannot ignore, the view summarized by Kaplan as follows: "It was certainly one of the bitter ironies of their marriage that after all those years he should be singled out by Livy's doctors and implicitly by Livy herself, as the chief external cause of the nervous states that went along with hyperthyroid heart dis-

1. *MTB*, p. 1212; and see *MTGF*, pp. 71–87 (see list of short references p. xiii).

ease." During his last months in Florence, Clemens could see his ailing wife briefly only once a day. The long, lonely hours were spent in part with Clara and Jean; dictating parts of his autobiography to Isabel Lyon; and working on his "half-completed" books with, it seems, the threat of mortality ever present. When Clara gave a concert in April, Mark Twain remarked in jest to William Lyon Phelps: "I am passing off the stage, and now my daughter is the famous member of the family."[2]

All this gives a special poignancy to Mark Twain's writing, at some time near or after Livy's passing, the well-known pages in which Forty-four proclaims, "*Life itself is only a vision, a dream.*" Tuckey's summary of the biographical significance of this fact[3] seems to me admirable and only in need of slight supplementation.

Around the middle of May, Livy's health began to fail drastically. On 12 May 1904, Clemens wrote to Richard W. Gilder:

> She remains what she always was, the most wonderful creature of fortitude, patience, endurance and recuperative power that ever was. But ah, dear, it won't last; this fiendish malady will play new treacheries upon her, and I shall go back to my prayers again—unutterable from any pulpit!

On 9 May, he had written to Muriel Pears that he would take himself "to the work which sweeps this world away, and puts me in one which no one has visited but me—nor will, for this book is not being written for print." Tuckey therefore suggested that late May was a period when Mark Twain was "mentally and emotionally disposed toward writing" chapter 34:

> Although he almost certainly did not think of Mrs. Clemens as the original of "44," he could easily have thought of her at the time of her death as the one whose spirit and force had sustained him and inspired his art; he could thereby have related his personal loss to his narrator's loss of the companionship of the mysterious stranger.

But in addition to making these biographical speculations, Tuckey also pointed out that the heading, "Conclusion of the

2. Justin Kaplan, *Mr. Clemens and Mark Twain: A Biography*, pp. 369–71.

3. I shall be paraphrasing *MTSatan*, pp. 62–64.

book," shows, "in fact, that it was explicitly a *story-solution*"—as well, perhaps, as a personal one. Gibson drew attention to the fact that the language of this chapter echoes that used in a personal letter to Twichell, dated 28 July 1904 (30), two weeks after Livy's funeral. "Unquestionably," as Gibson wrote, "Clemens endowed 44 with his own questionings and grievances and griefs," but even in his letters we find, not "unmixed autobiography," but also "a literary impulse" (31). And I should add that, as so often in his best writings, fictional and autobiographical elements were mingled throughout most of "No. 44."

End

After Livy's funeral in Elmira on 14 July, Clemens retreated for seclusion to a cottage in Tyringham, Massachusetts, owned by an old friend, Richard W. Gilder; and thereafter he moved for the winter, with Jean and Clara, to a New York City apartment on the corner of Fifth Avenue and Ninth Street. This was a season for him of indignations aroused by various political situations, and as a result he produced such powerful statements as "The Czar's Soliloquy," "King Leopold's Soliloquy," and "The War Prayer."[4] Early in May 1905, after a brief visit to Rogers, Mark Twain settled for the summer in the Copley Green house at Dublin, New Hampshire, where a summer colony of writers and artists, many from Boston, seems to have contributed to the health of his spirit as well as of his body. During this productive summer, Mark Twain wrote "Eve's Diary," a revision of "Adam's Diary," "A Horse's Tale," a complex satiric fantasy on the theme of microbes, and in two weeks early in July the concluding section of "No. 44" (chapters 26–32). "Three Thousand Years Among the Microbes" was characterized by A. B. Paine as a "scientific, socialistic, mathematical jamboree" (*MTB*, p. 1238), and writing it during June seems to have brought Mark Twain back to a mood in which he could more or less complete "No. 44" during July. Given the wildly fantastic, Swiftian and Rabelaisian, mood of "Microbes," we are not surprised to find similar quali-

4. Available in Janet Smith, ed., *Mark Twain on the Damned Human Race.*

ties, extravagant and apocalyptic, in these final chapters of "No. 44."

Basing his opinion on an autobiographical dictation of 17 July 1906, Tuckey suggested that Mark Twain dropped work on "No. 44" because of a visit by F. A. Duneka around mid-July 1905, since Duneka was a Roman Catholic and "wanted the priest reformed or left out."

When Clemens wrote to Clara that he was pleased by her plan to join him at 21 Fifth Avenue in the fall, he remarked that he himself had broken his bow and burned his arrows. As Tuckey suggests, he was probably identifying with Shakespeare's Prospero in *The Tempest* and paraphrasng the latter's valedictory speech: "I'll break my staff. . . ."

Dictating on 30 August 1906, Clemens spoke of *The Mysterious Stranger* as "more than half finished"; and as Tuckey has suggested, "in reckoning the degree of completeness that the book had attained, he may have been thinking not so much of additional wordage as of integration and revision."[5]

Tuckey has marshaled the manuscript evidence that establishes 1908 as the time of compostion of chapter 33, which was the final link necessary for completion of "No. 44." In addition, he cites a letter to Mrs. Hookway in Chicago about a children's theater movement in that city, reports of which had "stirred" Mark Twain (around September 1908) to his "deepest deeps":

> It is much the most effective teacher of morals and promoter of good conduct that the ingenuity of man has yet devised, for the reason that its lessons are not taught wearily by book and by dreary homily, but by *visible and enthusing action*; and *they go straight to the heart*, which is the rightest of right places for them. Book morals often get no further than the intellect, if they even get that far on their *spectral and shadowy pilgrimage*; but when they travel from a Children's Theatre they do not stop permanently at that halfway house, but *go on home*.
>
> The Children's theatre is the only teacher of morals and conduct and high ideals that never bores the pupil, but always leaves him sorry when the lesson is over. And as for history, no other teacher is for a moment comparable to it: no other

5. *MTSatan*, pp. 69–71.

> can *make the dead heroes of the world rise up and shake the dust of the ages from their bones and live and move and breathe and speak and be real to the looker and listener*; no other can make the *study of the lives and times of the illustrious dead* a delight, a splendid interest, a passion; and no other can *paint a history-lesson in colors that will stay, and stay, and never fade.*

Tuckey's italics draw attention to "the parts of this letter which most closely parallel, in their phrasing or in their ideas, certain elements" in chapter 33: the "Assembly of the Dead" there, as we shall see, is a pageant of history not unlike that provided by the Children's Theater.[6]

On the whole, Tuckey's arguments for a continuity of theme and plot at the end of "No. 44" seem to me persuasive and essentially right, as against Gibson's view that Mark Twain "wrote the pageant chapter as part of an effort—never fulfilled—to link the body of his story to the 'Conclusion of the book'" (11). The final link in "No. 44" was created at Mark Twain's last home, the "Stormfield" house in Redding, Connecticut. Clemens wrote from there to Mrs. Rogers on 12 October 1908: "Society and theology are sufficient for me"; and many of his last writings, including "Letters from the Earth," touch on problems of religion.

More to Say

My sole purpose in the foregoing has been to provide elementary background information about the situations in which "No. 44" was written: the winter and spring-summer of 1902–1903, the 1904 months in Florence, the 1905 summer in New

6. *MTSatan*, pp. 72–75. In his book-length study, *The Art of Mark Twain*, William M. Gibson more or less repeats with slight modifications the views previously published in the introduction to *Mysterious Stranger Manuscripts*. The concluding chapter, "Dreams and the Inner Life," is devoted chiefly to "The Chronicle of Young Satan," the version he feels "we could not do without" (p. 185). He thinks "No. 44" an incoherent work that "collapses in a general phantasmagoria" and is "notably diffuse" (pp. 12–13). I share Gibson's enthusiasm for "Young Satan," but disagree with him about the success of "No. 44." In his prefatory note, Gibson modestly presents his book as "one critic's choice of Mark Twain's 'best'" (p. viii); and I should like to think of my arguments for "No. 44" as supplementing (not contradicting) his for the more familiar tale.

Hampshire, and the period of 1908–1909 spent at Stormfield in Connecticut. Besides the human facts of age, family, and mortality, however, we need to seek insights into the mind and imagination of the writer; and the best place to do this is, of course, in his writings: as D. H. Lawrence put it, "Never trust the artist, trust the tale." There has been too much psychologizing and polemicizing about the last years of Mark Twain and not enough careful reading of what he actually wrote. For example, Hamlin Hill's description of the "literary activity" in Florence during the months before Livy's death barely mentions "No. 44"! Surely the most significant writing Mark Twain accomplished in Florence was the middle chapters of *The Mysterous Stranger* ("No. 44").

The writings and publications of Mark Twain's last decade were certainly uneven in quality and extremely varied. What had become of the author of *Huckleberry Finn*? To judge only from his published work, he seemed to have been transformed into a sort of "village-atheist" philosopher who wrote books on such melancholy and miscellaneous subjects as *What Is Man?*, *Christian Science*, and *Is Shakespeare Dead?*. Even so sympathetic a student of Mark Twain's literary development as Henry Nash Smith devoted the major part of his concluding chapter ("This Pathetic Drift") to *Pudd'nhead Wilson* and "Hadleyburg" and dismissed *Stranger* with three pages that concentrated chiefly on the "nihilistic" message of the conclusion to "No. 44." Smith's concluding paragraphs are as follows:

> Given this image of human society, a rational observer could have but one wish—to carry out Hank Morgan's impulse by hanging the race and ending the farce. Satan performs such an act in an early chapter of *The Mysterious Stranger*. He has created little men and women of clay and brought them to life for the amusement of Theodor and his friends. Two of the men quarrel and begin to fight one another. "Satan reached out his hand and crushed the life out of them with his fingers, threw them away, wiped the red from his fingers on his handkerchief, and went on talking where he had left off." When the wives of the dead men find the bodies of their husbands and fall to weeping a crowd collects about them, and the noise attracts Satan's attention; "then he reached out and took the heavy

> board seat out of our swing and brought it down and mashed all those people into the earth just as if they had been flies, and went on talking just the same."
>
> Satan's destruction of the mimic world he has created is the symbolic gesture of a writer who can no longer find any meaning in man or society. Mark Twain's only refuge is to identify himself with a supernatural spectator for whom mankind is but a race of vermin, hardly worth even contempt. And this marks the end of his career as a writer, for there was nothing more to say.[7]

But, as we have seen, the scene in "Young Satan" containing this "symbolic gesture" was written in Vienna during the winter of 1897–1898; and Mark Twain's career as a writer was far from over then, he had much "more to say." Other symbolic scenes of power that stand out in "No. 44," for instance, are the angel's farewell (written in 1904) and the "Assembly of the Dead" (1908–1909); the "Microbes" fantasy (1905), which deserves separate study, is a beautiful potpourri of real significance; and Twain in his very last year produced "Letters from the Earth."

The fictionalist Mark Twain, in other words, had neither vanished nor deteriorated into a drooling sentimentalist; those animal tales, for example, were written as anti-cruelty-to-animals propaganda and serve that purpose well. He had gone underground. What he now had to say was between Mark Twain and his Maker, between Clemens and his conscience, and required a certain amount of self-indulgence in the writing. As he said in the second preface to "Microbes," about his narrator (a cholera germ he called Huck): "His style is loose and wandering and garrulous and self-contented beyond anything I have ever encountered before, and his grammar breaks the heart. But there is no remedy: let it go" (*WWD*, p. 434) **[21]**.

The critical issue is whether in that final decade Mark Twain succeeded in writing a major work of fiction. It has become amply clear, I think, that the main keys to this question are to be found in three volumes: *Which Was the Dream?*, *Mysterious Stranger Manuscripts*, and *Fables of Man*; and in my judgment the two most considerable achievements in these

7. Henry Nash Smith, *Mark Twain: The Development of a Writer.*

volumes are "Three Thousand Years Among the Microbes" and "No. 44." When Henry Nash Smith wrote Mark Twain's literary biography, he obviously had no interest in, or patience with, much beyond "Hadleyburg." Others, following in Smith's excellent tradition of careful scholarship and critical sanity, many now find values Smith was not ready to grant in 1962 in some of the Mark Twain Papers he and other literary editors have so carefully preserved and published.

7

Confrontation and Interactions

(Chapters 2–13: "Life was become very interesting.")

Our chief justification for still yoking together "Young Satan" and "No. 44" is that they share the same opening chapter.[1] One may think of "No. 44," therefore, as a sort of sequel to the "Young Satan" in which Eseldorf bulked so large. But to experience "No. 44" properly the reader should try to put out of his mind all recollections of "Young Satan." The direction in the last part of the uncompleted story was centrifugal, outward from the village and toward the great world of China and India; in "No. 44," however, the direction is onward and inward. Though not without significant references to the fifteenth-century "great world," as well as satiric references (in the vein of the *Yankee*) ahead to the nineteenth century, "No. 44" emphasizes a new, closed, social situation that represents a further phase in a young Austrian's adolescence. Chapter 2 begins: "I had been familiar with that village life, but now for as much as a year I had been out of it, and was busy learning a trade." The village scene has been pushed firmly into the background and becomes less and less important as we move deeper into the world of the new story.

The tone, atmosphere, theme, and style of "No. 44" set it apart from its predecessor. It has qualities of lightheartedness, and even light-headedness, that run fairly consistently through the whole and find expression in burlesque situations, fantastic experiments, and a freewheeling style that includes extravagances such as an indulgent use of slang and rapid shifts within single paragraphs and even within sentences; always characteristic of Mark Twain's style, to a degree, these are now car-

1. See Appendix D: "Revisions of Chapter 1 for 'No. 44.'"

ried to a higher power, to an extreme. Gibson tells us Clemens wrote out the following "title-page" on a separate sheet:

No. 44
The Mysterious Stranger [22]
Being an Ancient Tale
found in a Jug, and freely
translated from the Jug
by
Mark Twain. (514)

The phrase "Ancient Tale" fits the earlier date of 1490; the "jug" suggests something like Aladdin's lamp, out of which jinns will come, and it suggests drunkenness; and "freely translated" (as well as the general style of the proposed title page) looks ahead to "Three Thousand Years Among the Microbes" (1905), which was similarly "Translated from the Original Microbic /By/ Mark Twain."[2] Indeed, these two works share many other elements of style and theme, including satire on Christian Science and Mary Baker Eddy. The direction of all the changes and additions in "No. 44" is to stress "magic" and "mystery"—with what artistic purpose we shall presently see.

Print-Shop World

It was with chapter 2 that the writing of "No. 44" began, and the rather slight links to "Young Satan" indicate chiefly that planning a new Austrian tale naturally sent Mark Twain back to his earlier effort. But these backward glances were few; and "No. 44" was properly launched when Clemens dictated to Jean elaborate notes, used almost verbatim in chapter 2, about his cast of characters (453–57).

In "Young Satan," chapter 2 introduces the angel with winning ways. In "No. 44," there is a different sort of contrast established in the two opening chapters: between the village world where "the Church was opposed to the cheapening of books and the indiscriminate dissemination of knowledge" (230) and the small castle community where the master, Heinrich Stein, is "a scholar, and a dreamer or a thinker," who

2. *WWD*, p. 433 (see list of short references p. xiii).

"loved learning and study," and who has a Xanthippe-like shrew for a wife. The variegated cast of characters also includes, in my summary:

Balthasar Hoffman, fake and parasitical "Magician"
Maria Vogel, evil and superstitious daughter of Frau Stein's first marriage
Frau Regen, the master's sister, a bedridden widow—and her daughter Marget, the master's niece, a lovely "kitten in a menagerie"
Katrina, cook and housekeeper, "independent and masterful," in conflict with the master's second wife
sundry minor servants

The printing force includes, besides August Feldner:

Adam Binks, the oldest worker, a proofreader
Hans Katzenyammer, 36, "drunk, quarrelsome" printer
Moses Haas, 28, egotistical printer
Gustav Fischer, 27, attractive printer, with "a good disposition"
Ernest Wasserman, treacherous apprentice, slightly older than August
Barty Langbein, 15, "sunny," affectionate cripple, "general-utility lad"

The setting, then, is the relatively closed world of a well-knit, if quarrelsome, group of people. There is a kind of parallel in the boardinghouse environment that played an important role in *The American Claimant* (1892) and that served as a sort of "microcosm of American society."[3]

As we have seen, one of the differences between "Young Satan" and "No. 44" is that in the latter the use of *devilish* and *devil* is on the whole conventional and does not create ambiguous references such as those to the angel "Satan" that we found in the former. But there is a complication implicit in the very name of a "printer's *devil*," which is defined by Gibson in his glossary as,

> The youngest or newest apprentice printer who performs much of the dirty work of a print-shop, such as washing type

3. Clyde L. Grimm, "*The American Claimant*: Reclamation of a Farce," p. 92. We are told in "No. 44" that the magician lived in the castle "on light salary *and board*" (230, my italics).

> or inking forms, and who is often black with ink. The name may be associated with the belief that Faust was in league with the devil. (476)

There are four candidates for this role in "No. 44": the youngest is Barty Langbein, but there is nothing "devilish" about him; another is Ernest Wasserman, "17, apprentice," who is in fact a proper villain ("braggart, malicious, hateful, coward, liar, cruel, underhanded, treacherous"); August, too, at the outset presents himself simply as "'prentice," it is not clear whether he is the newest, he is certainly not the youngest. Thus, when Forty-four is accepted by the master as apprentice (chapter 7), he is inheriting the role of "printer's devil" in the shop; though slightly older than August ("sixteen or seventeen"), he is clearly the newest of the group.

This hidden pun, however, is conspicuous by its absence from chapter 2, in which the "mixed family" (230) of the print shop is introduced; in fact, none of the references to "devils" are related to the characters we have mentioned.[4] In view of Mark Twain's conspicuous display of print-shop terminology and slang throughout this text and elsewhere,[5] his failure to apply this popular label is more significant than might have been his actual use of it. It seems to be part of the technique of mystification with which he is playing throughout.

Getting back to the contrast between the opening two chapters: the village life in chapter 1 may be a "paradise" for boys, but it is a kind of superstitious hell for adults—one in which the Devil's pressure is strong and a "good and gentle and truthful . . . good Catholic" like Father Peter is made to suffer. The print shop in chapter 2 is "more curiously than pleasantly situated," its castle—"prodigious, vine-clad, stately and beautiful, but mouldering to ruin"—has a "little household . . . near the center of the mass . . . a mixed family." The separation between the two worlds is emphasized: "Our villagers did not trouble themselves about our work, and had no commerce

4. So, Frau Stein is a "masterly devil" and Moses Haas is "as malicious a devil as we had on the place" (231) because of their evil characters; and Maria Vogel, whose eyes could shine with "hell-fire," is her mother's daughter, with no fears "except for Satan, and ghosts, and witches and the priest and the magician, and a sort of fear of God in the dark" (232). And so forth.

5. See Appendix E: "Mark Twain and Printers."

in it; we published nothing there, and printed nothing that they could have read, they being ignorant of abstruse sciences and the dead languages" (230). But if the master of the print shop, Heinrich Stein, is "a scholar, and a dreamer or a thinker, and loved learning and study"—a sort of proto-Enlightenment saint—the community over which he presides is anything but an utopia of learning. It too is a microcosm in which the struggle between light and darkness, good and evil, must be fought out.

There are two central rooms in which the main action takes place: "The printing-shop was remote, and hidden in an upper section of a round tower." And the large room "we used as dining room, drinking room, quarreling room—in a word, family room" (with adjoining spacious kitchen, Katrina's domain) is "a heaven of a place for comfort and contentment and cosiness, *and the exchange of injurious personalities*" (234, my italics); there is also an "apprentices' table in the corner" (253). All these assembled specimens of the "damned human race" (species: Austrian) are rather sharply divided into varieties of evilness and goodness. Aside from the master himself and little Barty, on the good side, there are the two Regens, paralyzed mother and enchanting daughter; the "towering" and "majestic" Katrina, yet another variation on the model of Aunty Cord, the Negro cook at Quarry Farm whose story was told by Clemens in "A True Story" (13); and Gustav Fischer, who "was about as much out of place as was Marget." The others, as we have seen, are a sorry lot.

Confrontation

This setting and cast of characters established, the first sequence of our fiction begins "one cold day, when the noon meal was about finished" (235) and continues through chapter 7; in it, the print-shop community is confronted by Forty-four, the remarkable "boy," as he is pretty consistently called. ("Satan" was somewhat older in character, if not in years; he was first introduced to us as a "youth" of superior mien and maturity, compared to the less graceful "boys" of Eseldorf—though he too was sometimes called a boy.) Forty-four at first appears pathetic and shy and tests the goodness of the castle community, each member of which responds according to his or her temperament and character.

Only Katrina befriends him, in spite of Frau Stein's opposition, and the master notices that the ordinarily vicious dog also accepts him without a bark or growl. In this first phase of confrontation, the "forlorn looking youth" seems to be part of an allegory of the verses in Matthew—"For I was an hungered, and ye gave me meat: I was thirsty, and ye gave me drink: I was a stranger, and ye took me in: naked, and ye clothed me" (25:35–36) [**23**]. This chapter of Matthew includes prophecies of Jesus' Second Coming, the End of the World, and the Final Judgment: "Inasmuch as ye have done it unto one of the least of these my brethren, ye have done it unto me" (25:40). Certainly Katrina here, in the terms of the parable, belongs with the sheep and has earned "life eternal," as has Herr Stein: "The boy is worn and tired," he says, "any one can see it. If he wants rest and shelter, *that* is no crime; let him say it and have it, be he bad or good—there's room enough." Though the boy is a "tramp" and "vermin" to Frau Stein, the master treats him with decent consideration and allows him to work.

This entire sequence thus explores the problems encountered by a stranger entering a closed community. Like David Wilson in *Pudd'nhead Wilson,* Forty-four gets off to a bad start. Some suspect that he is a jailbird, but he has a "good face," in Marget's opinion; some of his behavior "marks him for a fool," as Gustav says, "but it isn't the face of a fool." Gustav is puzzled: "I can't solve you that riddle, Fraulein—it's beyond my depth." A mystery is developing to which the evil characters respond with a note of "wonder mixed with maledictions—maledictions upon *the devil* that possessed the Jail-Bird" (240, my italics). Evil to him who evil thinks. The temporary solution in chapter 4 is a recourse to conventional opinion: "magic" must be the work of a magician.

Soon enough the situation develops into a sort of labor-union problem, however. The envious and cowardly apprentice, Ernest, who is "of his age," plays the traditional role of the bully testing the hero's mettle (as in chapter 2 of "Schoolhouse," where Forty-four crushed Henry's wrist). Forty-four's response here is Christian: "But I cannot fight you; I have nothing against you"; and when he "gently" offers to massage his opponent's bruise, the latter responds with unconscious humor: "You go to hell." The mystery seems to be mutual: why do human beings behave so irrationally? The Jail-Bird stands there, "looking as if it was all a puzzle to him and he couldn't make it out" (243).

All this happens quickly: as Twain put it in his working notes, "44 is persecuted in all ways the first day" (452)—though this might refer also to the first day of his apprenticeship, as we shall soon see.[6] The pace now slows down, "the days went along" (244), and the narrator, August, comes to the fore:

> Privately my heart bled for the boy, and I wanted to be his friend, and longed to tell him so, but I had not the courage for I was made as most people are made, and was afraid to follow my own instincts when they ran counter to other people's. The best of us would rather be popular than right . . . I should have been despised if I had befriended him; and I should have been treated as he was, too. It is not everybody that can be as brave as Katrina was. (244–45)

For Katrina, he is "a child to love"—to him she is "the salt of the earth" (Matthew 5:13). "What a devil to work the boy was!" He "seemed to find a high joy in putting forth his strange and enduring strength." Again, the theme of hypocrisy is taken up, dramatized this time by a peculiarly effective bit of "magic" (attributed to Balthasar) in which the dog "ducked its head piously, and said 'Yap-yap!—yap-yap!—yap-yap!' most reverently, and just as a Christian might at prayers" (246). This is followed by the dog mimicking obeisance, as if to royalty; and the effect is Swiftian in its simplicity and satiric power. When others kneel to Balthasar, overwhelmed by his magic, "I was amazed at such degraded idolatry and hypocrisy—at least servility—but I knelt, too, to avert remark." Both Balthasar and his presumed instrument, Forty-four, are now envied, even by Barty, though he too conceals his feelings in public.

The Mysterious Stranger is a sort of Bildungsroman, and the role of Forty-four will be to educate August Feldner; but

6. See Appendix F, "No. 44: Time Scheme," for a bird's-eye view.

henceforth this side of their relationship is kept strictly private. As in "Young Satan," there is a steady narrowing of focus toward a concentration on two figures and their growing understanding of one another; in the final chapters, August will begin to break out of his all-too-human limitations, while Forty-four will come to see the young Austrian as a "brother." The first step toward this eventual goal is taken in chapter 6, when the narrator seeks out Forty-four privately in his room at night; Forty-four arrives, somewhat surprisingly, "after midnight an hour or two." (Where has he been?) This corresponds to chapter 2 in "Young Satan," inasmuch as it is here that the stranger first reveals his superior powers, his secret—though not to a group of boys this time, but to one intimate friend. First, he reads August's thoughts; then, he mysteriously provides a hot drink ("it was nectar") to warm August's chilled body. All this puts fear into our narrator; and, after promising "to come again the next night," he thinks to himself "that I should break that promise *if I died for it*" (my italics). We are entering into a profounder, life and death, phase of our confrontation.

But August is easily won over and forgets his fears, and the next morning the two friends seal a sort of pact. August still thinks Forty-four a vagabond tramp (he uses the German name *landstreicher* [250]) but is happy to hear from him a bit of "sane and sensible" wisdom: "Why do you reproach yourself? You did not make yourself: how then are you to blame?"—this concept is new to August. Forty-four makes a sort of negative statement of his "omnipotent" powers: "What I don't wish, doesn't happen. I'm going to tell you various secrets by and by, one of these days. You'll keep them." August comments: "These things were dreadfully uncanny"; in general, "life was become very interesting" (246). Indeed, the rest of our fiction will be a working out of this promise to tell secrets and will display the interesting consequences it has for August's development.

Crisis

By now, "several weeks" (251) have gone by, and at breakfast that same day the master announces a decision that is received with great displeasure. Herr Stein, of course, does not know August's secret: "You have earned friends, and it is not your fault that you haven't them. You haven't one in the castle, except Katrina. It is not fair. I am going to be your friend myself" (251). He then raises Forty-four "to the honorable rank of apprentice to the printer's art, which is the noblest and most puissant of all arts"; he does this despite the fact that Forty-four is "a pauper and tramp without name or family" (252). And when the boy, "innocently and idiotically," denies ever having studied anything, the "generous" master rises to the emergency: "By the splendor of God I'll teach you myself!"

Why does August consider this "grand" decision a mistake? Why were the men opposed to it?

> He had struck at their order, the apple of their eye, their pride, the darling of their hearts, their dearest possession, their nobility—as they ranked it and regarded it—and had degraded it. They would not forgive that. They would seek revenge, and find it. This thing that we had witnessed, and which had had the form and aspect of a comedy, was a tragedy. It was a turning point. There would be consequences.[7] (253)

Whereas in chapter 39 of the *Yankee* Hank Morgan challenges and defeats the massed "chivalry of England," here Herr Stein symbolically challenges the hierarchy on which the craftsmen's guilds are based and, in a sense, moves in the direction of American-style universal education by offering to teach the pitiful stranger. In the village, the Hussite Frau Adler was challenging the Catholic priesthood; here in the print shop, the coming of Forty-four has precipitated a challenge to the monopolistic exclusiveness of feudal orders.

Forty-four's first day as apprentice is particularly trying. In addition to studying after hours, "he would now fill Barty's former place and put in a good deal of his time in drudgery and dirty work" (254). Barty, in other words, had formerly been the "devil," and Forty-four is next in line. Though drawing here upon his own experiences with the craft of printing in

7. The same phrase ("There will be consequences" [117]) occurs in the Nicky episode of "Young Satan": there the action seems inconsequential but leads to death. Here the action is by an adult and is momentous; the consequences will be "tragic," whatever that term could mean in this fantastic print-shop world.

America, Clemens was also interested in imagining what it might have been like in Austria to join a printers' "order" with ceremonies, insignia, and so forth (254–55). But the main point is that Forty-four is discriminated against, as a stranger or foreigner, and made to confront every conceivable obstacle. Unwelcomed, uninstructed, and friendless, he is a focus of hostility: "They were all waiting to see trouble come to him" (255). When the drunkard Katzenyammer uses a technical term the new apprentice has never learned, August secretly befriends Forty-four by thinking instructions—since he knows Forty-four can read his thoughts—that Forty-four then carries out successfully.

But success is just as bad for the stranger as failure. How could he have possibly known these things without prior instruction? Therefore: "The men took Forty-four for an old apprentice, a refugee flying from a hard master" (257). From the outset, the common denominator to all the reactions is hostility to the foreigner, whether he is thought to be a jailbird, tramp, pauper, orphan, ignoramus, or instructed refugee [**24**]!

This last accusation, along with Forty-four's earlier denial of ever having "studied" (which has, in a sense, precipitated the crisis), enabled Mark Twain to raise again the problem of kinds of knowledge, which had concerned him deeply in "Young Satan." What does Forty-four know? Or, rather, what kind of knowledge does he have? The distinctions made in the rest of chapter 7 might be variously formulated: lower versus higher, practical versus bookish, technical versus theoretical knowledge—with the stranger competent in the latter half of each of these polarities. The next expression of the collective hostility to the new apprentice is an oral examination to test his competence. Even August, partner to Forty-four's secret, fails now to understand: "Oh well, the boy was just an ever-fresh and competent mystery!" True, he had not studied Latin —"meaning in a school or with a teacher . . . I had only picked it up—from books—by myself."

As a result, when the eldest printer, Adam Binks, subjects him to inquisition, "44 took him out of his depth on every language and art and science, and if erudition had been water he would have been drowned" (258). Here Forty-four is the Admirable Crichton figure again, as he had been in "Schoolhouse." But for technical skills, those not printed in books or written down, he is still dependent on the "mentally telegraphed" instructions of the "experienced" August.

And again, Mark Twain is scoring points against his central target—human nature. "The examination scheme was a bad failure . . . , and the men hated the boy for being the cause of it, whereas they had brought it upon themselves. That is just like human beings." At this stage, August is much like the others: "I had saved 44, unsuspected and without damage or danger to myself, and it made me lean toward him more than ever. That was natural" (259). Here Mark Twain indulged (by describing the "marvelous" way in which Forty-four performs under August's "unspoken instructions") in a tour de force paragraph using a large number of printers' terms; when the stranger inked the form, he "came out of the job as black as a chimney-sweep from hair to heels," and these terms represent the kind of knowledge by experience that he lacks, though he is intellectually erudite. As to Forty-four's "blackness": we should note again how carefully Mark Twain avoids using the term *printer's devil,* though that is clearly the nature of the work now being described; instead Twain compares Forty-four to a chimney sweep. In fact, the only relevant use of the word *devil* we have found ("What a devil to work the boy was!" [245]) occurs before his apprenticeship began. The question of Forty-four's possibly "devilish" identity is thus left open, the mystery sustained.

This was as far as Mark Twain got in 1903. What is the nature of the crisis that has developed? As in the first phase of "Young Satan," the plot is double in focus: it is both social and private. On the social side, the mysterious stranger's confrontation of the established order of the print shop has produced a concentration of group hostility—in which the good figures of Katrina, Herr Stein, and August do not share, of course. But with August's secret help, Forty-four has managed to survive all the attempts to put him down.

On the private side, August has become intimate with Forty-four and begun to admire his wisdom, which includes a realization of the social tension: "It would injure you to befriend me in public, and I shall understand and not feel hurt" (250). Nevertheless, August's failure to stand up for his friend—in contrast to the behavior of Katrina and the master—is cowardly and immature. And this side of the crisis was precipitated when the villainous Ernest Wasserman "came out and told on me!" What will be the result of this disclosure? A possible clue to future developments is in the statement that appeared earlier, when the crisis first began to develop: "This thing that we had witnessed, and which had had the form and aspect of a comedy, was a tragedy." In any case, about half a year would elapse before Mark Twain would pick up the thread of his plot at this dramatic point. The knot he had tied was intricate and would not prove easy to unravel.

Union Trouble

Mark Twain was on familiar ground when, in Florence in 1904, he launched into the middle chapters of "No. 44" and began complicating them extravagantly and, sometimes, hilariously. He was treating, with a surer mastery and greater seriousness, issues about which he (along with Howells and other friends) had long been concerned and which he had tried to include in, first, a play he wrote with Howells in 1883 and, then, *The American Claimant* in 1891. As Colonel Sellers explained in chapter 3 of the *Claimant*, he had a plan to "materialize" the dead, who "shall walk forever, and never die again," and thus solve the labor problem: "I shall have a monopoly. . . . Two thousand policemen in the city of New York. Wages, four dollars a day. I'll replace them with dead ones at half the money." The fifteenth-century printers' guild was, in historical fact, another sort of monopoly, and Mark Twain does at various points speak of it as "the Union" (306, 307, 314). The entire potpourri of the *Claimant*—with its social theme, spiritualism, Europe-America polarity, scientific inventions, love story, artists, grotesque humor, and so forth—is a very crude prefiguring of parts of "No. 44" [**25**].

The device that, superficially at least, keeps the social side of the story moving (chapters 8–17) is a strike; but most of our attention is given to other matters involving August and Forty-four. Aside from temporarily solving the problems created by the strike through the use of "Duplicates," this sequence also works up to the "tragic" death (and secret resurrection) of Forty-four. From the point of view of the main action, this means that the latter is now thought dead by the entire print-shop community; he does not reappear after chapter 17 (except in his private relations with August and, a few times, disguised as Balthasar) until his transfiguration in the "transformation scene" in chapter 31, and then his next appearance is at the final departure. As is usual with Mark Twain, elementary exigencies of plot are observed; but the overall movement is thematic, episodic, and extremely interesting, once we have seen that the key to Twain's central intention lies in the "mystery" surrounding the stranger and his developing relations with our narrator.

Doangivadam

The first stage of this development, to the end of chapter 12, exhibits one of Mark Twain's characteristic tactics when he was having trouble with a story: he helped replenish his "tank" of inspiration by injecting new materials into the situation. Here there are two importations from his native state of Missouri: a set of miracles and a sermon he found in a 1902 pamphlet published by the convent of the Sisters of Perpetual Adoration at Clyde, Missouri [26], and, as a slangy American way of dismissing conscience and the Moral Sense, the colorful character of "Doangivadam," who is based on Wales McCormick. McCormick had shared Clemens's own apprenticeship in Hannibal, and Twain remembered him, Gibson reminds us, as a "reckless, hilarious, admirable creature," filled with a spirit of irreverence (14). The effect of bringing "Doan" (as we may call him) into the picture can be compared to that of bringing the Duke and the Dauphin onto the raft in *Huckleberry Finn*: he becomes a useful motivating force and a source of interest.

Because Twain's intention is to work up to a prayer scene in chapel on Sunday (chapter 10), we are carefully taken through the events of a week. The central contrast throughout this sequence is between genuine reverence and fake "magic." The bluffing Balthasar believes there is an elaborate "demonic" conspiracy against himself, involving "the very Prince of Darkness," and keeps at his charms and incantations. Meanwhile, we get an intimate glimpse of young August, watching for Doan's coming from "the Owl Tower" and experiencing private adolescent longings:

> Apparently all times are meet for love, sad ones as well as bright and cheerful ones. Down on the castle roof I could see two couples doing overtime—Fischer and Marget, and Moses and Maria. I did not care for Maria, but if I had been older, and Fischer had wanted to put on a sub—it was long ago, long ago, and such things do not interest me now. She was a beautiful girl, Marget. (270)

This is the only moment in August's narration that I have noticed Mark Twain falling back into the point of view he used with Theodor in "Young Satan" (109), that of an old man looking back to "long ago"; this passage tends to confirm an emerging hypothesis that the subsequent "comic" love affair with Marget is a re-creation of Clemens's courtship of Olivia Langdon (see Chapter 10). The magician's charms having failed, all the stops of prayer are pulled out on the Sabbath. This day is evoked in chapter 10: "It was a lovely Sunday, calm and peaceful and holy, and bright with sunshine. . . . The villagers had come over, and the seats were full." Mark Twain is displaying his usual mixture of true feelings and irreverence, putting into the mouth of Father Peter, who preaches the sermon, words from the Missouri pamphlet and ending as follows:

> There was not a dry eye in the house.
>
> At this moment the lightning struck the chapel once more and emptied it in a moment, everybody fleeing from it in a frenzy of terror.
>
> This was clearly another miracle, for there was not a cloud in the sky. Proof being afterward collected and avouched by Father Peter, it was accepted and consecrated at Rome, and our chapel became celebrated by reason of it, and a resort for pilgrims. (276)

A climactic point in the good father's argument is his explanation "that churches are not struck by lightning by accident, but for a worthy and intelligent purpose" (275); this is the old doctrine of providential design.

All the miracles cited occurred before 1490 (Turin, 1453; Marseilles, 1218; Bordeaux, 1322), and concerning the last one "the learned priest, Dr. Delort" gives expert testimony:

> "He now sees that the Sacred Host had, so to say, separated into two parts, in order to make room in the middle for the form

of a young man of wondrous beauty. The breast of Jesus projected beyond the circle of the monstrance, and He graciously moved His head whilst with His right hand He blessed the assembly. . . . The commemoration of this apparition is celebrated every year in this convent." (275–76)

This apparition of Jesus as a young man may perhaps be linked thematically both with the figure of Forty-four and with that of Doangivadam, who is "trim and graceful as Satan" and for whose coming August and Katrina actually are praying that Sunday [27]; and the splitting of the Sacred Host, which results in a sort of trinity, prefigures the theme of the Duplicates.

This is in fact the last time the village people figure largely in "No. 44"—except for a brief appearance in the "transformation scene" (chapter 31). Before getting on with his proper satiric business, one may say, Mark Twain wanted to establish once again a contrasting reality of powerful faith within the story, though this is seen as superstition by the reader when the seriousness of the sermon is undercut by, for example, the phrase, "there was not a dry eye in the house." Of course, August and Katrina are believing members of the congregation here; but there is more than light irony in the fact that the chapel's "new paint and gilding" (271) were contributed by "our Prince . . . to appease God on account of a murder he had done on an elder brother of his, a great Prince in Bohemia and head of the house" (261) [28]!

A bare summary of the action, as it relates to the consequences of the strike, would not begin to describe what happens in our story when Doan breezes into it. Simultaneously, Mark Twain has been working heavily on the theme of miracle, implicitly posing the questions: What is a true miracle? What is the nature of Forty-four's power? How is it distinct from Balthasar's "magic"? And in the middle of Father Peter's sermon, which is for the most part quoted verbatim from the Clyde pamphlet, there is a passage that is given as if it were Theodor's paraphrase of part of the sermon but that probably represents Mark Twain's own thinking:

He said that an occurrence could be extraordinary without necessarily being miraculous, that indeed a true miracle was usually not merely extraordinary, it was also *a thing likely to*

> *happen*. Likely, for the reason that it happened in circumstances which showed that it was not idly sent, but for a solemn and sufficient purpose. (273, my italics)

This sort of discourse puts us into the world of rationalist discussion of religious questions that had long occupied Clemens's mind.

In the initial characterization of Doan there is an interesting ambivalence: "He was a good son of the Church, faithful to his religious duties," on the one hand; but as his nickname suggests, "he didn't give a damn, and said so," on the other. His master faculties seem to be rebelliousness, especially against tyrannical power and in defense of the underdog; gay irreverence, he is "trim and graceful as Satan" and "a born masher"; and learning in the new "humanism," he is "possessed of a wide knowledge of the arts in general, and could swear in nine languages" (268). In other words, he appears to be an embodiment, in human terms, of some of the qualities and values represented by Forty-four and his "mystery."

We know that the figure of Doan is modeled on Wales McCormick; and on 29 March 1906, two years after he created Doan, one of Clemens's autobiographical dictations filled in the story of Sam's own apprenticeship to a Hannibal printer, which he was certainly recalling as he wrote "No. 44." Sam was then twelve or thirteen, while Wales was "seventeen or eighteen years old, and a giant"; and there was also a third apprentice named Ralph. Among the relevant associations is a story of Wales "elaborately making love" to the "very handsome and bright and well-behaved young mulatto daughter" of the "old slave cook"—the latter may have entered into the characterization of Katrina. This particular dictation is usually cited for its amusing anecdote describing how Wales printed the name of Jesus Christ first as "J.C." and finally as "Jesus H. Christ"; it also contains an anti-good-boy story involving Twain's brother Henry and a watermelon shell.[8]

But, what has generally been overlooked is the fact that the sermon in which Wales printed "the Saviour's name" was delivered by Alexander Campbell, the famous revivalist preacher,

8. *MTA*, 2:275–85. See also the concluding pages of "Autobiography of a Damned Fool" (*S&B*, pp. 160–61), which make use of Alexander Campbell.

who, as Ernest Lee Tuveson has shown, was prominent among the many preoccupied in those days "with the millennium and with history as apocalyptic"—which is the general conclusion toward which the last part of the "No. 44" tends, as we shall see. Tuveson has argued persuasively, I think, in "A Connecticut Yankee in the Mystical Babylon,"[9] that "Campbell's conception of history had much that might well appeal to the grown man, Clemens" and that the "mystery of iniquity," making "mysteries of plain facts" and creating a "long night of apostacy and darkness" opposed to "what we call experience," is part of a world view capable of explaining many elements in *A Connecticut Yankee in King Arthur's Court*, especially "puzzles about the conclusion of the book—the failure of progress."

Doangivadam-Wales, in other words, lent himself well to Mark Twain's purpose of playing satirically with problems of religion and history. His name suggests, without the theorizing of "Young Satan," a lighthearted release from the demands of conscience and the Moral Sense. He also has some of the adventurous spirit and boldness of a Western hero, as when he paraphrases a well-known boast usually associated with the Texas Rangers: "I'll be the right wing of the army, and you'll be the left" (279). But rather striking is the fact that his leadership is also associated with "wisdom, good and sound" (284, and also 295). The adolescent youth August needs a hero to worship: at first, it looked as though Gustav Fischer was billed for that role, but in 1904 the superior "wandering comp" Doan took over. It is as if Mark Twain could not get on with his Austrian tale unless he used the vivid recollections of his own Hannibal days [29], which he transposed, more or less, into a European key.

9. Ernest Lee Tuveson, *Redeemer Nation: The Idea of America's Millennial Role*, appendix; quotes in this paragraph on pages 217, 219–20, 215.

8

Mysteries, Mastery, and Salvation

(Chapters 14–22: The Duplicate emerges: "The Dream Self . . . could he be saved?")

About one-third of the way through "No. 44," the reader may be growing impatient with an involved plot that does not seem to be getting very far (much ado about very little, perhaps) and with a shifting focus that dwells on details with no apparent purpose. The relations between Forty-four and the narrator, August, which had begun to seem intriguing to the reader in chapters 6–9, have been shunted aside for a Sunday chapel spectacular, more strike troubles, ghosts, and the distracting figure of Doangivadam. Early in "Young Satan" the fascinating angel is established as a center of interest and motivation; but here the impact of the stranger has begun to be dissipated by too many scattered episodes that are hard to perceive as part of a single action.

But this method of developing a story through accretion and variation on a central situation was, for better or for worse, Mark Twain's usual way of creating a fictional world. The strike plot and its complications do not disappear from August's narrative, remaining as a part of the background till as late as chapter 30. The strike gradually becomes less important in itself, coming to serve more as an excuse for treating various aspects of the basic theme of mystery, developed by means of Forty-four, and for treating a remarkable array of supernatural, or at least hard to explain, phenomena. The problem of the Duplicates gradually becomes central.

The issues of magic and of Forty-four's superior powers have been present almost from the beginning; and the rush printing job is completed, despite the strike, by a number of specters or ghosts, whose character has not been explained to us. After the magician is tricked into threatening Forty-four and taking a public oath, August (along with Katrina) wants to pray again, this time for his friend's safety, which is defined as keeping him from the temptation of defying Balthasar. In chapter 15, August takes Forty-four to his room for this purpose and is shocked when he sees "that 44 was not minded to pray, but was full of other and temporal interests"; it seems Forty-four is really "indifferent to religion. . . . In that paralysing moment my life changed, and I was a different being; I resolved to devote my life . . . to *the rescuing of this endangered soul*" (my italics). As the emphasis of the satire moves from labor trouble to religion, we naturally recall that one of Mark Twain's early ideas had been to write about Satan's conversion to Christianity.

"Heathen" Mysteries

The keynote at this point, in an increasingly wild farrago, is Forty-four's "frivolity" and his "heathen" behavior. This goes along with a device, which will take over completely toward the end, of playing fast and loose with the time dimension: Forty-four says, "I am not living in the present century, but in one which interests me more, for the time being"—whereupon he takes out "a jew's harp—the niggers use it" and begins

> to buffet out of it a most urgent and strenuous and vibrant and exceedingly gay and inspiriting kind of music, and at the same time he went violently springing and capering and swooping and swirling all up and down the room in a way to banish prayer and make a person dizzy to look at him; and now and then he would utter the excess of his joy in a wild whoop, and at other times he would leap into the air and spin there head over heels for as much as a minute like a wheel, and so frightfully fast that he was all webbed together and you could hear him buzz. And he kept perfect time to his music all the while. It was a most extravagant and stirring and heathen performance. (299)

We understand that Mark Twain is describing a kind of nineteenth-century American Negro jazz session; or more precisely, perhaps, a minstrel-show routine, with a white man performing in blackface. But to August this is an "insane exhibition," and Twain explores a series of ironies concerned with whether August enjoys this sort of "fiendish orgy" and whether Forty-four gets tired when he "performs" this way. August wishes "he would sit down and act civilized, and give me a rest" (300); and when August wants to avoid telling his friends how he feels, he tries to do so by "grabbing at an imaginary spider inside my collar," which turns into "three spiders—real ones, . . . quite unusual . . . at that time of the year, which was February." As in their first private meeting, August's wishes and imaginings are being realized—or at least they are when Forty-four is concerned about him and paying attention. But "religious conversation" is "squelched" (301).

August and Forty-four are then magically transported to Forty-four's room and launch into a discussion of the latter's relation to Balthasar. "I know every trick he knows," says the stranger, and "some that he doesn't know," tricks "bought" from "a bigger expert than he is." (God, or the Devil?) Forty-four later justifies his building up of the magician's reputation: "At home we don't care for a small vanity like that" (he does not let August ask where "home" is, though that it is a world of hierarchy is clear from Forty-four's use of *bigger* and *smaller*). What follows suggests more parallels to the story of Jesus. August foresees that "you will bring a tragedy upon yourself" and suggests that Forty-four ought to prepare by becoming a Christian:

> He shook his head, and said—
> "I should be too lonesome."
> "Lonesome? How?"
> "I should be the only one."
> I thought it an ill jest, and said so. But he said it was not a jest—some time he would go into the matter and prove that he had spoken the truth.[1] (302)

A concern with the contrast between vain reputation and true righteousness and "glory" is an essential element in Protestant

1. Gibson draws attention (explanatory note to 302.13) to two relevant Pudd'nhead Wilson maxims: "If Christ were here now, there is one thing he would *not* be—a Christian"; and "There has been only one Christian. They caught Him and crucified Him early" (480).

Christianity; and the magician's entire career in "No. 44," through chapter 32, is an extended parable of vanity and hypocrisy. But at this stage August is still uninstructed: "I wished in my heart I could have that gorgeous reputation which he so despised!" (302).

August's weakness from the start has been an excessive concern with reputation that has made him afraid to make public the fact of his friendship with Forty-four. Now, to help cure August of his fears, Forty-four teaches him how to become invisible, whenever he pleases, by thinking a magic word: "Utter it in your mind, for you can't do it with your tongue, though I can." August's delight in his newfound gift is boyish:

> I was very proud, and considered myself the superior of any boy in the land; and that was foolish, for I did not invent the art, it was a gift, and no merit to me that I could exercise it. Another boy with the same luck would be just as superior as I was. But these were not my thoughts, I got them later, and at second hand—where all thoughts are acquired, 44 used to say. (302–3)

I should characterize the ironies throughout these chapters as rich but not particularly subtle; Mark Twain had given utterance to similar ideas throughout his career, and they became obsessive in the writings of his final phase. Here they emerge naturally enough, though unevenly, from a fictional situation. Some of the complexities may seem *voulu*, contrived; but for the most part, the effect is one of power.

Chapter 15 ends with the "good Christian" (so to speak) going "to sleep happy and content, without saying one prayer for 44, and he in such danger. I never thought of it." Is August simply exhibiting normal human selfishness here, or is he becoming infected with Forty-four's "heathen" amorality? A bit of both, perhaps; but the main point is that he is changing. And we now move fairly rapidly to what, on one level, is made to seem like a denouement of "strange and uncanny tragedy" (311) in which most of the elements of the earlier plot will be skillfully used.

Masters and Servants

The pages that follow (chapters 16–22) are in various respects transitional and may have caused Mark Twain some trouble [30]. As so often, he seems to be using the very act of writing and of playing imaginatively with his characters to help him work out his problems with the story. With chapter 16, the emphasis moves back to the social situation and Forty-four's foreign "strangeness" in it. Because of his newly acquired status as an apprentice, we are told, he is now "legally a gentleman" and decides to dress the part, which August thinks foolish because it increases the antagonism against Forty-four, which of course was the original cause of the strike.

A theme of masters versus servants—the latter are later modulated into slaves—gradually emerges. The legal master in the print shop, of course, is Heinrich Stein. But Forty-four speaks of Balthasar as "the master" (and of himself as "humble servant") of the dark powers of magic and sorcery. On one level, the relationship between the stranger and the magician, established early, can be seen as a convenient device to enable Forty-four to produce a variety of "wonderful" effects without revealing the mystery of his own identity; but we know, from his conversations with August, that he has some purpose in building up Balthasar's reputation and pretending to work with him.[2] In chapter 19 "he could not seem to care for anything but building up the magician's reputation. He said he was interested in that, and in one other thing, *the human race*" (318).

On a deeper level, a complex struggle for some sort of mastery is being dramatized in which the theme of Negro blackness will later become fairly strong. At this stage, it is still relatively submerged, but it is clearly present in the description of Forty-four, who "carried himself like a princeling 'doing a cake-walk,'[3] as he described it."

When the evil Katzenyammer gives Forty-four a "cruel slap," the latter (as always, in the name of the magician) utters a "darkling vague threat" that puts the entire print-shop community into a depressed and demoralized state of suspense. Toward midnight, "at half past eleven . . . it happened": a "*duplicate Katzenyammer*" (italics in original) appears—this is the first time this term has been used; when

2. See "Turn Backward, O Time" (Chapter 12).

3. *Webster's New World Dictionary* (1957): "An elaborate step or walk formerly performed by Negroes in the South competing for the prize of a cake."

used as a noun it is capitalized: "Duplicate" [**31**]. At first, this theme is developed humorously, in terms of the strike situation. The original Katzenyammer attacks his own Duplicate as a "bastard of *black* magic" (my italics) and denounces him as a "scab." All the struggles, between pairs and groups of Originals and Duplicates, come to a draw, "for each Duplicate fought his own mate, and was his exact match, and neither could whip the other" (306)! The logic of this situation is drawn out with amusing consistency and leads to a deadlock: "If the Duplicates remained, the Originals were without a living . . . they deserved some punishment, but to take their very bread was surely a punishment beyond the measure of their fault."

At this point, Doan again proves his superior wisdom by working out "a fair and honorable compromise . . . Doangivadam's idea was, for the Duplicates to do the work," which they are better fit to do; and because "to eat or drink or sleep" could only be done by the Originals, they would "take the pay, and fairly and honorably eat and sleep enough for both" (307)! However, this supremely rational arrangement (with obvious satiric implications) runs aground on the reef of man's irrational social conventions: "It would not be *lawful* for unions and scabs to have dealings together" (my italics). Another aspect of the deadlock is that each of the parties gets only "half drunk," an alcoholic touch that prepares us for a comic denouement in chapter 25.

So far, the Duplicates have been used to create comically satiric effects; but now, with the entry of the magician, we move rapidly toward what Mark Twain calls "tragedy"—though the situations, largely because they are described from the outside as spectacles and not experienced in their inwardness, would better be characterized as pathetic. Balthasar is maneuvered (by Forty-four himself, we presume, who is "dainty and gay in his butterfly clothes") into keeping his pledged word and burning the stranger "to ashes for misusing his enchantments" (308). This scene, in which Forty-four is "transformed to a core of dazzling white fire" (309), is brief, but effectively serious; when Katrina says the traditional blessing, we are told, "it was the faithful Christian parting with its [his?] all, yet still adoring the smiting hand."

The problem of mastery, as we have called it, is implicit in a great deal of this part of "No. 44" and is worked out on many levels. Between the Originals and the Duplicates, there is a deadlock. In the situation involving Forty-four and the magician, the latter appears to be master, but we were made aware very early that this is only a heavily sarcastic pretense. Mark Twain wanted his readers to see Balthasar as a fake; but he also wanted August and Katrina, at least at the beginning, to believe in Balthasar's powers. Hence the "tragedy" of Forty-four's death is treated pathetically in chapter 17, which depicts all the stages of mourning and remorse felt by Katrina, and by the others as well; she was heartbroken at Forty-four's having gone "unassoiled to judgment and the eternal fires of hell." In general, Katrina has begun to emerge as a peculiarly vivid and rich character, comparable to Roxana in *Pudd'nhead Wilson*. I find that I have linked her to Negro servants in the Clemens's household (Aunty Cord and others), as well as to the quasi-maternal figure of Aunt Polly. It would be more just, perhaps, to take her as "an original."

The "death" of Forty-four is sincerely mourned by August: "I was trying to excuse myself for my desertion of him in his sore need; when my promised prayers, which might have saved him, were withheld, and neglected, and even forgotten." But as for the Duplicates, "they were not affected, they did not seem interested." It is probably significant that Forty-four, in his presumed death, has been invested with a dignity superior to whatever went before: for one thing, he is referred to now as "a youth" (311), rather than "a boy." And in fact the stranger proves to be a master of death.

Another major form of mastery in the Austrian setting, of course, involves the Catholic Church. But Father Adolf is frustrated in his persecutions, for every time he chains the Duplicates to the stake "they vanished and left the stake empty before the fire could be applied" (317); and "Doangivadam, to show how little he cared for Adolf's pretensions, took out a fire insurance policy upon his Duplicate"! The Duplicates "fell to making love to the young women, and in such strenuous fashion that they soon cut out the Originals and left them out in the cold"! Such frivolities make August try again "to interest 44 in the life eternal," and in one of their conversations the latter says he is "not a human being"; but again he does not name what he in fact is. Instead Forty-four says:

> "I will use the language of my country, where words are not known. During half a moment my spirit shall speak to yours and tell you something about me. Not much, for it is not much of me that you would be able to understand, with your limited human mentality."
>
> While he was speaking, my head was illuminated by a single sudden flash of lightning, and I recognized that it had conveyed to me some knowledge of him, enough to fill me with awe. Envy, too—I do not mind confessing it. (318–19) **[32]**

August clings to his notion that man is "the noblest work of God," but to Forty-four the study of man is a "small study" (of "the human race or other bugs"), "in many ways amusing." August reacts bitterly:

> "As 'amusing' as a basket of monkeys, no doubt!"
>
> It clean failed! He didn't know it was a sarcasm.
>
> "Yes," he said, serenely, "as amusing as those—and even more so, it may be claimed; for monkeys, in their mental and moral freaks show not so great variety, and therefore are the less entertaining." (320)

We recall that in "Young Satan" a major purpose was "study" of the human race; but in "No. 44" the emphasis seems to have shifted to the amusement and entertainment to be derived from observing human behavior. The two are related, of course; the change is one of degree.

These and other problems of "mastery" were carried on into later chapters; their multiplicity and confusion here may be the result of difficulties Mark Twain had in deciding what direction to give to his story. The Church, the striking "union," the evil and ridiculous magician—these were rather obvious targets. But his deepest insights in "No. 44" were private, as we have characterized them, or psychological; and without abandoning the social conflicts, he shifted, by means of the Duplicates and other devices, to the more psychological problems as soon as he could.

Tragedy and Comedy

Another basic duality in this middle part of "No. 44" is that of "tragedy" versus comedy—this duality is bridged, perhaps, by the art of satire. Mark Twain began with the bitter-satiric, romantic-serious, tone of chapter 1; but after chapter 7 he shifted, rapidly and unmistakably, to the more exuberant style we have been analyzing. He never lost the basic seriousness of his concern, however, and it would be a gross oversimplification to characterize the later development as merely lighthearted comedy. The mixture that emerges is sui generis, characteristic not only of the late writings of Mark Twain in general, but peculiar in some ways to this particular work.

Among the dimensions August associates with "tragedy" are the problems of saving Forty-four's soul and the familiar but inadequate notions that suffering and death are tragic [33]. We have seen how speedily Mark Twain "resurrected" the corpse of Forty-four and followed a chapter of deep pathos with one of lighthearted entertainment and discussion; and we are naturally reminded here of the rhythm found in "Young Satan," where the angel "liked to rough a person up, but he like to smooth him down again just as well" (168).[4] Something of the same sort is clearly happening now, but on a larger scale that extends over many more pages and chapters. In any case, the "tragedy" of Forty-four's death, though evoked at some length by August in chapter 17, persists only for Katrina, Herr Stein, and a few others, since August soon learns that his friend is actually alive and well. One way to describe this development is to say that, having pushed the "tragic" problem of the stranger into the background, Mark Twain could proceed to develop certain related satiric-comic themes with which his imagination was more deeply involved.

But along with this humorous vein, there remain the graver questions concerning the mysterious reality that Forty-four seems to represent:

4. See above, "The Sense of Humor" (Chapter 5). It seems relevant to this entire development that a similar "rough-smooth" pattern had long been central to the planning of Mark Twain's lectures, and later his readings, as described in an 1871 letter to Livy: "*Any* lecture of mine ought to be a running narrative-plank, with square holes in it, six inches apart, all the length of it, and then in my mental shop I ought to have plugs (half marked "serious" and the other half marked "humorous") to select from and jam into these holes according to the temper of the audience" (Franklin R. Rogers, *Mark Twain's Burlesque Patterns*, p. 26). The analogy is not perfect, but Clemens's "serious" ideas were often quite "rough"; and humor, at least in some of its manifestations, might be thought of as a way of smoothing over tragic or painful truths.

> He was always doing and saying strange and curious things, and then leaving them but half explained or not explained at all. Who was he? what was he? where was he from? I wished I knew. Could he be converted? could he be saved? (320)

Despite whatever instruction August has already received, he thinks like an orthodox Christian at this stage, and the question of Forty-four's identity still remains unanswered.

Especially in these chapters, we must grant Mark Twain his *donnée* of a believing Catholic world and take the details that flow from it with some measure of seriousness. For example: "Of course the destruction of a youth by supernatural flames summoned unlawfully from hell was not an event that could be hidden" (311). The same seriousness is necessary with the repetitious business of Balthasar's inflated reputation and with the fact that Forty-four's ashes are buried "in waste ground half a mile from the castle, without prayer or blessing" (311–12).[5] But for Mark Twain, clearly, the fact that these traditional formulations were not acceptable as solutions to the problems of the story led to rapid transitions between the sublime and the comic. Father Adolf's "becoming ridiculous and a butt for everybody's private laughter" (317) epitomizes the central tendency.

One aspect of the many shifts between "tragedy" and comedy is the play with time dimensions. Tragic action must produce effects of inexorable necessity; and though it often proceeds by digging into the past, this is usually done on a level of knowledge and awareness (the Aristotelian *anagnorisis* or "recognition") and not as a frivolous sort of flitting about "in the past, in the present, and in the future" (315). In this connection, one aspect of the complex pattern of "No. 44" emerges when we step back from the whole with the help of our Time Scheme (Appendix F). We begin with a strongly emphasized sense of calendar time, culminating in a traditional Sabbath observance (chapters 10–11). Thereafter, the time element, while still present, gradually becomes less important; days flow

5. The working notes (458–59) make certain indications even clearer: "No consecrated ground—they lacked absolution." And the introduction of the cat, at the opening of chapter 18, has two dimensions, I think: cats traditionally have nine lives, in that sense they "die" and go on living, like Forty-four; and they are without immortal souls. Nevertheless, "Katrina and others grieve for cat and others."

into weeks, and the Sabbath is no longer mentioned. Finally, in the concluding dozen chapters or so, we seem to enter a dream world in which the time dimensions expand and contract and melt into one another; this dream world culminates in an apocalyptic Assembly of the Dead and in "the eternities." At this stage, of course, it becomes impossible to think in terms of tragedy, in its usual human connotations [**34**].

However, the strongest basis of the tragic-comic shift is as old as the Greek satyr plays and Roman comedy: sex. The lovemaking aspect of the Duplicates is introduced by Forty-four: "These Originals are in love with these women and are not making any headway: now then, if we arrange it so that the Duplicates . . ." The suggestion is left hanging at this point, but it has intriguing possibilities!

We have already noted various aspects of the difficult chapter 19, in which a remarkable balance between seriousness and frivolity is maintained. August persists in his efforts to save Forty-four's soul, to interest the stranger "in the life eternal" as he understands it; and he is struggling against the novel and heretical ideas constantly insinuated by the latter. When "the Duplicates fell to making love to the young women, . . . the castle was no better than a lunatic asylum," and it is hard to say what is the predominating tone and tendency.

> Forty-four and I went about, visible to each other but to no one else, and we witnessed these affrays, and 44 enjoyed them and was perfectly charmed with them. Well, he had his own tastes. I was not always invisible, of course, for that would have caused remarks; I showed up often enough to prevent that. (317)

The discussion of the human race that follows is sharply dramatic, with August reacting at times "acidly" (318) and "coldly" (320).

The difference in point of view has two dimensions, not unlike those already developed in "Young Satan." First, Forty-four makes clear that he is not "human": "It is a new and strange and fearful idea: a person who is a person and yet *not a human being*" (318). But, as already suggested, the lightning flashes of information do not begin to satisfy our curiosity about the precise nature of the stranger: god or angel? angel or devil? reality or vision? This margin of mystery, even more effectively than the ambiguity created by "Satan's" name in "Young Satan," serves to complicate and deepen our response.

Second, we encounter the problem of scale: "The difference between the infinitely trivial and the infinitely sublime!" This leaves us suspended between August's "mixed" emotions, in which a desire for reverence persists, and Forty-four's mockery: "Put it away; the sun doesn't care for the rushlight's reverence, put it away. Come, we'll be boys together and comrades!" August's response—"I said I was too much wounded, just now, to have any heart in levities" (319)—is almost a perfect parallel to that of Theodor in "Young Satan"—"I said I was too much hurt to laugh. I said our religion was our stay our solace and our hope" (167). Forty-four speaks "in his kindest and thoughtfulest manner" to the effect that "I have no prejudices against the human race or other bugs, and no aversions, no malignities." Just as "Satan" is clearly represented as "unfallen," so Forty-four here speaks (and since he is talking privately with his friend, we have no reason to expect anything but the unvarnished truth) without "malignity." The "emotions" he expresses are pity for the human race—"*out of my heart* I can say that I have always felt more sorry for it than ashamed of it" (my italics)—and a combination of "interest" and amusement (320).

Thus, we have here a part of the emotion roused by tragedy (an unmotivated pity, but no terror) and a predominance of the sort of intellectual comic sense we found in "Young Satan." There too, in the later chapters written in 1900, a central tension involved the exceedingly complex problem of the relation between thought and feeling; and here we may be similarly puzzled to find this person-who-is-not-a-human-being speaking "out of my heart." But, as we shall see, the major difference between the two treatments is, in fact, that the personal aspects of Forty-four, and his relationship to the narrator, are much more fully and successfully developed than were the parallel elements in "Young Satan." These are related to the alternating presence and absence of Forty-four, the rhythm of which is evident from our Time Scheme. In "Young Satan," a similar alternation was motivated chiefly by the errands for which the angel absented himself; in "No. 44," no explanations are given of this mystery, but one of the periods of absence will coincide with the activities of August's Duplicate **[35]**.

The Pathetic Brinkers

In chapters 20–22 Mark Twain continues to walk the tightrope between tragedy and comedy. Forty-four speaks "lightly" as he invites August on an outing to "a small town fifty miles removed" (321). Part of the relatively superior integration of "No. 44" results from the fact that, in spite of all the suggestions that Forty-four travels through time and space, we stay for the major episodes within the limited "world" of the castle, Eseldorf, and environs; there are no digressive excursions to France, China, India, and the like.

The episode of Johann Brinker and his family, which happened thirty years earlier, is presented as an exemplum of the character of the human species as it has been described by Forty-four. The young Johann has rescued Father Adolf from drowning and as a result is paralyzed for life. His tale is predominantly pathetic, even touched with terror, and only with the greatest difficulty could be called "amusing." The double edge of Mark Twain's intention is evident from the preliminary statement: "I'll show you a really creditable thing. At the same time I'll have to show you something discreditable, too, but that's nothing—that's merely human, you know."

Significantly, this "parable of human suffering," as Gibson characterized it (10), tells of "a rising young artist," who "had exhibited a picture in Vienna that had brought him great praise" and enviable celebrity. There is a brief thematic counterpointing here, on the level of normal experience, against Balthasar's exaggerated, caricatured concern with the vanities of "reputation." Johann's fate is roughly that designed for Nicky in "Young Satan" before "Satan" changes his life plan—had he saved Lisa from drowning he would have caught cold and spent forty-six years "in his bed a paralytic log, deaf, dumb, blind" (117–18)—and Gibson reminds us that it is "similar to that of Tom Nash of Hannibal" (14).

In the case of Brinker, the ironies are multiplied by the fact that, first, it is the evil Father Adolf who is rescued; and that, second, the lives of the entire family of four sisters are ruined "ministering to this poor wreck." Only "his mother's heart broke, and she went mad." When August seeks to formulate the traditional comfort of reward in the next world for virtue in this, Forty-four responds "indifferently." August himself suggests an attitude derived from one of the ideas taught by "Satan" when he perceives the mother's fate as relatively easy: in Forty-four's words, "the madness was a mercy, you think?" (323).

But the end is yet to come: a further twist of irony and pathos is reached the next day when August is shown an old, miserable woman about to be burned at the stake as a witch. This is Johann's mother, who had escaped into madness thirty years ago but had not been granted the grateful oblivion of an early death as August had assumed. Instead, she is now to be executed, condemned by the very person her son had rescued at such great cost! When August pleads for her life, Forty-four says, "No . . . that which is not foreordained will not happen" (325). There is thus no hopeful changing of life plans in this part of "No. 44."[6]

After all this, the picture of the old "gray head" asleep, and then set ablaze at the time of her death, comes as a powerfully pathetic climax; and there is an acme of horror in the simple act that breaks the stillness "in a way to make any being with a heart in his breast shudder—a man lifted his little child and sat her upon his shoulder, that she might see the better!" This is one of Mark Twain's stronger moments; and the entire episode may be compared—with respect to content, treatment, and successful blending of idea, narrative, and style to create dramatic action—to the death of Nicky and its sequel, in "Young Satan." It might well have been the stuff of genuine tragedy, but the treatment—including Forty-four's "serene" comments and his "faint spiritual cackle" (323)—as well as the other contexts established by the rest of "No. 44," prevent this from happening.

Instead, Mark Twain shifts his tone immediately, taking advantage of the presence of Father Adolf and bringing in Balthasar the magician for burning at the stake. "The crowd woke up! this was a show to their taste." Adolf confronts Forty-four, who is in the shape of Balthasar: "Yield—in His Name I command!"—and when the latter yields, August "rejoiced for that at last he had learned the power of that Name at which he had so often and so recklessly scoffed" (328). But

6. But see below, "Turn Backward, O Time" (Chapter 12).

just after the flames have been applied—as "the forlorn creature stood weeping and sniffling and pleading in his fantastic robes, a sorry contrast to that poor humble Christian who but a little while before had faced death there so bravely"—Forty-four-Balthasar vanishes, "leaving his robes empty and hanging collapsed in the chains!" The intention is to humiliate Adolf, but August again is shocked:

> So all his pretence of being struck down by the Name was a blasphemous jest. And I had taken it so seriously, so confidingly, innocently, exultantly. I was ashamed. Ashamed of him, ashamed of myself. Oh, manifestly nothing was serious to him, levity was the blood and marrow of him, death was a joke; his ghastly fright, his moving tears, his frenzied supplication—by God, it was all just coarse and vulgar horse-play! The only thing he was capable of being interested in, was his damned magician's reputation! I was too disgusted to talk, I answered him nothing, but left him to chatter over his degraded performance unobstructed, and rehearse it and chuckle over it and glorify it up to his taste. (329)

Some of the attitudes displayed by Forty-four are out of the *Yankee*, of course, but there are important differences: the narrator's point of view here does not correspond to Hank Morgan's, and Forty-four's miracles are presented as real, not faked.

This sequence is rounded out with a private session over breakfast (chapter 22) at which August's cupidity is revealed by his thinking that "the rich and costly table-service" is "presently quite likely to be mine" (330). Forty-four uses nineteenth-century delicacies and slang ("It's a jag!"), but when asked for more explanations,

> He reflected a while, then he said he was in a mood to enlighten me, and would like to do it, but did not know how to go about it, because of my mental limitations and the general meanness and poverty of my construction and qualities. He said this in a most casual and taken-for-granted way, just as an archbishop might say it to a cat, never suspecting that the cat could have any feelings about it or take a different view of the matter. (331)

Forty-four is not impressed by August's heated reply: "I must remind you that I am made in the image of God." Forty-four reminds August that "you are an animal," whereas

> "with my race it is different; we have no limits of any kind, we comprehend all things. You see, for your race there is such a thing as time—you cut it up and measure it; to your race there is a past, a present and a future—out of one and the same thing you make *three*; and to your race there is also such a thing as *distance*—and hang it, you measure *that*, too!. . . . . Let me see: if I could only. . . . if I. . . . oh, no, it is of no use—there is no such thing as enlightening that kind of a mind!" He turned upon me despairingly, pathetically, adding, "If it only had *some* capacity, some depth, or breadth, or—or—but you see it doesn't *hold* anything, one cannot pour the starred and shoreless expanses of the universe into a jug!" (331–32)

There may be an echo intended here of the line, "Ancient Tale found in a Jug," which appeared on the original title page.

To summarize: in these chapters, the pathetic scenes are subjected to a sort of comic irony; the comic situations are tinged with a pathos ("I reveled in these alien wonders; truly I was in Paradise!" [330]) that hovers between the sentimental and the "tragic"; and the whole succeeds somehow in making satiric points that militate against Forty-four's conversion to Christianity.

9

The Complex Self and Mr. Clemens

Out of the proliferating details of Mark Twain's text, two sets of problems have emerged as central: What is the nature of the stranger called Forty-four? What are his relations to August—or more generally, to the various aspects of the self, especially the Duplicate? Since "No. 44" is not a philosophical or psychological treatise but rather a work of fiction in which the chief character is "mysterious," the simultaneous concealment and gradual unfolding of elements in his mystery is inevitably bewildering. We need, therefore, at this point, to digress from our examination of the narrative and attempt a brief survey of the more theoretical and speculative aspects of our complex subject.

A close reading reveals that there is a clearly structured analysis underlying the action and having its own peculiar blend of comedy and pathos, its mixture of "moods and modes." This analysis was formulated, as we have seen, by Clemens in 1898 in the 7 January notebook entry and in the July passages (cut in revision) of the "My Platonic Sweetheart" manuscript. In January, Clemens's triad was one of the waking self, the dream self, and the soul; and the problems were concentrated in the dream self, the "other person" (alter ego) that emerges during sleepwalking and can be recalled only by hypnotism. These phenomena, clearly different from ordinary dreams usually remembered upon waking, had recently been studied by Charcot and others. By July (as we saw in Chapter 3), this "other person" had become the "dream-*artist*," "another and spiritualized self" that lives with "dream-creatures," who are "real creatures and immortal." In "No. 44," Clemens was trying to make up his mind about the reality and permanence of such "artistic" creations.

How are these interests related to the Duplicates? Some of

the complexities of this growing mystery are explored in chapter 18, when Forty-four ("the corpse!") reappears in August's room in a gay mood and treats him to a supper of "canvas-back" duck, "hot from America" and "beyond praise for toothsomeness." The Duplicates, August is told, though "solid enough," are not "*real* persons"; in some ways they may remind a generation familiar with modern science fiction of Isaac Asimov's robots. Indeed, "they are fictions":

> "You know, of course, that you are not one person, but two. One is your Workaday-Self, and 'tends to business, the other is your Dream-Self, and has no responsibilities, and cares only for romance and excursions and adventure. It sleeps when your other self is awake; when your other self sleeps, your Dream-Self has full control, and does as it pleases. It has far more imagination than has the Workaday-Self, therefore its pains and pleasures are far more real and intense than are those of the other self, and its adventures correspondingly picturesque and extraordinary. As a rule, when a party of Dream-Selves—whether comrades or strangers—get together and flit abroad in the globe, they have a tremendous time. But you understand, they have no substance, they are only spirits. . . . it is only fictitious flesh and bone, put upon them by the magician and me. We pulled them out of the Originals and gave them this independent life." (315)

Forty-four is still pretending to August that the magician's powers are real; but here his use of *we* implies that the two have worked in partnership, instead of in a relationship of master and servant, as previously.

As fictions, the "measureless imaginations" (316) of the Duplicates are one secret of their "independent life":

> "If they imagine there is a mystic clog upon them and it takes them a couple of hours to set a couple of lines, that is what happens; but on the contrary, if they imagine it takes them but half a second to set a whole galleyful of matter, *that* is what happens! . . . the easy match of a thousand real printers!" (316)

This is a clear formulation of the potency of "Thought," to be restated later with variations by Forty-four, most notably in the concluding chapter. As bodies, the Duplicates are "flesh and bone"; but this is merely "fictitious" and subject to "mystic" influences. The usual duality of body and soul is being complicated here. The central fact about the Duplicates is that they appear in materialized form; they are problematic because they seem to partake, in nineteenth-century parlance, of both the flesh and the spirit.

Waking, Dream, Soul

How did Mark Twain make his transition in "No. 44" from the usual dualistic view of the self? The two troublesome issues are freedom and immortality, and both come to a focus in the ancient problem of the body.

At first, in using the Duplicates, Mark Twain had based his fiction on the duality of the waking ("workaday") and dream selves (personified in the story as Waking-Self and Dream-Self). Later, chiefly because of the implications of Forty-four's gift of invisibility to August, he needed to introduce a third factor:

> There was another thing which I had learned from 44, and that was this: each human being contains not merely two independent entities, but three—the Waking-Self, the Dream-Self, and the Soul. This last is immortal, the others are functioned by the brain and the nerves, and are physical and mortal. . . . When I was invisible the whole of my physical make-up was gone, nothing connected with it or depending upon it was left. My soul—my immortal spirit—alone remained. Freed from the encumbering flesh, it was able to exhibit forces, passions and emotions of a quite tremendously effective character. (342–43)

Body and soul are linked, so to speak, in different ways, by the nature of dreams and by the existence of the Duplicate.

In the tragicomedy of love (chapters 23–25), which will be further analyzed in our next chapter, we begin with August using his gift of invisibility in order to make *contact* with his beloved Marget: "As she passed through me the contact invaded my blood as with a delicious fire!" This is an intimation of the intense love of spirits, the clearest poetic statement of which within my ken is by Milton's angel, Raphael, in book 8 of *Paradise Lost*:

> Whatever pure thou in the body enjoy'st
> (And pure thou wert created) we enjoy
> In eminence, and obstacle find none
> Of membrane, joint, or limb, exclusive bars;
> Easier than air with air, if spirits embrace,
> Total they mix, union of pure with pure,
> Desiring. (lines 662–68)

Mark Twain's version of this in "Young Satan" had been: "An angel's love is sublime, adorable, divine, beyond the imagination of man—infinitely beyond it! But it is limited to his own august order" (114). Now he is experimenting with mortal, human sensations by imaginatively premising invisibility—in other words, temporary spirituality of a kind—and other special conditions. In this scene, Marget shares August's sensations; but she has in fact been dreaming and behaves quite differently when she encounters him "in the flesh." August is puzzled: "Why should she be glad to dream of me and not glad to meet me awake?" (336).

There follows a rather clever, comic-pathetic, episode showing two young people who are seeking and yet avoiding one another—she wanting to renew that brief, dreamlike moment; and he burning with "the fever born of that marvellous first contact." August has an advantage because he can become invisible and follow her to "feast my eyes upon her loveliness"; but, with proper Victorian restraint—even in this manuscript not written for publication!—August resists the temptation of voyeurism: "When at last she entered her apartment and closed the door, I went to my own place and to my solitude, desolate." But he does not resist the desire to contact Marget again in a dream:

> My passion rose and overpowered me and I floated to her like a breath and put my arms about her and drew her to my breast and put my lips to hers, unrebuked, and drew intoxication from them! . . . Her body trembled with each kiss received and repaid, and by the power and volume of the emotions that surged through me I realized that the sensations I knew in my fleshly estate were cold and weak by contrast with those which a spirit feels. (338)

This is effectively, and delicately, evoked.

The comedy of love that follows seems at first to be based on dualities of personality similar to those in *The Comedy of Errors, A Midsummer Night's Dream,* and other Shakespearean romances involving disguise—which is a dramatic convention by no means confined to Shakespeare or the Elizabethans, of course. Each of the lovers, in the world of dream, becomes another person: Marget Regen is Elisabeth von Arnim;[1] and part of the comedy springs from the fact that August does not know his own dream identity until it is spoken by Marget-Elisabeth: his other name is Martin von Giesbach. The two dreamers enjoy their lovemaking, until they are interrupted by August's Duplicate, who addresses Elisabeth as *Marget*! When she fails to take notice of the Duplicate, the latter assumes "she's walking in her sleep!" August himself, of course, is invisible; and when "Lisbet" kisses "Martin" goodnight, the Duplicate assumes "she was dreaming of me."

As a result of these complications, August now experiences intense jealousy "for the first time," and when his own Duplicate kneels to kiss the place where Marget has stood: "I flew at him and with all my *spirit-strength* I fetched him an open-handed slat on the jaw" (my italics). There is a delicious humor, I find, in the picture of the Duplicate "rubbing his bruises" as he "went limping away, saying—'I wonder what in hell that was!' "

A diagram may help clarify the triadic situation that is emerging:

WAKING	DREAM	SOUL
Marget Regen ⟷	Elisabeth von Arnim	immortal spirit
	↕ (spiritual contact, unencumbered by flesh)	
August Feldner ⟷	Martin von Giesbach	invisible

There are many unresolved problems in this web of relationships: to begin with, the soul is invisible, but dreams are not. Because August can make himself invisible, there is an asymmetrical relationship between him and Marget; he has also an

1. This is the full name of "Bettina" (1785–1869), the young admirer of Goethe who published *Goethes Briefwechsel mit einem Kinde* (1835). The *Encyclopaedia Britannica,* 14th ed., comments: "Possibly Bettina herself had so woven the real story into her dreams that she could no longer disentangle truth from fantasy" (2:420).

exceedingly active, fleshly Duplicate, and she has neither of these "gifts." The closest she gets to the world of spirit is in dreams—more exactly, in somnabulistic states—and, as we have seen, these can be induced by hypnosis.

In their first thrilling contact, August is invisible:

> She was coming toward me, walking slowly, musing, dreaming, heeding nothing, absorbed, unconscious. . . . as she passed through me the contact invaded my blood as with a delicious fire! . . . "I was surely asleep—it was a dream—it must have been that—why did I wake?" . . . I believed she loved me, and had been keeping her secret, as maidens will. (336)

But thereafter, when August makes himself visible and approaches Marget ardently, she is shocked. The key to the "enigma" is that in August both states are under the control of the same personality, he deliberately and consciously assumes the invisible state; but the conscious Marget and the unconscious Lisabet (her dream nickname is spelled in various ways) are separate, disassociated personalities [**36**].

The Problem of the Duplicates

The first three pages of chapter 24 are a complex analysis of this tragicomic situation, part of which has already been quoted; the whole is presented through August's thoughts, which are based on "information garnered from 44's talks" (342). For example: "My presence as a spirit acted upon her hypnotically—as 44 termed it—and plunged her into somnabulic sleep." Further, the brain and nerves may be "paralysed by a temporary hurt or stupefied by narcotics" (342). "It seemed to me that I had now ciphered the matter out correctly" (343), but the problem of the Duplicates remains. The Duplicate corresponds in August's experience to the sleepwalking self in Marget's:

> To me he was merely a stranger, no more no less; to him I was a stranger; in all our lives we had never chanced to meet until *44 had put flesh upon him*; we could not have met if we had wanted to, because whenever one of us was awake and in command of our common brain and nerves the other was of necessity asleep and unconscious. (my italics)

Unlike the situation of Siamese twins, whose nervous systems are merely linked, these have a common body separated only by the differentiation between consciousness and unconsciousness:

> All our lives we had been what 44 called Box and Cox lodgers[2] in the one chamber; aware of each other's existence but not interested in each other's affairs, and never encountering each other save for a dim and hazy and sleepy half-moment on the threshold, when one was coming in and the other going out, and never in any case halting to make a bow or pass a greeting. (343)

What has developed, then, is a struggle for mastery, so to speak, among three selves of August. Where does the Duplicate belong in the diagram we have made? That its status is hard to fix precisely may be the result of Clemens's uncertainties; or it may in fact be the very point he wanted to make in these chapters! We have been told that Forty-four (with the help of the magician—but that is probably a pretense) has "pulled" the Duplicate out of the Original and given it "independent life" (it is a sort of golemlike creation) and that the "flesh and bone" is fictitious," but "solid enough!" (315). Now we are told that they are, in a way, both brothers and strangers:

> And so it was not until my Dream-Self's fleshing that he (my Duplicate) and I met and spoke. There was no heartiness; we began as mere acquaintances, and so remained. Although we had been born together, at the same moment and of the same womb, there was no spiritual kinship between us; spiritually we were a couple of distinctly independent and unrelated individuals, with equal rights in a common fleshly property, and we cared no more for each other than we cared for any other stranger. My fleshed Duplicate did not even bear my name, but called himself Emil Schwarz. (343)

In the scene after the meeting of the two dream-lovers, Lisabet and Martin (341), August's jealousy is directed, as we have seen, against his own Duplicate!

This absurd situation makes good psychological sense, however, since both the Duplicate and the Dream-Self are, in

2. Gibson explains, about "Box and Cox": "The comparison is especially apt since Box was a journeyman printer in John Maddison Morton's farce of 1847, *Box and Cox*" (481).

various ways, superior to the ordinary Waking-Self. The Duplicate "had all the intensities one suffers or enjoys in a dream! . . . But my Soul, stripped of its vulgar flesh"—as August's had been when invisible—"what was my Duplicate in competition with that?" Flesh, in other words, is arrayed against spirit. The result in our story is a sort of classic dilemma:

> Ah, there could be no help for this, no way out of this fiendish complication. I could have only half of her; the other half, no less dear to me, must remain the possession of another. She was mine, she was his, turn-about.
>
> These desolating thoughts kept racing and chasing and scorching and blistering through my brain without rest or halt, and I could find no peace, no comfort, no healing for the tortures they brought. Lisbet's love, so limitlessly dear and precious to me, was almost lost sight of because I couldn't have Marget's too. By this sign I perceived that I was still a human being; that is to say, a person who wants the earth, and cannot be satisfied unless he can have the whole of it. Well, we are made so; even the humblest of us has the voracity of an emperor. (344)

In other words, we mortals want to eat our cake and have it too. And the chief trouble we usually have with our "other selves" is their tendency to "vulgar" fleshliness, which has obvious Freudian implications, as we shall see.

The Problem of Forty-four

In the contest between the Duplicate and the soul, however, soul is superior. (This probably is the explanation of Forty-four's absence during chapters 23–25 and elsewhere: when the Duplicate comes to the fore, the stranger temporarily falls away and seems to be forgotten.) In chapter 22, Forty-four's exposition anticipates some of the ideas of the book's well-known "dream" conclusion. August is asked: "Can't you comprehend eternity?" And he is told: "Your race cannot even conceive of something being made out of nothing," for in fact the world itself "was built out of *thought*." This gives a somewhat different emphasis, as we shall see later, to the "vagrant Thought" that is a man: this "Thought" is akin to that of God, which created the universe:

"I don't mean *your* kind of thought, I mean my kind, and the kind that the gods exercise. . . . A man *originates* nothing in his head, he merely observes exterior things, and *combines* them in his head—puts several observed things together and draws a conclusion. His mind is merely a machine, that is all —an *automatic* one, and he has no control over it; it cannot conceive of a *new* thing, an original thing, it can only gather material from the outside and combine it into new *forms* and patterns. But it always has to have the *materials* from the *outside*, for it can't make them itself. That is to say, a man's mind cannot *create*—a god's can, and my race can. That is the difference. We need no contributed materials, we *create* them—out of thought. All things that exist were made out of thought —and out of nothing else." (332–33, italics in original)

We are less concerned here with Mark Twain's orthodoxy or "theories" than with the workings of his creative imagination. He was wrestling with a genuine mystery; and at this stage August is represented as still failing to understand Forty-four:

In my private heart I judged—and not for the first time—that he was using magic learned from the magician, and that he had no gifts in this line that did not come from that source. But was this so? I dearly wanted to ask this question, and I started to do it. But the words refused to leave my tongue, and I realized that he had applied that mysterious check which had so often shut off a question which I wanted to ask. (333)

An affinity may be intended here between August's attitude and the humility of the true believer, who is forbidden to ask, or restrains himself from asking, about the ultimate mysteries of his faith. But, in terms of Mark Twain's art of fiction, the effect is to tease the reader! Questions are being dramatized and explicitly formulated, but answers are being withheld. There are no easy solutions.

Not only is August restrained from asking about the source of Forty-four's powers, but he may also be radically wrong about the next world, especially about the realities of heaven and hell. Similarly, when "Satan" gives Theodor and Seppi a brief taste of heavenly wine in chapter 8 of "Young Satan," he leaves them uncertain about their own ultimate destiny: "It is best not to inquire too far, in some matters, if you want to be comfortable" (139). August assumes that Johann Brinker's mad mother will be recompensed for her earthly suffering by the eternal delights of heaven; but Forty-four shows him the truth: "That poor creature is in hell; see for yourself!" There is power in the simple statement, "Before I could beg him to spare me, the red billows were sweeping by, and she was there among the lost." And there is an analogous foreshadowing of the book's final conclusion in the sentence, "The next moment, the crimson sea was gone, with its evoker, and I was alone." This is essentially the same scene, in little, as the later one.

There is some excellent writing in chapters 16–22; and the somewhat zany, high-spirited irreverence that began to make itself felt in chapter 15 makes excellent sense once we see it as a fantastic correlative of the serious problem involved in Forty-four's possible conversion to Christianity—and also, by implication, of the problem concerning the salvation or damnation of August's soul. The characterization of Forty-four has certainly deepened and grown in complexity, and August still has a lot more to learn from the stranger. The tragic–comic, rough-smooth rhythm and the use of the episode of the Brinker family indicate that Mark Twain was harking back to methods familiar throughout his lecturing and writing careers and recently used to good purpose in "Young Satan"; these are now being managed skillfully within an even more complex design. The problem of Forty-four's true identity, and hence our understanding of the full nature of his mastery, seems to be related to the question of whether the story in which he is a prime mover will be a tragedy or a comedy or some complex blend of satire. Forty-four is associated primarily with the spiritual aspects of the duality represented by the Duplicate; but he also indulges in frivolous and "heathen" behavior, leaves August to cope with his Duplicate alone, and remains "mysterious" to the end.

Know Thyself?

At a later stage of his love drama, August comes to see that his Duplicate offers opportunities for self-knowledge. Emil Schwarz is courting Marget, and his villainous plans must be foiled. The extent to which August's "education" by Forty-four has progressed at this point is evident from the ease with which he now rationalizes his behavior. "Having reached solid ground by these logical reasonings, I advised my conscience to go take a tonic, and leave me to deal with this situation as a healthy person should" (363); and "being human accounts for a good many insanities, according to 44—upwards of a thousand a day was his estimate" (364). Another healthy symptom is that he takes a good look at his own Duplicate:

> It is actually the truth that I had never looked this Duplicate over before. I never could bear the sight of him. I wouldn't look at him when I could help it; and until this moment I couldn't look at him dispassionately and with fairness. But now I could, for I had done him a great and creditable kindness, and it quite changed his aspects. (364)

In order to facilitate this self-examination, Mark Twain invents (from the point of view of the fifteenth century) a phonograph and a camera, so that August can hear and see himself as others hear and see him:

> In the figure standing by the door I was now seeing myself as others saw me, but the resemblance to the self which I was familiar with in the glass was *merely* a resemblance, nothing more; not approaching the common resemblance of brother to brother, but reaching only as far as the resemblance which a person usually bears to his brother-in-law. Often one does not notice that, at all, until it is pointed out; and sometimes, even then, resemblance owes as much to imagination as to fact. It's like a cloud which resembles a horse after some one has pointed out the resemblance. You perceive it, then, though I have often seen a cloud that didn't. Clouds often have nothing more than a brother-in-law resemblance. I wouldn't say this to everybody, but I believe it to be true, nevertheless. For I myself have seen clouds which looked like a brother-in-law, whereas I knew very well they didn't. Nearly all such are hallucinations, in my opinion. (364–65)

This is more of Mark Twain's zany late style, but there is a method in its madness; we are concerned at this stage with "merely" physical resemblances and differences. The problem of hallucinations was much discussed in psyhcological writings around the turn of the century; and the "cloud" example, of course, may be an echo of *Hamlet* (act 3, scene 2, line 401 ff.) [37]. As August says: "Well, there he was; that is to say, there *I* was and I was interested; interested at last."

The self-examination soon passes from externals to "mentality" and proceeds by way of a conversation between August and his Duplicate that is reminiscent in many ways of the dialogue in "The Facts Concerning the Recent Carnival of Crime in Connecticut" (1876), that early Poe-esque allegory of "a man WITHOUT A CONSCIENCE!"—as the narrator there described himself at the end. In order to justify such dialogue in "No. 44," some contrast must be established; here we find Schwarz answering all of Herr Feldner's logical reasonings with a "vacant," "placid" sort of rambling elusiveness. The Duplicate finally explains the differences between them—related to Forty-four's earlier statements about his unidentified "race" (318–20)—in an eloquent speech:

> "Oh, not *that*! I care nothing for that—it is these bonds"—stretching his arms aloft—"oh, free me from *them*; these bonds of flesh—this decaying vile matter, this foul weight, and clog, and burden, this loathsome sack of corruption in which my spirit is imprisoned, her white wings bruised and soiled—oh, be merciful and set her free! . . . Oh, this human life, this earthly life, this weary life! It is so groveling, and so mean; its ambitions are so paltry, its prides so trivial, its vanities so childish; and the glories that it values and applauds—lord, how empty! Oh, here I am a slave—slave among little mean kings and emperors made of clothes, the kings and emperors slaves themselves, to mud-built carrion that are their slaves!" (369)

The problem of freedom, the conflict between flesh and spirit, and the theme of brotherhood come together and are fused at this point. (There is even a hint of the problem of blackness in the image of the *white* wings of the spirit "bruised and soiled" by the imprisoning body.)

In this long speech, the tone of which is a peculiar blend of mockery and seriousness, the Duplicate pleads for a spirit of fraternity: "Say you will be my friend, as well as brother! for brothers indeed we are; the same womb was mother to us both. *I live by you, I perish when you die*" (my italics). This is yet another prefiguring of the concluding chapter, though Schwarz will not survive even until then. He goes on:

> "To think you should think I came here concerned about those other things—those inconsequentials! Why should they concern me, a spirit of air, habitant of the august Empire of Dreams? *We* have no morals; the angels have none; morals are for the impure; we have no principles, those chains are for men. We love the lovely whom we meet in dreams, we forget them the next day, and meet and love their like. They are dream-creatures—no others are real. Disgrace? We care nothing for disgrace, we do not know what it is. Crime? We commit it every night, while you sleep; it is nothing to us. We have no character; no *one* character, we have *all* characters; we are honest in one dream, dishonest in the next; we fight in one battle and flee from the next. We wear no chains, we cannot abide them; we have no home, no prison, the universe is our province; we do not know time, we do not know space—we live, and love, and labor, and enjoy, fifty years in an hour, while you are sleeping, snoring, repairing your crazy tissues; we circumnavigate your little globe while you wink; we are not tied within horizons, like a dog with cattle to mind, an emperor with human sheep to watch—we visit hell, we roam in heaven, our playgrounds are the constellations and the Milky Way." (370)

This is fully as important, I submit, for our view of the aged Mark Twain, as some of the better-known, more cynical passages in "Young Satan." It is the first place where "the angels" are mentioned in "No. 44"; and it suggests, again, the close links intended among the Duplicate, the Dream-Self, and the artistic imagination. (There are quite possibly confusions here: the notion of "purity," for example, might suggest also the immortal soul, as previously described.)

But Mark Twain is being neither a precise philosopher or theologian, as I have already said, nor a clinical psychologist: he is releasing—to a degree indulging—his own imagination. And he is stating once again, in one of its richest contexts, a paradoxical idea he had long held most ardently: "Morals are for the impure." The illustrations of dream-freedom here include the dramatic ("we have *all* characters") and the cosmic ("our playgrounds are the constellations"). As Arnold put it in his "Shakespeare" sonnet, in a statement about imaginative freedom at its highest human pitch,

> Others abide our question. Thou art free,
> We ask and ask: Thou smilest and art still,
> Out-topping knowledge.

Mark Twain's Duplicate represents a sort of chaotic approximation of this—chaotic because it is not governed by human purpose and personality and seems to exist in a limbo between infinite possibility, on the one hand, and the imprisoning body, on the other. And again paradoxically, we are reminded by August that the Duplicate, whose name is *Black* and who desires release from "odious flesh," has been flinging "scoffs and slurs" at the former's "despised race"; he is referring to the human race, of course, but there are undertones of Negro-white conflict. Their relationship emerges, on the whole, as a complex mixture of ambivalences.

But Schwarz's speech does awaken August's pity, and the result is that these "brothers" do indeed become friends: "He could not speak, for emotion; for the same cause my voice forsook me; and so, in silence we grasped hands again; and that grip, strong and warm, said for us what our tongues could not utter" (370). Mark Twain characteristically undercuts this pathos immediately by referring to "that gushy and sentimental situation" (371).

Twain's use of the cat in the first half of chapter 28 is a masterpiece of comic evocation, as we shall see. After she is properly christened—rather, just named, for "she's no true Christian cat, if I know the signs" (372)!—and finally put tenderly to bed, the "brothers" carry on their dialogue in chapter 29, as they wait for the magician. Again, the Duplicate tells "about his life and ways as a dream-sprite." He also thinks like a dream: "His talk was *scatteringly* seasoned with strange words and phrases, picked up in a thousand worlds, for he had been everywhere" (376, my italics).

It is not easy to summarize just what our narrator has learned, so far, from "looking over" this particular Duplicate of his Waking-Self. The result has been general, rather than specifically concerned with Herr August Feldner, giving us an awareness of the differences between men's conceptions of themselves and others' conceptions of them and an awareness of the random, elusive, incoherent, capricious behavior of our various other related, "brother," personalities.

At this point, the Duplicate is intended to be very close to the Dream-Self: "He did wish he was back in my skull, he would sail out the first time I fell asleep and have a scandalous good time!" (380). And this is something the magician—that is, Forty-four—has to take care of: just as he pulled the Duplicate out of its Original, so only he can put it back. The Duplicate is the Dream-Self "abstracted" (literally) from the Waking-Self and materialized ("you imprisoned me" in the Duplicate's body) and thus given an "independent life" of its own, as we have seen; but it never wholly loses its dependence, in some ways, on the Original.

The difference can perhaps be compared to that between normal dreams, on the one hand, and the fiction-creating dreams of an artist's imagination, on the other. Schwarz "side-tracked" abruptly (379) when he wished himself back in August's skull; and he boasts that escaping therefrom—in his dream aspect, so to speak—he would see "wonders, spectacles, splendors which your *fleshly* eyes couldn't endure" (380, my italics). Thus, we can finally locate the Duplicate in our diagram of the self, in terms of his relative bondage to the flesh:

Soul	pure spirit
Dream-Self	temporarily freed, but bound to return to the body
Duplicate	a fictional abstraction, but imprisoned in a second body
Waking-Self	

Now Forty-four returns, and we get the Duplicate's limited view of the stranger's mysterious nature:

> "It's the magician; he's coming. He doesn't always let that influence go out from him, and so we dream-sprites took him for an ordinary necromancer for a while; but when he burnt

> 44 we were all there and close by, and he let it out then, and in an instant we knew what he was! We knew he was a . . . we knew he was a . . . . a . . . a . . . how curious!—my tongue won't say it!"
>
> Yes, you see, 44 wouldn't let him say it—and I so near to getting that secret at last! (380)

Suspense is thus maintained till the very end; at this point, August says: "It was a sorrowful disappointment." The only hint Schwarz drops during his plea to Forty-four, who is "still in the disguise of the magician," is that "you possess *all* the powers, all the forces that defy Nature, nothing is impossible to you." These might be the attributes of Deity, but on other levels might be applied also to the creative imagination, as some conceive it. We never are told which they are, unless the farewell statement by Forty-four in chapter 34 is taken, in a rather simpleminded interpretation, as the unraveling of the mystery. But we must leave that discussion for a later chapter.

A Tribute to Livy?

Given the fact that Mark Twain had the foregoing anatomy of the self in mind as he was writing "No. 44," we are still left with the question of its artistic purposes. What was the author of *Huckleberry Finn* trying to say or do with these curious devices? Gibson could find only "a dramatic vacuum" (10); and the difficulty any reader, along with Gibson, may feel is one of encountering too many things, too many diverse kinds of literary "moods and modes," proliferating in rapid succession—though I find that the central tendency does emerge unmistakably for an attentive and sympathetic reader. The main purpose of the Duplicate in chapters 23–29, though he plays many roles, is to create a tragicomedy of love and courtship, the denouement of which comes when Forty-four helps August dispose of Emil Schwarz.

As our Time Scheme (Appendix F) makes clear, after chapter 18 the movement away from calendar time leads toward a return to the past, involving both personal memory and universal history. This general tendency, the fact that most of the text was written in the shadow of Livy's final illness, and many of the details of the text suggest that "No. 44" is some sort of allegory of Mark Twain's most private experiences and convictions. This is only a hypothesis, no doubt, that has to be tested by much biographical study; but it is the only theory that makes sense of the work and its biographical contexts.

John S. Tuckey was right, I think, when he linked the writing of chapter 34 in Florence (1904) with the death of Olivia; and it seems to me natural, by extension, to see the entire middle part of "No. 44" as an indirect tribute to the woman Clemens loved. The death of Susy had been too horrible and too sudden to permit Clemens to view it with any of the detachment of art —though even then he escaped into months of work on the manuscript that became *Following the Equator*. When Livy and Jean passed away, however, the nature of their illnesses made it inevitable that their deaths had been long anticipated; and Hamlin Hill has commented on the ways in which "The Death of Jean," which was one of the last things Mark Twain wrote and which he intended to be the final chapter of his autobiography, linked up biographically with "the most recent preceding one in his family, Olivia's" (*MTFG*, p. 254). The later piece is a somewhat sentimental, conventional eulogy, however, as compared with this deeper tribute from an artist to the woman who has been rightly characterized as his muse: "No. 44" is a sort of re-creation in the comic-satiric mode he loved best of the happier days of their complex courtship. And his awareness of what he had in fact accomplished also explains why he made the later effort to bring "No. 44" to completion.

Though it is an Austrian village, "Eseldorf" is clearly related to Hannibal—as are St. Petersburg, Dawson's Landing, and other of Clemens's fictional small towns; and the many scattered elements and episodes that echo details from his biography and themes from earlier writings suggest that this work was shaped by a sophisticated variant of the autobiographical impulse, so strong throughout his works, to which he was giving himself more directly during his last years. We recall, for instance, that in "Young Satan" many of the passages cut by Paine and Duneka involve Theodor's family, who in some ways resemble Clemens's, and that the young Samuel had been a sleepwalker. Twain's choice of a print-shop setting for "No. 44" brings Hannibal to mind and suggests that both August and Forty-four may be surrogates of Clemens's youthful self and may reflect various influences on his "education." The theory of humor and the rough-smooth rhythms in both

"Young Satan" and "No. 44" obviously derive from his experiences as a writer and lecturer and are rooted deep in his temperament, as are many of the ideas about religion, history, miracle, science, and the like with which he is working.

The many allusions to private experiences, especially those involving Twain's family, are necessarily elusive; but most of these should be clear enough to the student of Clemens's life. Only a few striking parallels may be noted here. When Herr Stein says, "I am going to be your friend myself" (251), we inevitably recall Clemens's anecdote in the *Autobiography* about Livy's father's reaction to adverse letters of recommendation that he received when Clemens was seeking his daughter's hand in marriage.[3] The young apprentice-writer from the West was similarly challenging, and seeking entry into, the social and financial "hierarchy" of Elmira, New York. The entire sequence in which the Duplicate is seen as a "brother" and sought as a "friend" certainly reminds us of Clemens's lifelong problematic involvement with his elder brother, Orion. And in creating Forty-four Clemens may have had in mind some person (or persons) who influenced his spiritual and imaginative life—someone such as Captain Stormfield, the Reverend Joe Twichell, William Dean Howells, or Livy herself. (Because of the large amount of psychological analysis and spiritualistic terminology, some members of the Psychical Research Society, centered in London, might have been intended.)

At the end, Forty-four will say: "I am but a dream—your dream, creature of your imagination" (404). This somewhat puzzling statement might be paraphrased: "I am only mortal, after all, but in your creative imagination (based on 'nothing,' in a sense) you made of me a divine instructor." In our present literary study, however, these biographical implications must be kept subordinate and allowed to remain hypothetical.

3. Justin Kaplan, *Mr. Clemens and Mark Twain: A Biography*, p. 91.

10

A Tragicomedy of Courtship

(Chapters 23–25: "I had only ruined myself!")

As if bored by "cosmic" issues, in chapters 23–25 August shifts back to the social scene, the Duplicates, and a seventeen year old's love life, as we have seen. August is on his own now, but he is putting into practice ideas and knowledge acquired from Forty-four and using the power of invisibility bestowed upon him by the stranger. The result is a "French" comedy of love intrigues, with painful implications and pathetic treatment that at certain points give it some qualities of tragicomedy. In the previous chapter, we have considered some of its more theoretical aspects as they involve August's Duplicate and the difficulties of self-knowledge. We return now to the dramatic action in its early phases.

To our post-Freudian minds, there are no startling revelations or novelties in Mark Twain's analyses, and we must put ourselves back in 1904 to fully appreciate his achievement. In Vienna in the late 1890s, Sigmund Freud had made the world-shaking breakthrough of *Die Traumdeutung* (*The Interpretation of Dreams*, 1900). But he was not yet internationally famous at the time Mark Twain was writing; Freud's visit to the United States took place in 1909, and widespread interest in his ideas came after 1910. There are profound insights in Mark Twain's work, nevertheless, that constitute a significant chapter in the history of the relations between modern psychology and literature.

The involved plot is constructed around two central focuses: first, the denouement reached at the end of chapter 25 ("Good heavens! in trying to ruin the Duplicate, I had only ruined myself"); and second, various love complications, comically absurd on the whole but leading to a "sorrowful thought": "All three of my Selves were in love with the one girl, and how could we all be happy?" (343). How indeed? As compared with the usual boy-meets-girl plot in which two or more young men may be in love with one woman, this is certainly a more sophisticated situation.

The existence of the Duplicates has earlier opened up intriguing sexual possibilities and is now leading August into deep waters:

> Young as I was—I was barely seventeen—my days were now sodden with depressions, there was little or no rebound. My interest in the affairs of the castle and of its occupants faded out and disappeared; I kept to myself and took little or no note of the daily happenings; my Duplicate performed all my duties, and I had nothing to do but wander aimlessly about and be unhappy. (335)

Our adolescent apprentice is secretly in love with Marget, "the master's niece," but has little hope that she "should ever give me an actual thought—any word or notice above what she might give the cat" (335). The dramatization of relations between the flesh and the spirit, however, as we saw in our last chapter, soon leads to psychologically profound consequences.

Rationalization, Repression, Ambivalence

Twain associated the body with limitation, necessity, mechanistic laws, and even "slavery"; and he associated the spirit with infinite possibilities and freedom. The situation between August and Marget is asymmetrical: she has no Duplicate, and it is her "Waking-Self" who is "the slave of that reptile" Emil Schwarz. August is thus the rival of his own Duplicate! Emil ("the devil Schwarz") and Marget are lovers and engaged to be married; and the next day Emil tells her gaily how he has seen her walking in her sleep. The invisible August spies on them, while they talk of the "happy days" ahead and then gradually rise to "love's true and richer language, wordless soul-communion: the heaving breast, the deep sigh, the unrelaxing embrace, the shoulder-pillowed head, the bliss-dimmed eyes, the lingering kiss" (346). Racked with jealousy, August "swept forward and enveloped them as with a viewless cloud! In an instant Marget was Lisbet again"—and in love with her Martin. "That dream-mash" who is the Duplicate again thinks she is sleepwalking; and this time he is rejected out of hand.

Thereupon August takes Emil's place in "sofa-scene" lovemaking, which shows how much he has been learning from Forty-four:

> But with an important difference: in Marget's case there was a mamma to be pacified and persuaded, but Lisbet von Arnim had no such incumbrances; if she had a relative in the world she was not aware of it; she was free and independent, she could marry whom she pleased and when she pleased. And so, with the dearest and sweetest naivety she suggested that to-day and now was as good a time as any! The suddenness of it, the unexpectedness of it, would have taken my breath if I had had any. As it was, it swept through me like a delicious wind and set my whole fabric waving and fluttering. For a moment I was gravely embarrassed. Would it be right, would it be honorable, would it not be treason to let this confiding young creature marry herself to a viewless detail of the atmosphere? I knew how to accomplish it, and was burning to do it, but would it be fair? Ought I not to at least tell her my condition, and let her decide for herself? Ah . . . . . She might decide the wrong way!
>
> No, I couldn't bring myself to it, I couldn't run the risk. I must think—think—think. I must hunt out a good and righteous reason for the marriage without the revelation. That is the way we are made; when we badly want a thing, we go to hunting for good and righteous reasons for it; we give it that fine name to comfort our consciences, whereas we privately know we are only hunting for plausible ones. (348)

This is an excellent explanation of the psychological process we now label *rationalization.*

I have said that *August* takes the place of Emil in this lovemaking because of a rather curious fact; though we have been given to understand that Lisbet loves only Martin, in all of this chapter (after the initial explanation) the name of Martin is not mentioned—it is as if the Waking-Self and Dream-Self have combined, or fused, in opposition to the Duplicate. And this is the solution, or rationalization, that August works out:

> I seemed to find what I was seeking, and I urgently pretended to myself that it hadn't a defect in it. Forty-four was my friend;

> no doubt I could persuade him to return my Dream-Self into my body and lock it up there for good. Schwarz being thus put out of the way, wouldn't my wife's Waking-Self presently lose interest in him and cease from loving him? That looked plausible. Next, by throwing *my* Waking-Self in the way of *her* Waking-Self a good deal and using tact and art, would not a time come when . . . . . oh, it was all as clear as a bell! Certainly. It wouldn't be long, it couldn't be long, before I could retire my Soul into my body, then both Lisbet and Marget being widows and longing for solace and tender companionship, would yield to the faithful beseechings and supplications of my poor inferior Waking-Self and marry *him*. Oh, the scheme was perfect, it was flawless. (349)

The possible pairs now appear as follows:

Marget (Waking)	August (Waking)
Marget (Waking)	Emil (Duplicate)
Lisbet (Dream)	Martin (Dream)

But Twain did not plan to lock up the Dream-Self in the body until later in the story—here it is Martin and Emil who will be fused (along with August's soul), rather than Martin and August. Meanwhile, August-Martin uses hypnotic "suggestion" to get Lisbet to marry him before an "imaginary altar and priest," and they are finally "alone, immeasurably content, the happiest pair in the Duchy of Austria!" (349)—in the world of dream [**38**].

After the dream marriage, the newlyweds are interrupted on their honeymoon; she becomes Marget again, and the odious Emil takes over:

> The astonished and happy bullfrog had her in his arms in a minute and was blistering her with kisses, which she paid back as fast as she could register them, and she not cold yet from her marriage-oath! A man—and such a man as that—hugging my wife before my eyes, and she getting a gross and voracious satisfaction out of it!—I could not endure the shameful sight. (350)

The "scheme," in other words, has not worked because the voracious Duplicate has not yet been locked up by Forty-four.

Is not this an excellent statement and dramatization of the problem that Freudians call *repression*?

August goes on, in chapter 25: "I was so unutterably happy and so unspeakably unhappy that my life was become an enchanted ecstacy and a crushing burden. I did not know what to do, and took to drink. Merely for that evening. It was by Doangivadam's suggestion that I did this" (350–51). We are not going back here to our social theme with Doan, however; he has just been introduced briefly as a means of getting August drunk to "the heedless stage," in which stage our young lover forgets to make himself invisible. Through the bedroom door,

> I saw an enchanting picture and stopped to contemplate it and enjoy it. It was Marget. She was sitting before a pier glass, snowily arrayed in her dainty nightie, with her left side toward me; and upon her delicate profile and her shining cataract of dark red hair streaming unvexed to the floor a strong light was falling. Her maid was busily grooming her with brush and comb. (351)

Thus, August succumbs to the temptation of voyeurism only when he is drunk. "Supposing that I was invisible"—and therefore, also, that he is gazing upon his "wife" Lisbet!—August steps into the room just as "Marget's mother appeared in the further door," whereupon "three indignant women" begin to shriek at once! (At this point, the name of Martin, whose identity August has forgotten to assume, gets mentioned again.)

The satire at this point is cleverly pointed; it takes the form of a boudoir comedy with intrigues that are both logical and ridiculous. Master Stein assumes that the indiscretion was committed by the Duplicate, Emil, and comes to August to confirm this view, which the latter is glad to do. Marget accuses August, but her uncle calls this "nonsense, in the face of the other evidence and your denial. She is only a child—how can she know one of you from the other?" When the uncle threatens Emil ("he'll not compromise my niece again"), August misunderstands and lies like a trooper:

> It had always cost me shame to tell an injurious lie before, but I told this one without a pang, so eager was I to ruin the

> creature that stood between me and my worshipped little wife. The master took his leave, then, saying—
>
> "It is sufficient. It is all I wanted. He shall marry the girl before the sun sets!"
>
> Good heavens! in trying to ruin the Duplicate, I have only ruined myself. (353)

This was the point to which Mark Twain had unraveled his plot when he put aside this manuscript in 1904; except for writing the dream ending he would not pick it up again until the middle of 1905. The paradoxical outcomes of emotionally ambivalent attitudes and activities, related to what E. A. Poe in a famous story called "The Imp of the Perverse," is, once again, a phenomenon with which Freudian psychologists are very familiar. Thus, we may find ourselves doing the opposite of what we think we intend, or something we know must prove fatal (as in Poe's story). Or the actual result of our actions, whatever was in our minds, may be different from what was intended, as in tragic or comic irony.

The Problem of Freedom

Once we have granted Mark Twain this rather absurd comic machinery, we find that he has in fact carried out its implications with a madly humorous, grotesquely ridiculous consistency. But what is he driving at? What is the idea underlying the complex intrigue? On a fairly obvious level, there are the many insights into the relations between body and soul, Waking-Self and Dream-Self, Original and Duplicate, that are formulated in a triadic view of the self and revealed in a variety of love situations. But in chapter 24 this develops into an exploration of the more limited problems of courtship and marriage; and with this the problem of freedom becomes central, in a variety of ways.

First, there is the excess of freedom, the extraordinary license, that is achieved in dreams by August-Martin or in the sleepwalking state by Marget-Lisbet. This is not true freedom, however, because the self then comes back to the waking state and finds its world completely changed again. Also, the hypnosis used to induce Marget-Lisbet's sleepwalking states is a form of mental slavery in that it imposes an external control over the will [**39**].

Second, we have what might be called freedom by "rationalization," that is, by way of a scheme that takes into account the role of each of the three selves, attempts to control them, and places the other two in proper subordination to the Waking-Self. Mark Twain's psychology of love seems remarkably perspicacious and roughly parallel—very roughly so—to the Freudian anatomy of the self. The Waking-Self is clearly the ego; the Dream-Self, with its great imaginative freedom and tendency to chaos, points in the direction of the id and libido; and the Duplicate, with its complex suggestions of sensuality and fleshliness (implying also their opposites), points in the direction of the superego. Or, with a change of emphasis, one might see Forty-four as a dramatization of the problem of the superego—or conscience, in Clemens's terminology. Interestingly enough, in the Freudian scheme, which is ultimately naturalistic, it seems hard to find room for pure soul, completely "stripped of its vulgar flesh."

Striking, certainly, whatever the possible sources of his ideas, is the effectiveness with which Mark Twain has also dramatized the mechanism of repression, which contains just a hint perhaps of sublimation as well. Here, the final, normal freedom and health of the Waking-Self will be achieved by controlling, or "locking up," the various other selves: dream (and Duplicate) and soul. In the brief compass of a frivolous-seeming little comedy, the entire problem is necessarily simplified, of course. And the tendency of this part of the allegory is to move away from a mature view of freedom, as a Freudian might formulate it: the ego does not achieve healthy freedom so much by "retiring" as by understanding and using the forces revealed in dreams, self-analysis, and the like; the "solution" offered at this stage is obviously too pat. But we do feel that the anatomy of the self (or selves) adumbrated in these chapters begins to approximate a true psychology. No resolution of psychic conflict could really be accomplished so easily, but the elements of the love situation have been effectively sketched.

Third, a fuller achievement of a more mature freedom comes later in our story, when August exemplifies the ancient doctrine of "know thyself" by taking a good look at his own Duplicate; and for this to happen, Forty-four has to come back into the story. By chapter 25, Mark Twain had established only the general terms of the problem; in order to do so, it seems, he had had to let his imagination play freely for a period with some of the dramatic possibilities inherent in the Duplicates and to push Forty-four into the background. The resulting tragicomedy of love seems to me a lively, at times brilliant, success. But in what senses has August "ruined" himself? Most simply, his Duplicate will now be engaged to Marget. But there seems to me to be overtones also of the general pathos of all courtships: which self gets married, which achieves satisfaction, which must be repressed?

A final question is hard to avoid: how was it that Mark Twain came to write chapter 34 at this point? That important "Conclusion of the book" needs careful, detailed analysis; but, in relation to chapters 23–25, we here note merely its references to the Dream-Self and the problem of freedom. Two of the key sentences are: "But I your poor servant have revealed you to yourself and set you free. Dream other dreams, and better!" (404). One aspect of this richly significant statement and command is the notion of achieving freedom by "revealing you to yourself"; and one device by which this was accomplished is the Duplicate, as we have seen. In addition to this striking example, there are many other links, of course, between chapter 34 and the body of manuscript that Twain had accumulated by 1904.

11

August and his Duplicate

(Chapters 26–29: Know Thyself: "Brother, be my friend!" Winding up the comedy.)

The skillful plotter who called himself Mark Twain did not forget, in the nine chapters with which "No. 44" concludes, to complete and weave together all the important figures in his elaborately wrought tapestry. The style and the fantasy, however, are if anything wilder than in the middle part. Though written at various times (1904, 1905, 1908), these final chapters pay careful attention to the overall scheme and purposes that had governed the earlier writing, and the effect is one of a continuation and climax to what has gone before. Gibson's feeling about chapter 33 was negative: "He wrote the pageant chapter as part of an effort—never fulfilled—to link the body of his story to the 'Conclusion of the book' " (11). But I find the concluding sections, in their own way, aesthetically satisfying: the link is there, I think, and strong enough for us to say that this version of the "Stranger" was actually and successfully completed. Of course, such a statement does not pretend to settle the large question of the literary value of "No. 44" as a whole.

Forty-four now returns to the scene and becomes very active. Chapter 26 begins with August in despair because his Duplicate-rival seems to have won the girl: "Oh, why didn't he [Forty-four] come . . . and I so in need of his help and comfort!" Though the mysterious stranger was a very substantial physical presence in the first part of his story, since chapter 17 he has been officially dead, invisible to all but the narrator or present only in the guise of Balthasar the magician. Now August, after a period in which he "took little or no note of the daily happenings," comes back to the social world of the printshop community; and Forty-four is very much with August in all that transpires (except in chapters 28–29, where he is replaced by August's Duplicate).

The Power of Blackness

A theme earlier present involving images of night and blackness, linked with references to the Negro, now emerges to take the center of our stage for a while, then to undergo curious permutations. In chapter 26, there is an especially effective sequence in which Forty-four takes the shape of a Negro minstrel, speaks dialect, and sings some of the old plantation songs; and what I have been calling the characteristic zany style of Mark Twain's last decade—mixing wit, fancy, slang, and the grotesque in a freewheeling way—comes out strongly here:

> It was awfully still and solemn and midnighty, and this made me feel creepy and shivery and afraid of ghosts; and that was natural, for the place was foggy with them, as Ernest Wasserman said, who was the most unexact person in his language in the whole castle, foggy being a noun of multitude and not applicable to ghosts, for they seldom appear in large companies, but mostly by ones and twos, and then—oh, then, when they go flitting by in the gloom like forms made of delicate smoke, and you see the furniture through them—.(353)

Like the Connecticut Yankee, this is a sort of grown-up Huckleberry Finn, and he takes aesthetic delight in working up various "boney" skeletal and spectral effects. Later, Forty-four addresses August:

> "Bress yo' soul, honey, I ain' no dread being, I's Cunnel Bludso's nigger fum Souf C'yarlina, en I's heah th'ee hund'd en fifty year ahead o' time, caze you's down in the mouf en I got to 'muse you wid de banjo en make you feel all right en comfy agin." (355)

In other words, he is from the year 1840, when Sam Clemens was five—roughly the period of Tom Sawyer and his comrades! Finally, when Forty-four comes out of his "Swanee River" blackface routine, he says: "Your eyes are wet; it's the right applause. But it's nothing, I could fetch that effect if they were glass. Glass? I could do it if they were knot-holes. Get up, and let's feed" (356). To this reader, this is a most delightful section.

Other indications as well point to a major thematic dimension of August's Duplicate, to the "blackness" implied by the

German name Emil *Schwarz*. In the very first notes for "Young Satan," the good priest, who later became Father Peter, was called "Father Kitchelt (Black)" (417); and in the first manuscript, he appeared as "Mr. Black" (523—note on 53.32), which is, incidentally, a curious name for a priest. The evidence of Clemens's deep love for the Negro people and their music is well known; it is no exaggeration to say that at times it went almost as far as a complete, psychological identification [**40**]. This is one reason, I think, that one of his fictional surrogates, Forty-four, takes such delight in the role of a Negro minstrel: "And so on, verse after verse, sketching his humble lost home, and the joys of his childhood, and the black faces that had been dear to him, and which he would look upon no more" (356). Though today we tend to regard the songs of Stephen Foster as expressing a stereotyped sentimentality, there is no doubt of the genuine feeling being expressed by Mark Twain here.

It is a natural transition for Mark Twain from ghosts and skeletons to Negro superstitions and then to the Negro more generally; and the references to "the joys of his childhood" and "a cabin of logs" make this one of a number of passages in "No. 44" where the writer may be felt to have lost aesthetic distance from his imaginative creation and spoken out in the voice of Samuel Clemens. There is a textual link, also, to the concluding chapter: the music fades away and "with it faded the vision, like a dream"; similarly, Forty-four will later tell August: "*Life itself is only a vision, a dream*" (404). In sum, the web of Negro associations is rich and complex, involving Forty-four, as we have seen; the Duplicate (the name *Schwarz*); and, initially, the good priest Mr. Black.

The Duplicate, as we have seen, is a "fiction" created by Forty-four, "pulled out" of the original August; and soon the stranger will come up with the "insane" idea of making "some more Schwarzes, then Marget would not be able to tell t'other from which, and couldn't choose the right one" (358). A sort of comedy of identities is implied: many variations on an individual are possible, so to speak, to the imagination. This is presented as a "scheme" for unraveling the love complication, the word *scheme* sending us back to August's earlier scheme for "locking up" and "retiring" all the other selves into the body (349).

But, despite his name, the Duplicate's relation to the Original is far from being consistently one of a mirror copy; we find the resemblance between "myself as others saw me" and "the self which I was familiar with in the glass . . . not approaching the common resemblance of brother to brother, but reaching only as far as the resemblance which a person usually bears to his brother-in-law" (364). That is, as it seems to August at this moment, the resemblance is not even hereditary, but merely one of common membership in the human race. This difficulty had been established at the outset, in chapter 24: though "born together, at the same moment and of the same womb, . . . we cared no more for each other than we cared for any other stranger" (343). Now the relation of brotherhood is taken more seriously for a while, until the Duplicate exclaims: "brother, be my friend!" (369).

Without forcing the text, I think, one can see in this entire sequence a subdued, perhaps even unconscious, statement about the general problem of the brotherhood of man and the more specific problem of achieving brotherly relations between races divided by the "color line." To find this only in the names *Schwarz* and *Black* would be going beyond a reasonable use of evidence; but the vigor with which Forty-four anachronistically plays something like Negro jazz on a jew's harp, and so forth, amply justifies this broader interpretation. And Twain's wavering among various versions of the relations between Original and Duplicate, from photographic copy to "brother-in-law" resemblance, may be seen as a dramatization of the difficulties of self-knowledge. "O wad some Pow'r the giftie gie us/To see oursels as others see us!"

There are two especially problematic characters, from the point of view of plot: "the first and main necessity was to silence the maid," and the next step was to "stop Schwarz from proceeding with his marriage" (357). It is possibly relevant that August mentions the blondness of both: "that poor little blonde-haired lady's maid" (362); and concerning the Duplicate: "complexion—what it should be at seventeen, with a blonde ancestry: peachy, bloomy, fresh, wholesome" (365). But the Duplicate's name is *Schwarz*: *Black*.

All in all, the racial touches are not especially emphasized but are part of the larger tragicomedy of freedom and love. And, in a fuller sense, one may see this fantastic plotmaking and play with ministrel-show material as an expression, or displacement, of Mark Twain's deeper concern with religion; he is writing about the relations, not only among the various aspects of the self, but between the secular and the sacred. Another overall aspect of pattern in "No. 44" then (related to the shifts in the time dimensions already noted) involves the developing manifestations of the various mysteries: the wonder-working stranger, the Sabbath service and its miracle, the ghostly and psychological Duplicates, shifting attitudes toward prayer, and so forth. To explore such "mysterious" phenomena in depth is what the entire book is about, it is the central core and essential action of "No. 44," in yet another formulation.

Of Cats and Women

When August explains his "marital" difficulties to Forty-four, he runs into an old problem: "To my grief I soon saw that he was settling down into one of his leather-headed moods. Ah, how often they came upon him when there was a crisis and his very brightest intelligence was needed!" (357). The stranger's first "bland" proposal is to kill the gossiping maid and the rival Schwarz! "We don't need those people, you know. . . . There's a plenty of them around, you can get as many as you want. Why, August you don't seem to have any practical ideas —business ideas." After some heated debate, this "insane" idea is dropped and,

> the idea this time was to turn the maid into a cat, and make some *more* Schwarzes, then Marget would not be able to tell t'other from which, and couldn't choose the right one, and it wouldn't be lawful for her to marry the whole harem. That would postpone the wedding, he thought. (358)

The plan for the multiplication of Schwarzes is temporarily dropped; but the cat idea enabled Mark Twain to launch into one of his more delightful creations, the "cataclysmic" Mary G., which is short for "Mary Florence Fortescue Baker G. Nightingale," as she is later named (375); this in turn will be the springboard for comic treatment of the founder of Christian Science, Mary Baker Eddy (chapters 30–32). (I suppose, to see all this in a humorous way, one should share Clemens's passion for cats and his critical reservations about Christian Science.) At this point: "She came sauntering sadly in, a very pretty cat," alive to the tips of her paws and tail. She has long conversations "in catapult, or cataplasm, or whatever one might call that tongue" (362)—and is a fitting climax to Mark Twain's satiric thesis, in the *Stranger Manuscripts* and elsewhere, about the superiority of the "lower" animals:

> "Christians go—I know where they go; some to the one place some to the other; but I think cats—where do *you* think cats go?"
>
> "Nowhere. After they die."
>
> "Leave me as I am, then; don't change me back." (361)

This wonderfully feminine cat enables Mark Twain to make such statements as these on the problems of immortality and of heaven and hell; but she also develops into a humorously rich character with a variety of other functions. We have seen how Forty-four (like "Satan") earlier followed a pattern of alternating moods, serious and gay, heavy and light, "roughing up" and "smoothing down" his friend. Now, in the second half of "No. 44," the stranger, without revealing his secret, seems to have developed increasingly human dimensions, displaying various emotions and weaknesses. "Satan" does something like this when he takes the shape of Philip Traum and enters into the village plot; but Forty-four in these last chapters is engaged almost entirely with August and displays his growing humanity only in relation to him. We find a reversal of roles in August's description of Forty-four:

> He was crushed, and looked it. It hurt me to see him look cowed, that way; it made me feel mean, and as if I had struck a dumb animal that had been doing the best it knew how, and not meaning any harm; and at bottom I was vexed at myself for being so rough with him at such a time; . . . but I just *couldn't* pull myself together right off and say the gentle word and pet away the hurt I had given. I had to take time to it and work down to it gradually. But I managed it, and by and by his smiles came back, and his cheer, and then he was all right again, and as grateful as a child to see me friends with him once more. (358)

Put another way: though the ultimate nature of Forty-four remains mysterious, in terms of behavior he and August move steadily toward one another. And it is at this point that the idea for transforming the lady's maid into a cat is suggested.

To Mary, who is all cat and all woman, Forty-four appears in the guise of Balthasar. She provides another variation on the theme of servitude:

> "I would rather be a cat than a servant—a slave, that has to smile, and look cheerful, and pretend to be happy, when you are scolded for every little thing, the way Frau Stein and her daughter do, and be sneered at and insulted, and they haven't the right to, *they* didn't pay my wage. I wasn't *their* slave—a hateful life, an odious life! I'd rather be a cat." (360)

As we shall see, even in her feline metamorphosis, Mary will remain concerned about the "union" strike. Here she chatters along like a "liberated" American feminist: "What larks! I never knew what nuts it was to be a cat before" (362). August too has been changing: "In her place," he says, "I should feel about it just as she does." There are many dimensions to this metamorphosis: cats are not "slaves," they are well treated, they "do not carry anger" (360), they go "nowhere" after death, they "wail" in a beautiful tongue, and they enjoy having kittens. This is, then, yet another step in August's "heathen" education: it may be significant that the next time he speaks of "prayers" the reference is not to church, but to pleading with the magician—that is, with Forty-four (370).

The evocations of feminine felinity—cathood or cattiness, so to speak—in chapters 28 and 30–31 are well managed. Restricting ourselves to chapter 28: there is a lovingly careful description of Mary's behavior, which demonstrates that August-Clemens was indeed "fond of cats, and acquainted with their ways" (371–72). The "translation" of her soliloquy out of cat language is also delicious and helps advance the plot involving the Duplicate: "I would rather be a cat and not have any Duplicate, then I always know which one I am" (373). One of the high points in her characterization comes at the end of this chapter when "Mary Florence" (she has such a big name that it keeps changing!) insists on privacy and a snug bed, saying: "I have never roomed with any person not of my own sex" (375). And knowing Mark Twain's love of the German language, we sense the depth of feeling in August's final words: " 'Good-night, Mary G., und schlafen Sie wohl!' and passed out and left her to her slumbers. As delicate minded a cat as ever I've struck, and I've known a many of them" (376).

Thematically, the feminine cat is counterpointed against the grossly masculine Duplicate, Emil Schwarz. More generally, Mary G. is one of Mark Twain's most delightfully effective tributes to the fair sex.[1] And if in "Young Satan" the angel could only ameliorate the human condition by having people killed or driven insane, with Marget's maid we encounter the less drastic procedure of turning them into animals. A "heathen" idea, certainly, but one with many precedents in the literature of satire—the most notable, of course, is Swift's rational horses, the Houyhnhnms, in part 4 of *Gulliver's Travels*; whatever the ironies, Mark Twain had achieved a positive, even gay, solution.

Disposing of the Duplicate

In chapter 29 [**41**], another theme of blackness begins to develop, which will reach its climax in chapter 33: "invisible black planets swimming in eternal midnight and thick-armored in perpetual ice, where the people have no eyes nor any use for them"; and "*general space*—that sea of ether which has no shores, and stretches on, and on, and arrives nowhere; which is a waste of black gloom and thick darkness through which you may rush forever at thought-speed" (377); and so forth. We may associate this with *Captain Stormfield's Visit to Heaven*, extracts from which were published in 1909, though its ideas had lived in Mark Twain's imagination since the 1860s;[2] with "The Great Dark," to use DeVoto's title; and with other texts. This particular blackness seems more astronomical than apocalyptic or psychological; but the latter formulations, though relegated at this stage to the "groping

1. He was harking back, in a sense, to a *jeu d'esprit* he wrote for Susy and Clara in 1880, "A Cat-Tale" (included by Bernard DeVoto in *Letters from the Earth*). On the subject of cats and women, see "The Fourth Life" in Louis Untermeyer's *Cat O'Nine Tales*, entitled "How I Became Human." The man this cat marries observes: "I've always heard that there's something of a woman in every cat and something of a cat in every woman" (p. 40). My guess is that Mark Twain would have said "amen" to that.

2. See S. L. Clemens, *Report from Paradise*; the full texts were reproduced by Ray B. Browne in a later edition: *Mark Twain's Quarrel with Heaven*.

Mortal Mind," will emerge later. Indeed, there is "*nothing* permanent about a dream-sprite's character, constitution, beliefs, opinions, intentions, likes, dislikes, or anything else; all he cares for is to travel, and talk, and see wonderful things and *have a good time*" (my italics). But the "sprites" do feel limited in the body, "because they had to communicate through the flesh-brothers' Waking-Self imagination" (378), which is earthbound.

On the positive side, this might be thought of as an experiment—one that eventually fails—with bringing together aspects of the self. This experiment parallels the gradually increasing intimacy of August and Forty-four; and, as we have seen, the ambiguous, shifting status of the Duplicate reflects profound pre-Freudian insights into complexities Mark Twain is exploring, perhaps without understanding them fully himself. On the other hand, we recall also August's earlier scheme for *locking up* the Dream-Self *and* the soul (349) and possibly the Duplicate as well, and we recall that the "chances" of the Duplicate's survival are linked to the mortal body: "I perish when you die" (369).[3] The satire here is coruscating:

> He went to discussing my health—as coldly as if I had been a piece of mere property that he was commercially interested in, and which ought to be thoughtfully and prudently taken care of for *his* sake. And he went into particulars, by gracious! advising me to be very careful about my diet, and to take a good deal of exercise, and keep regular hours, and avoid dissipation and religion and not get married, because a family brought love, and distributed it among many objects, and intensified it, and this engendered wearing cares and anxieties, and when the objects suffered or died the miseries and anxieties multiplied and broke the heart and shortened life; whereas if I took good care of myself and avoided these indiscretions, there was no reason why he should not live ten million years and be hap—
>
> I broke in and changed the subject, so as to keep from getting inhospitable and saying language [profanity]. (378–79)

3. There is a parallel here to the situation of the cholera microbe named "Huck" in "Three Thousand Years Among the Microbes," who exists within the universe of the Hungarian tramp Blitzowski: "What would become of me if he should disintegrate?" (*WWD*, p. 458, see list of short references p. xiii).

The chief point here is that August's Waking-Self is still "a good deal tried" by his amoral, frivolous Duplicate.

The same is true in the following paragraph, in which Schwarz (sounding more and more like "Satan") discusses the Christian and Jewish Sabbaths. This obviously comes out of the same complex of philo-Semitism, sharpened by the encounter with virulent anti-Semitism in Vienna, that led Twain to write "Concerning the Jews" in 1898. There is a touch of the envy of excellence (which is illustrated throughout the opening chapters of "No. 44" and which Mark Twain saw as the root cause of anti-Semitism) in the Duplicate's saying, "along in the twentieth century somewhere it was going to be necessary to furnish the Jews another Sabbath to keep, so as to save what might be left of Christian property at that time" (379). Mark Twain's satire was wide ranging, magnificently ambivalent, and magnanimously scornful, at most times, and it was directed toward all targets, including himself. But it was no accident, it seems, that anti-Semites could use quotations from his philo-Semitic essay as part of their propaganda.

For the final disposition of the Duplicate, Forty-four goes back to his earlier idea of multiplying Schwarzes: "He said . . . he would let this one go, and make some fresh ones for the wedding, the family could get along very well that way. So he told Schwarz to stand up and melt" (281). Thus, the "devilish" idea of a harem, which as we noted is found in the very first "Stranger" notes (415), was kept almost to the end, but here the sexes are reversed: there are multiple men, instead of women. This is the last mention we find of the love plot. In fact, Marget herself is mentioned only once more, and that is when time is made to run backward to the scene of the drunken invasion of her bedchamber; however, when "I was due to appear drunk in Marget's chamber, I took the pledge and stayed away" (399)!

Clearly, the entire love complication was used to provide a dramatization of the complex structure of the self; in a sense, Marget (as well as the Duplicate) has already served her purpose in our story and can be dismissed. Whether or not a wedding (with the Original, of course) will take place need not concern us; that would make another story of a different kind. The "very pretty" thinning out of Schwarz into "the delicatest soap-bubble stuff . . . then—poof! and it was gone!"

is similar to the disappearance of "Satan" in chapter 2 of "Young Satan," after his first long meeting with Theodor and his friends (56). So much for the "brothers" and ardent "friends" of the preceding chapters. *Sic transit gloria fraterni*!

One final note, with respect to Emil Schwarz and the Negro minstrel sequence. Does not the writing of those pages in Florence harmonize perfectly with the well-known fact that, on the day of Livy's death, Clemens "went to the piano and sang the old songs, the quaint negro hymns" (*MTGF*, p. 84) of his childhood? In their lost Hartford home, he and Livy had cherished the humanity of George Griffin, Aunty Cord, and others of their race; and it was in the Langdon family of Elmira, New York (Livy's maiden name was Olivia Langdon) that he had first learned to carry abolitionist ideals over into programs for the amelioration of the lot of the Negro.

12

Farewell to Forty-four

(Chapters 30–34: "Turn backward, O Time"—"I your poor servant have revealed you to yourself and set you free.")

There is a double (at least) tendency in the last five chapters of "No. 44." On the one hand, with the Duplicate gone,[1] the direction of August's story goes back to social and, later, to historical matters, the latter tending toward the apocalyptic. The feminine interest, too, has changed drastically: August's love for Marget, and her possible marriage to one of the *other* Schwarzes Forty-four has promised to create, is not mentioned again; however, the delightful cat, after her "lady's-maid curtsy" and "quite Cheshirely" smiling (381), is a lively, not at all romantic, presence. What we have been calling the psychology of adolescent love is well-nigh forgotten.

On the other hand, Forty-four, our mysterious stranger, and his relationship to August become central. More of his teaching remains to be conveyed, by means of discussion and dramatization that includes some extremely spectacular "effects." This aspect of Twain's work involves a drastic critique of the language, and other characteristics, of Christian Science: the second part of Mark Twain's book on that highly controversial subject was written in 1903, and other "Eddypus" satires had been penned [**42**]; chapters 30–31 of "No. 44" came in 1905; *What Is Man?* was privately published in 1906; and the *Christian Science* volume itself appeared in February 1907. Obviously, some sort of intellectual-religious summing-up was being attempted. But merely in terms of the plot of "No. 44"

1. Though August's Duplicate has vanished like a bubble, Mary G. continues to refer to August as "Duplicate" (387): she has not had the benefit of Forty-four's instruction. Nor have the strikers, who work up a conspiracy "to kill the Duplicates" (387). The general fact and problem of the Duplicates persist, but not for August.

one might say that, having more or less disposed of the Duplicate and the problems it presented, Mark Twain was now preparing to do the same with Forty-four. We naturally ask, yet again: What are the relationships among Forty-four, the Duplicate, and August? Who, or what, is the "mysterious stranger"?

Disposing of the Crisis

Getting back to the social scene involves a return to the situation that precipitated the original crisis of the strike: the tension between Forty-four and the print-shop "union." This requires that Forty-four reappear, in the guise of Balthasar, since his youthful self is supposed to be dead; and again the pattern of "roughing up" and "smoothing down" is followed. Cosmic issues, and the questions of war and peace, are put aside by Forty-four: "I think we can have a good time. I have shut down the prophecy-works and prepared for it." The point is the same as that already made in chapter 9 of "Young Satan": foreseeing all of the future eliminates the pleasurable element of surprise; and Forty-four confesses: "That is one of the main reasons that I come here so much. I do love surprises!" (386). He is saying, in essence, "I don't know a thing that's ahead, any more than you do," which results in a sort of meeting of the two levels of being: August has been making good progress in the mysteries, on the one hand; and Forty-four is temporarily indulging in the limitations of "humanity," on the other.

This meeting of minds, or of levels of being, between August and the stranger may be seen as one of the main outcomes of our fiction. August and his Duplicate, "brothers" and "friends," have exhibited a "gushy and sentimental" relationship that soon disappears like a bubble; but the developing companionship between August and Forty-four, at the center of the plot, is much more complex, real, and substantial. Thus, when Forty-four invites August to one of his delicious "alien meals, raked up from countries I had never heard of and out of seasons a million years apart," the latter overcomes "habit and prejudiced imagination" and "enjoyed what came, asking *few* or no questions" (382, my italics). He is thus almost completely won over and educated by the stranger, though he is still anxious to know where the latter comes from: *God or the Devil?* remains the unspoken question. Forty-four, on his part, desires to be rid of his foreknowledge:

> "Where I came from we have a gift which we get tired of, now and then. We foresee everything that is going to happen, and so when it happens there's nothing to it, don't you see? . . . I do love surprises! I'm only a youth and it's natural. I love shows and spectacles, and stunning dramatics, and I love to astonish people, and show off, and be and do all the gaudy things a boy loves to be and do; and whenever I'm here and have got matters worked up to where there is a good prospect to the fore, I shut down the works and have a time! I've shut them down now, two hours ago . . . I had plans, but I've thrown them aside. . . . I will let things go their own way, and act as circumstances suggest." (386)

Forty-four wants to be less free, in other words, in order to be more human—in the style, roughly, of Tom Sawyer.

As Forty-four has said, "things are working"; and the cat now comes in to report developments, going on and on in a state of breathless excitement:

> "Everybody is searching for me, and for you, too, Duplicate, and for your Original; they've been at it some time, and are coming to think all three of us is murdered . . . and laws bless me, *there's a conspiracy* . . . . It's the strikers, going to kill the Duplicates." (387, my italics)[2]

What we have been calling a meeting of levels is also a sort of crossing of roles: Forty-four appears in his usual disguise as magician ("I'm going just so"), and August again becomes invisible (388).

We start on a "dark, sour, gloomy morning," and to intensify the effect, Forty-four works up an eclipse [**43**]; in addition, that night will be a "Ghost-Night," a special one of the "Hundredth Year," when "the best ghosts from many other castles come by invitation, . . . and take a hand at the great ball and banquet at midnight." This time Forty-four is "inviting A 1

2. We recall that one of the last attempts by Mark Twain to use Tom and Huck was called "Tom Sawyer's Conspiracy" (1897–1900) and made elaborate use of printers and printing.

ghosts from everywhere in the world and from all the ages, past and future, and each could bring a friend if he liked—any friend, character no object, just so he is dead" (389)!

When Forty-four appears, disguised as the magician, Katrina wants to kill him in revenge for the "death" of her darling boy. She charges at him

> through the gathering darkness—
>
> Then suddenly there was a great light! she lifted her head and caught it full in her swarthy face, which it transfigured with its white glory, as it did also all that place, and its marble pillars, and the frightened people, and Katrina dropped her knife and fell to her knees . . . and there where the magician had stood, stood 44 now, in his supernal beauty and his gracious youth; and it was from him that that flooding light came, for all his form was clothed in that immortal fire, and flashing like the sun; and Katrina crept on her knees to him, and bent down her old head and kissed his feet, and he bent down and patted her softly on the shoulder and touched his lips to the gray hair—*and was gone!*—and for two or three minutes you were so blinded you couldn't see your next neighbor in that submerging black darkness. (390–91)

We have just witnessed a "great transformation scene"—literally, a transfiguration. But Forty-four, like the Yankee, undercuts his own "miracle":

> He said himself it beat Barnum and Bailey hands down, and was by as much as several shades too good for the provinces—which was all Sanscrit to me, and hadn't any meaning even in Sanscrit I reckon, but was invented for the occasion, because it had a learned sound, and he liked sound better than sense as a rule. There's been others like that, but he was the worst.

A conversation follows between August and the cat in which we have yet another crossing of roles—somewhat like the one in *Huckleberry Finn* where Huck on the raft establishes a relationship with Jim that is analogous to the one Tom had previously had with Huck. Mary speaks with August's former naivety about her news that Balthasar is not dead, while August this time reacts with superior knowledge and sophistication. Her "proof" is the Boston newspaper previously mentioned; and August plays along with Mary's catlike (or feminine?)

"reasoning," saying: "It proves he is alive—nobody else could bring this paper." They get involved in a disagreement, however, based on a misunderstanding of a statement by August:

> "It was a supposititious case, and literary; it was a figure, a metaphor, and its function was to augment the force of the—"
>
> "Well, he *isn't*, anyway; because I've noticed, and—"
>
> "Oh, shut up! don't I tell you it was only a *figure*, and I never meant—"
>
> "I don't care, you'll never make me believe he's cross-eyed and left-handed, because the time he—"
>
> "Baker G., if you open your mouth again I'll jam the bootjack down it! you're as random and irrelevant and incoherent and mentally impenetrable as the afflicted Founder herself."
>
> But she was under the bed by that time; and reflecting, probably, if she had the machinery for it. (394)

We are reminded of some of Hank Morgan's exasperated conversations with Sandy in *A Connecticut Yankee.*

As our narrative gets wilder—surrealistic, perhaps—Mark Twain seems to care less and less about consistency. For example, where did that "American clock on the wall" (395) come from, and how does August know what it is? In the past, Forty-four has taken pains to explain such "futuristic" details, but now he has ceased to bother. The same inconsistency is apparent in the entire strike situation, which has rapidly dissolved in the middle of nowhere, like the pack of cards in Lewis Carroll's *Alice in Wonderland.* The new "conspiracy" is evoked in terms of nightmare:

> I glanced back, by chance, and there was also a living fence *behind*! dim forms, men who had been keeping watch in ambush, and had silently closed in upon the magician's tracks as he passed along. Mary G. had apparently had enough of this grisly journey—she was gone. (389)

And after the transformation scene, August goes back to his private room and "puts on" his "flesh":

> I judged it would take those people several hours to get over that, and accumulate their wits again and get their bearings, for it had knocked the whole bunch dizzy; meantime there wouldn't be anything doing. I must put in the time some way

> until they should be in a condition to resume business at the old stand. (391)

Life, as we say, will carry on; but, except for the humorous dialogue between August and Mary G., this is the last we hear, in this text, of the village and print-shop communities. They have served their purposes both in Mark Twain's fable and for August's education. Forty-four himself has spoken no word, but merely stands revealed "in that immortal fire"; and the "great light" shines on Katrina's "swarthy face, which it transfigured with its white glory, as it did also all that place, and its marble pillars, and the frightened people" (390).

Probably, these Austrians of Eseldorf have found a new saint to worship; but in any case the conspiracy, the strike, and the original antagonism to the stranger have now shrunk into insignificance. Only Mary G. continues to find the event "interesting," but in our last image of her, she is "under the bed . . . reflecting, . . . if she had the machinery for it."

"Turn Backward, O Time"

There is a kind of crazy logic to the reversal of time in chapters 32–33. If Forty-four is "the master" (395) of space and time, like "Satan" (150 ff.), and has been displaying this mastery by taking August into the nineteenth- and twentieth-century future, why should he not likewise explore the past? His relationship to time is more coherent than that of the Duplicates. The latter "don't measure time at all" (378), and they love to travel, indiscriminately, learning phrases that

> come from countries where none of the conditions resembled the conditions I had been used to; some from comets where nothing was solid, and nobody had legs; some from our sun, where nobody was comfortable except when white-hot, and where you needn't talk to people about cold and darkness, for you would not be able to explain the words so that they could understand what you were talking about. (377)

Their "science-fiction" world is extremely remote from the Earth and normal human time. Forty-four's use of time here, by way of contrast, is measured and significant.

The very idea of a "Ghost-Night" is linked to a unit of chronology: instead of the traditional thousand years (millennium), we find the modern concept of the century. Clemens, of course, sharing the fin de siècle mood, had recently written his memorable "Greeting from the Nineteenth to the Twentieth Century," which ends with a well-known comment on Christendom: "Give her soap and towel, but hide the looking glass." Now in the course of a fifteenth-century fiction, Mark Twain is holding a mirror up to the moving picture of human history, as well as to that of the pre-Adamite generations. In "Young Satan," he sketched "a history of the progress of the human race" (134–37), which was less skillfully managed. Here, the spectacle comes after Forty-four's "transformation scene," and it is linked with traditional ideas of ghosts emerging in the dark on the stroke of midnight.

The excuse given for turning time backward is comic, and even a bit silly, springing from a much-quoted line in a popular poem by William Allen Butler (483): "Flora McFlimsey—nothing to wear"; this is the sort of sophomoric humor that Mark Twain too often could not resist: "Eve, ditto; Adam, previous engagement, and so on and so on; Nero and ever so many others find the notice too short" (395). With the "show . . . due to begin in an hour," Forty-four-Balthasar explains:

> "Now there are two ways to manage. One is, to have time stand still—which has been done before a lot of times; and the other one is, to turn time backward for a day or two, which is comparatively new, and offers the best effects, besides.
>
> " 'Backward, turn backward, O Time, in thy flight—
> Make me a child again, just for tonight!'—" (395) **[44]**

The decision is to take the second course: "We will make the hands of the clocks travel around in the other direction."

What follows is an ingenious tour de force in which the implications of this idea, including the sun's "rising up out of the west," are systematically—too systematically?—worked out. As Forty-four says, "It will be the only perfectly authenticated event in all human history. All the other happenings, big and little, have got to depend on minority-testimony, and very little of that—but not so this time, dontcherknow. And this one's patented. There aren't going to be any encores" (396). The plan is to go backward "two or three days or a week; long enough to accommodate Robert Bruce, and Henry I and such, who have hearts and things scattered around here and there and yonder, and have to get a basket and go around and collect; so we will let the sun and the clocks go backward a while, then start them ahead in time to fetch up all right at midnight to-night . . . and . . . round out, and perfect the reputation I've been building for Balthasar Hoffman, and make him the most glorious magician that ever lived, and get him burnt, to a dead moral certainty." (396)

This being the last mention of Balthasar and his tiresome reputation, we should pause to reflect why Mark Twain harped so persistently on this theme. One reason may have been its sheer convenience as a plot device that enabled him to "turn on" magical effects whenever he pleased. But there is an especially tart tone in this passage: "I've spared neither labor nor thought, and I feel a pride in it and a sense of satisfaction such as I have hardly ever felt in a mere labor of love before" (397). Mark Twain's "cool" profane style is telling us, by understatement and controlled sarcasm, that this has been indeed a labor of hate. The puffed-up, pretentious, hypocritical, cowardly, and parasitical magician represents, as an almost too obvious and easy target, all the petty human traits Mark Twain heartily despised. The magician will be "hoist with his own petard"; and there is poetic justice in having this prime product of (Mark Twain's conception of) the feudal system burned at the stake for witchcraft—though we never actually witness this consummation.

At Forty-four's command, the clock strikes eleven again; and in a rather funny section, the events and speeches of the previous chapters are retold and written out in reverse order! "There she goes striking eleven again." becomes "again. eleven striking goes! she There," and so on. After a long paragraph of this, Forty-four relents: "I see it is too much for you, you cannot endure it, you will go mad," and he relieves August (and the thankful reader also) "of your share in this grand event. . . . Go and come as you please, amuse yourself as you choose" (398)—an excellent example of Mark Twain's literary tact. August chose, in fact, "to see the grand transformation repeated backwards"; but when "I was due to appear drunk in

Marget's chamber, *I took the pledge and stayed away*" (my italics)! "Everywhere weary people were re-chattering previous conversations backwards and not understanding each other."

The Possibility of Freedom

Now, without getting too metaphysical about it all, this seems to be a significant turning point in our story, with respect to the problem of freedom. The chief reason for running our fictional film backward (to use a cinematic metaphor) is to give a demonstration of determinism: "perfectly authenticated" history. But, at the crucial moment in August's love story, we find a swerving from the inexorable march of events: "I took the pledge and stayed away." Strictly speaking, then, we should have a rewritten text, an alternate version—in the phrase used in "Young Satan," a different "life-plan." Of course, we do not get this, and the point is made very lightly, without emphasis, almost as if the problem had ceased to bother Mark Twain. But the resulting difference between "No. 44" and "Young Satan" is profound: in "Young Satan" only the angel could change a career, and only from the outside; here August, simply and spontaneously reliving the past, makes a different choice [**45**].

The novelty here is a matter partly of tone: this chapter has been managed with such wit and ease that the effect is humorous. But it is building up toward a seriousness that is genuinely apocalyptic (as in the conclusion of the *Yankee*):

> Always there were groups gazing miserably at the townclocks; in every city funerals were being held again that had already been held once, and the hearses and the processions were marching solemnly backwards; where there was war, yesterday's battles were being refought, wrong-end-first; the previously killed were getting killed again, the previously wounded were getting hit again in the same place and complaining about it; there were blood-stirring and tremendous charges of masses of steel-clad knights across the field—backwards; and on the oceans the ships, with full-bellied sails were speeding backwards over the same water they had traversed the day before, and some of each crew were scared and praying, some were

> gazing in mute anguish at the crazy sun, and the rest were doing profanity beyond imagination. (400)

This, I find, is Mark Twain at his superb best; and I imagine the Chinese setting is essential to the full effect. He shared with Henry Adams, and with many others at the turn of the century, a concern about the problem of Asia; so it is "millions of yellow people" who are "gazing in mute anguish at the crazy sun." The evocation of a disoriented sense of time is more general, of course. I find particularly depressing the "weary people . . . re-chattering previous conversations backwards and not understanding each other, and oh, they did look so tuckered out and tired of it all!" And again, the mechanical fixity of a deterministic scheme is breached, on this occasion by the awareness that the normal order has been reversed, yielding misery and anguish.

A critical question remains, as we have seen, as to whether chapter 33, written in 1908, succeeds in bridging the gap between this apocalypse and the 1904 conclusion. Mark Twain gives indirect expression to the problem by criticizing Forty-four's flightiness:

> Nothing interested him long at a time. He would contrive the most elaborate projects, and put his whole mind and heart into them, then he would suddenly drop them, in the midst of their fulfillment, and start something fresh. (400)

Thus, chapter 33 does seem to begin in the middle of nowhere; and the return to the midnight hour of the "Ghost-Night" ("when everything was ready for the exhibition") is taken for granted. Also, this time the exploration of the past is less systematic, not oriented to chronology but to theme; it begins enthusiastically with the "handsome and exciting" incident of "the Egyptians floundering around in the Dead Sea" (this should be the Red Sea, of course).

The Assembly of the Dead takes the form of a forlorn procession. "First, there was an awful darkness," into which gradually come the "dry sharp clacking" and "spidery dim forms of thousands of skeletons marcing!" The light "paled to a half dawn," and "Forty-four had enlarged the great hall of the castle, so as to get effects. . . . Some of the names were familiar to me, but the most of them were not," belonging as they did to "six hundred thousand years ago." August's report, however, concentrates on familiar names, from Adam and Eve on; and, consciously or not, he echoes the descriptions of Hades found in the works of Homer and Virgil:

> And there were skeletons whom I had known, myself, and been at their funerals, only three or four years before—men and women, boys and girls; and they put out their poor bony hands and shook with me, and looked so sad. Some of the skeletons dragged the rotting ruins of their coffins after them by a string, and seemed pitifully anxious that the poor property shouldn't come to harm. (402)

Pathos is eternal:

> There was a slim skeleton of a young woman, and it went by with its head bowed and its bony hands to its eyes, crying, apparently. Well, it was a young mother whose little child disappeared one day and was never heard of again, and so her heart was broken and she cried her life away. It brought the tears to my eyes and made my heart ache to see that poor thing's sorrow. (402)

Though this had happened five hundred thousand years before, "I suppose such things never grow old, but remain always new."

Mark Twain revives an old favorite: "King Arthur came along, by and by, with all his knights. That interested me, because we had just been printing his history, copying it from Caxton"—whose version was, indeed, printed in 1485. "They talked about Arthur's last battle, and seemed to think it happened yesterday, which shows that *a thousand years*[3] *in the grave is merely a night's sleep, to the dead,* and counts for nothing" (my italics). The biblical history mingles with the Darwinian:

> The skeletons of Adam's predecessors outnumbered the later representatives of our race by myriads, and they rode upon undreamt-of monsters of the most extraordinary bulk and

3. The year when the *Yankee* begins is 528 A.D., making almost a millennium to the time of "No. 44." August is echoing 2 Peter 3:8: "One day is with the Lord as a thousand years, and a thousand years as one day." This in turn echoes Psalms 90:4.

> aspect. They marched ten thousand abreast, our walls receding and melting away and disappearing, to give them room, and the earth was packed with them as far as the eye could reach. (403)

Mark Twain drags in a satiric description of "the Missing Link," the subject of much debate, and popular humor, at the beginning of our own enlightened century. Then comes the paragraph that links this final "show" to the "Conclusion of the book":

> For hours and hours the dead passed by in continental masses, and the bone-clacking was so deafening you could hardly hear yourself think. Then, all of a sudden 44 waved his hand and we stood in an empty and soundless world. (403)

This "empty and soundless world," appropriately, returns us to the "deep stillness" out of which the procession initially emerged.

All this may be read, despite its brevity, as a sort of "hellish" counterpart to the version of heaven in *Captain Stormfield*. The similarities are in the enormous dimensions of time and space and in the mingling of all classes and conditions of men and women and children. But it is no doubt significant that Mark Twain never produced either a Dantesque or Calvinistic hell after the model of Milton's in *Paradise Lost*. He was less interested in sin and punishment and more interested in the simple, unrelieved pathos of common human suffering; and to express this, perhaps by instinct, he avoided creating an inferno—which he would probably have treated satirically [**46**]—and evoked instead a pagan assembly of the dead. He did so love processions!

And though Mark Twain had been concerned (especially when writing "Young Satan," as we have seen) with speculating about the chronology of hell and devils, here he went beyond the biblical account and included "kings and kings and kings till you couldn't count them—the most of them from away back thousands and thousands of centuries before Adam's time" (401–2). In fact, the random mingling of biblical and pagan, historical and Darwinian, elements is precisely the point here, which suggests that all may be equally true, or untrue, versions of the past.

Poor Servant of Truth

The effective evocation of the Assembly of the Dead leads smoothly into Forty-four's final teaching that *"there is no other"* life. In other words, if Mark Twain's fictions truly revealed his beliefs, and I think they did, he had made up his mind to be annihilated, like Melville. His youthful narrator, August Feldner, is thankful to be relieved of the threat of hell, or the promise of heaven, in equal measure; this gives him "great hope" (404). This attitude is like that of Mary G., the lady's maid transformed into a cat (361).

Is there no contradiction, however, between the two chapters? In one, "the dead passed by in continental masses"; and August says, "we have *seen* that future life—seen it in its actuality, and so—." But in the other, "it was a vision—it had no existence" (404). Clearly then, the former chapter was written to provide a thematic link to the "Conclusion," if only by contrast. And however sound, or unsound, the latter may be as metaphysics or theology, we should at least pay careful attention to all of what August is saying—and "realizing" with such emphasis at the end—to be "true" in chapter 34. It is not as simple as most critics have made it out to be [**47**].

The two main questions still remain to be perennially restated: who or what is the mysterious stranger, and what is his relationship to August? And further: what has been the purpose of his coming to Eseldorf, what truth or truths has he come to teach? Considering the latter first: "all" Forty-four "had said was true," but unfortunately he seems to have said many, and sometimes contradictory, things. The final image we have is of August "appalled" at his statement that the "Dream" of life is "grotesque and foolish" and that the "Thought" that is "You" is "a vagrant Thought, a useless Thought, a homeless Thought, wandering forlorn among the empty eternities!" The "philosophy" of this chapter has been called both solipsistic and nihilistic; and there is indeed something rather terrible—even if we attribute it to a temporary mood of despair induced by the death of Livy—in the utter loneliness of this final image. But if "you have existed . . . through all the eternities"—according to the ancient doctrine of the transmigration of souls, the metempsychosis—why is it "companionless"? This was manifestly, in Mark Twain's fiction as well as his life, not true.

It seems clear to me that Forty-four's final message is not a doctrine of nihilism, because his statement that "nothing exists" is immediately followed by "all is a dream" or, in the earlier formulation, "a vision." What does exist is "empty-space—and you!" In other words, Forty-four is, consciously or not, adopting something like the radically skeptical position of the Cartesian cogito—"you are but a *thought*"; his is an imperfectly understood version, perhaps, of the starting point of modern philosophy. We shall return to this central question in our Epilogue.

As to the stranger: August, in some sense, was Forty-four's creator, though this may seem hard to reconcile with his various roles earlier in the story. Now it is August who will "banish" his own creation from his "visions," having created him ex nihilo, that is, with a godlike power; as Forty-four says, "I shall dissolve into the nothingness *out of which you made me*" (my italics). True, when Forty-four departs he will leave August alone: "But I your poor servant have *revealed you to yourself* and *set you free*. Dream other dreams, and *better*!" (my italics). What a world of optimism these two sentences contain!

First of all, compared to August, the angel—though never named as such in "No. 44," as we have seen—has been a "poor servant." The ultimate mystery of Forty-four's identity is never explicitly solved, and I suppose it is theoretically possible to contend—as some critics using the Paine-Duneka text, with its ambiguous "Satan" angel, have done—that he is really the Devil, or a devil, in disguise or that he is just part of a dream or nightmare, as Gibson has suggested. But I think these solutions are incompatible with the entire "No. 44" text and probably with the sentences just quoted. The idea that a dream, in and of itself, can set one free—and go on to exhort one to dream better dreams!—seems to me an inadequate statement of what August's story is about.

Of course, August has been our narrator from the start, but he has told us about an entire community of other people with whom Forty-four has been involved. This then would seem to be yet another point at which Mark Twain has briefly, but significantly, lost his aesthetic detachment and merged August and himself into a Prospero-like creator of the entire story. Certainly, if he "made" Forty-four, August could just as well have "made" Herr Stein and all the rest. But this would simply convert the entire story into a hoax, as Pascal Covici, Jr., in fact tried to do in his chapter titled "The Hoax as Cosmology": "The world, then, is a gigantic hoax—it pretends to exist, but it doesn't."[4] This would be, indeed, a parody of an "extreme Platonic" position; and we do, of course, in the last analysis, accept that there is some element of truth in the Platonic view that all works of the imagination—those by Homer, Dante, Shakespeare!—are "only" fictions, "lies," ultimately inadequate "representations" or "imitations" of the inaccessible reality, the metaphysical *Ding an sich*.

Unresolved Conflicts

Nevertheless, as with any critical discussion, if we are to preserve our sanity and avoid an infinite regress into the void, we must accept as our initial (usually unspoken) premise the universe of discourse established by the art or science concerned. In the fictional world of "No. 44," August and Eseldorf and the print-shop community *are* the reality into which the mysterious stranger enters. As we have said, our essential plot has been the elaborate confrontation of, and interaction between, the two; and it is therefore disconcerting to be told that Forty-four is only August's creation!

This discrepancy, I fear, cannot be read out of the text entirely, but it should probably be seen as relative, not absolute. Since the basic mode of our story has been one of satiric fantasy, we have been granting all along a dreamlike, unreal quality to August's experience. To the extent that this is true, and within the framework of our Austrian "romance" (though it includes a good deal of realistic ballast), these final statements make sense. Since the role of Forty-four as August's "servant" has been to reveal August to himself, the stranger has been responding to his whims, as well as guiding him into new areas of awareness. The fact that August has all along been creating Forty-four (in this sense August is providing the

4. Pascal Covici, Jr., *Mark Twain's Humor: The Image of a World*, p. 241.

education he himself needs) does not negate Forty-four's superior reality, his ultimately mysterious existence.

This attempt at rationalization, however, does not take into account the "nothingness" out of which August is said to have made the stranger. This could only make sense if the narrator were thought to have godlike powers (as in Poe's "The Power of Words"). But August in the story is merely an adolescent Austrian printer's apprentice, not an idealized poet. This discrepancy, therefore, remains.

Returning to Forty-four's farewell message: his sentences imply that our visionary, fictional exploration has indeed accomplished one of its purposes, that of self-exploration and revelation. And further, it has set "you" free, however ultimately, metaphysically lonely you may be in the empty eternities and infinities of the modern astronomical universe.

What does this last sentence mean? It does not, I feel, refer to the negatively presented, incoherent freedom of the Duplicate, which finally melted away into nothingness: "poof! and it was gone!" This dramatized a release from the bonds of the body; but the Duplicate, however useful as a device, and whatever vaguenesses remain in the way it was presented, never went beyond the status of a "materialized" fiction. We are on an entirely different level when August is now given a *positive* injunction by Forty-four: "Dream other dreams, and better!"—in other words, this is *not* a last event, or work of fiction, or vision, not a literal end of the world.

Whatever Mark Twain may have meant precisely at this point by *better*, it seems to me that the word is not used cynically. It corresponds in a way to the message embodied, so much less imaginatively, in *What Is Man?*, the "gospel" he humorously deprecated as "wicked." There the Old Man formulated his "plan" as an admonition: "Diligently train your ideals *upward* and *still upward* toward a summit where you will find your chiefest pleasure in conduct which while contenting you, will be sure to confer benefits upon your neighbor and the community" (*WIM*, chapter 5). This statement, from the same years when he was completing "No. 44," candidly puts into a formula what Mark Twain thought was at the heart of all the great religions: enlightened selfishness.[5] This is not

5. Enlightened selfishness is also at the heart of the philosophy that provides the basis for the Declaration of Independence, the Constitution,

an easy doctrine; it neither sentimentalizes man nor abandons him to negation and despair.

The vehicle by means of which Mark Twain conveyed this hard-won truth includes two remarkable fictional creations. "Young Satan," the first of these, even in the poorly edited *Stranger* version, succeeded for half a century to trouble the thoughts and dreams of many excellent readers and critics. And like Tom Sawyer's companion, Huck, August's comrade, Forty-four, is indomitably alive, though here he says "I am perishing already—I am failing, I am passing away." There are some final hints, in the long statement that follows, that must enter into our full sense of the stranger's mystery. Critics of the old Paine-Duneka text made much of one such hint, namely the "dream-marks" attributed to "your universe and its contents" (404)[6]—though in the *Manuscripts* the reference is to the universe of August Feldner, not that of Theodor Fischer. Again, we suspect a lapse of artistic detachment in the views expressed: Clemens is speaking out, through his persona, about a God

> "who mouths justice, and invented hell—mouths mercy, and invented hell—mouths Golden Rules, and foregiveness multiplied by seventy times seven, and invented hell; who mouths morals to other people and has none himself; who frowns upon crimes, yet commits them all; who created man without invitation, then tries to shuffle the responsibility for man's acts upon man, instead of honorably placing it where it belongs, upon himself; and finally, with altogether divine obtuseness, invites this poor abused slave to worship him!" (405)

This is part of a tirade that restates, in words of fire, ideas upon which Mark Twain had been brooding for decades; and to really understand them we need a full-scale study of his re-

---

and the American philosophy of government, as shown by Arthur O. Lovejoy, *Reflections on Human Nature.* A recent essay by Ellwood Johnson, "William James and the Art of Fiction," draws attention to one possible source of this formulation of the melioristic doctrine. Johnson quotes from the 1890 *Principles of Psychology* by William James (which Clemens read) the admonition to "dream better dreams," by which means the will would be moved to "faith" or "belief" (p. 287).

6. See especially Edwin S. Fussell's essay, "The Structural Problem of *The Mysterious Stranger,*" in *Critics*, pp. 75–83.

ligion, comparable to those we have had of his social thought. I note here merely that, again, more explicitly, Mark Twain is rejecting the Calvinist version of hell; that he is thinking of God as a person with whom he can quarrel, as Father Abraham and others do in the Old Testament; and that the divine traits here are in some respects like those of Forty-four: "obtuseness," for one; and the tendency to commit "crimes"—though in the story these traits were attributed to the Duplicate, as we have seen (370).[7]

There is a limit to the degree of precision one should expect in a fantasy, and an unrevised one at that. Unresolved conflicts and an aura of mystery, these certainly remain at the end. However, it seems significant that the truth August finally accepts is based on, among other things, a contrast between the lots of mortals and angels. This is only the second time that the latter word has been used in the text of "No. 44":

> "who gave his angels eternal happiness unearned, yet required his other children to earn it; who gave his angels painless lives, yet cursed his other children with biting miseries and maladies of mind and body. "

Is there any responsive reader who does not realize, by this time, that Forty-four—of course, also a "dream," a "creature" of August's imagination, a "poor servant"—is actually intended to suggest an angel of some sort? Was not Shakespeare's Ariel veritably an "airy spirit"?

Forty-four himself speaks here, I think, as an unfallen angel who has formed ties with one of God's "other children" on Earth and who at this moment (if we grant Mark Twain the drift of the concluding chapters of his fiction) has reached the highest point of identification with his human friend and the mortal lot. We cannot expunge from his farewell statement the view that "there is no God, no universe, no human race,

7. Or are these ideas intended to suggest that Forty-four has all along actually been the Devil, since the attack on God may indeed be read as satanic doctrine? Must we, as readers, decide—if Mark Twain did not? The subsequent writing of "Letters from the Earth," with its echoes of the Book of Job and satiric view of "The Creator" may seem to give support to a devilish view; but even there we end with a search for balance: "The Beatitudes and the quoted chapters from Numbers and Deuteronomy ought always to be read from the pulpit together; then the congregation would get an all-round view of Our Father in Heaven."

no earthly life, no heaven, no hell," but neither can we ignore the earlier parts of that same statement. The identical imagination that created August's interlocutor and put these negative words in his mouth was also responsible for the exactly contrary "silly creations" of a mysterious God and his eternally happy angels; and it is one of these angels that is speaking!

Since it is impossible, for one who has read and understood everything in chapter 34, to accept either extreme as exclusive truth, we must obviously accept both sides of this polarity as parts of a total vision ("*all* he had said") that leaves August "appalled."

Epilogue

The Dream of Mark Twain

Our analysis is finished, the tale of Mark Twain's *Mysterious Stranger Manuscripts* is substantially told. The texts, despite all their unrevised imperfections, have rewarded close attention and will certainly continue to engage readers, scholars, and critics in future generations. As I have tried to suggest at various points, for full comprehension they must be related to the entire corpus of Mark Twain, especially to the other writings of his final phase; and till this is done, we cannot really generalize adequately about Mark Twain's last dozen years. But I should like nevertheless to speculate briefly about what was happening, with special reference to chapter 34 of "No. 44."

We have seen how naturally the "Conclusion of the book" follows chapter 33 and how many of the threads of the "plot" the former succeeds in tying into a rather neat knot. But at the very end of our text is the word *true*; and however richly complex, sometimes self-contradictory, we find Mark Twain's "literary solution" (Tuckey's phrase), it may also leave us, like August, "appalled"; certain ultimate issues remain to bother the reader and tease the critic. Since this is an impressive last chapter in Mark Twain's last major work, it has the air of being Clemens's personal testament of belief, and many have read it as such—though the generalizations stated by the departing Forty-four may be understood just as well simply in terms of that fictional character and the problems he has presented and dramatized for August by means of the Duplicates. The distinction between "personal" and "literary" here becomes finally unreal, since Mark Twain–Clemens was an imaginative creator of fictions in his deepest being. As he wrote in one of his last essays, "The Turning-Point of My Life":

"To me, the most important feature of my life is its literary feature. I have been professionally literary something more than forty years." Man and writer (and legend too, as one of his biographers put it) were inextricably united.

The issue, then, is not so much one of truth versus fiction as one of the nature of the truth expressed. What was it, after all, that Mark Twain succeeded in saying in "No. 44"? We must accept the legitimacy of nuanced variety in interpretations, but we must insist also on the primacy of Mark Twain's own text. Though chapter 34 has been much read and analyzed, this has usually been done in misleading contexts. We have noted most of the previous interpretations—nihilism, solipsism, "extreme Platonism," the magic of art, hoax, escape from reality—and we have seen that there is some justification for all of them in words Mark Twain actually wrote. I should like, however, to suggest yet another framework, one basic to the history of modern thought and truer on the whole to the fundamental character of Clemens's mind.

I think of Mark Twain as a sort of archetypal modern American, exquisitely sensitive to many of the currents of religion, philosophy, science, society, and culture that made the nineteenth century so exciting and upsetting. And in "the revolution from the medieval to the modern universe," the combination of radical skepticism with the mathematical-mechanical logic displayed by Descartes was both a climax and a new beginning.[1] Whether or not Clemens read Descartes, and I have found no mention of Descartes in the literature about Clemens, there are advantages in placing him in the large Cartesian contexts: a surprising number of aspects of "No. 44" are lit up by Descartes's *Discourse* and *Meditations*. To paraphrase T. S. Eliot in his "Shakespeare and the Stoicism of Seneca": "I propose a Mark Twain under the influence of Descartes' rationalism. But I do not believe that Mark Twain was under the influence of Descartes directly."[2] Whether he was influenced by the Cartesian tradition, of course, is another matter.

1. John H. Randall, Jr., *The Making of the Modern Mind*, pp. 239–42. For a more thorough philosophical discussion see Albert G. A. Balz, *Descartes and the Modern Mind*.

2. T. S. Eliot, *Selected Essays*, p. 109.

Cartesian Science and Skepticism

Jacques Maritain concluded an important essay, "The Dream of Descartes," by writing about "the idea of what the modern world calls The Science" and "the emotional and reverential compliments evoked by this word," which "plays in the mythology of modern times a role as majestic and as formidable as Progress itself." But Maritain emphasized, from his perspective as a believing Catholic in the twentieth century, that this is "not the true science, science such as it exists and is brought about by scientists, science submissive to things and to extra-mental reality." It is instead a sort of phantom caricature, characteristic of the "sorrowful" many "who have lost the good of the intellect" (Dante's *Inferno*, 3:18), it is "the Mid-Autumnal Night's Dream conjured up by a mischievous genius in a philosopher's brain."[3] Maritain's version of Descartes supplies an ambience for the problems we have found to be at the heart of "No. 44."

I do not mean to exaggerate Clemens's philosophic learning or sophistication when I contend that there are fundamental affinities between the dream of Descartes and what we may call "the dream of Mark Twain." I mean by this phrase not just the actual dreams reported by Clemens, nor even his use of dream materials in his writings, though these are included. I mean rather, to use his own word, the entire "vision" of life and death that might be taken as summing up his life's work. This aspect of any writer's achievement is at once the most important and the most difficult to state; and it is the final battleground, the area of ultimate controversy, on which generations of critics will struggle to articulate their fullest and truest judgments about, in this case, Mark Twain's oeuvre. Until fairly recently, the tendency has been to make light of his intellectual concerns, even while acclaiming the truth and profundity of his art. But during the last decade, partly as the result of the wider availability of the writings of Mark Twain's last years, increasing numbers of critics have been taking him more seriously as a thinker. They have been thinking of him not as a technical philosopher, but as a "true wit" and a "man of judgment," in S. J. Krause's formulation.[4]

3. Jacques Maritain, *The Dream of Descartes*, p. 29.
4. See my review essay, "The Real Mark Twain: School of Tuckey,"

There is no need to rehearse in detail the well-known autobiographical passages[5] in Descartes's *Discourse on Method* (1637), which is usually considered to mark the beginning of a distinctively modern philosophy in Europe. Coming to these after study of Mark Twain, we are struck by many analogies: Clemens's lifelong education through travel is paralleled by Descartes's summary of his youthful observation of the "extravagant and ridiculous" things approved by "great peoples," discovered by "mingling with people of various dispositions and conditions in life, . . . collecting a variety of experiences," and so forth. The Frenchman restricted himself to Europe, whereas the American began by "learning the river" and eventually girdled the entire globe; but the principle was the same. And with reference to the "Stranger" texts: there is an analogy between Descartes's education and "Satan's" plan to study the human race; and the movement in Descartes from the outside social world to "within myself" is like the central pattern we found in "No. 44."

In part 2 of the *Discourse,* Descartes tells of the famous winter day in Germany spent "shut up in a room heated by a stove" holding "converse with my own thoughts," which led to his determination to rely on "the plain reasoning of a man of good sense in regard to the matters which present themselves to him." This historic moment may be paralleled, in a sense, by Mark Twain's Austrian sojourn, during which he decided to retreat into the "self-reliance" of writing his own thoughts, for himself, in fictions "not for publication." Further, the effort of many of Mark Twain's later writings—the elaborate critical examination poured into *What Is Man?*; autobiographical dictations; a wealth of essays; as well as more imaginative, satiric, and fantastic, works—may be thought of as his personal effort to go beyond the "opinions" he had en-

---

in which I consider, among other recent studies, S. J. Krause's *Mark Twain as Critic* and the first volumes in the Mark Twain Papers (*Jahrbuch für Amerikastudien* [1969], esp. p. 303 ff.). In addition to many articles, especially noteworthy and characteristic books that add to this growing scholarship are Roger B. Salomon's *Twain and the Image of History,* Louis J. Budd's *Mark Twain: Social Philosopher,* and Arthur L. Scott's *Mark Twain at Large.*

5. Quoted in Arther K. Rogers, *A Student's History of Philosophy,* pp. 260–61 (Torrey's translation).

countered as a youth and those that had been pressed upon him all his life by an all-too-friendly environment.

Finally, consider for example the paragraph in chapter 34 that gives the details ("hysterically insane—like all dreams") of conventional belief: "a God who could make good children as easily as bad, yet preferred to make bad ones," and so forth. This, as well as Forty-four's act of stripping away all external reality ("God—man—the world,—the sun, the moon, the wilderness of stars"), can be readily understood as an act of ultimate doubt, not unlike Descartes's act of imagining the deceptions of an "evil genius":

> I shall suppose, then, not that God, who is very good, and the sovereign source of truth, but that a certain evil genius, no less wily and deceitful than powerful, has employed all his ingenuity to deceive me. . . . I persuade myself that nothing has ever existed of all that my memory, filled with illusions, has represented to me; I consider that I have no senses; I assume that body, figure, extension, motion, and place are only fictions of my mind. What is there, then which can be held to be true? Perhaps nothing at all, except the statement that there is nothing at all that is true. But how do I know that there is not something different from those things which I have just pronounced uncertain, concerning which there cannot be entertained the least doubt? Is there not some God, or some other power, who puts these thoughts into my mind? That is not necessary, for perhaps I am capable of producing them of myself. Myself, then! at the very least am I not something? . . . But there is I know not what deceiver, very powerful, very crafty, who employs all his cunning continually to delude me. There is still no doubt that I exist if he deceives me; and let him deceive me as he may, he will never bring it about that I shall be nothing, so long as I shall think something exists. Accordingly, having considered it well, and carefully examined everything, I am obliged to conclude and to hold for certain, that this proposition, *I am, I exist*, is necessarily true, every time that I pronounce it or conceive it in my mind. (*Meditations*, 1)[6]

Just as Descartes actually assumed "God, who is very good," so Mark Twain prefixed to Forty-four's statement that "God"

6. Ibid., pp. 265–67.

has "no existence," an exclamation by August: "*By God* I had had that very thought a thousand times in my musings!" (my italics).

I am well aware that the parallels or affinities I have been suggesting are literary, not philosophical or logically precise. But they could be multiplied and would add up to a fairly coherent world view. One may conceive of the last dozen years of Mark Twain's writings as constituting an almost separate career—a new start, a distinct "final phase."[7] What his "dreams," loosely considered, share with those of Descartes is a spirit of search for religious truth. A flash of lightning in Descartes's second dream led to "the admirable science"; for the American, a more gradual accession of independence led to a burst of fresh creativity and truth saying.

It needs only a slight shift to put both Descartes and Mark Twain into a psychological perspective. Very easily, we can understand Descartes's God and "evil genius" as analogous, for example, to angels and devils, principles of good and evil, heroes and villains, and we can move thereby into the world of modern literature. So Georges Poulet, concentrating on "human time," wrote an essay of a different sort than Maritain's but also titled "The Dream of Descartes."[8] What emerged as especially important for Poulet were the notes of terror and alienation in Descartes. He showed the connection between the first dream, the "Spiritus malus" (as it appears in the original Latin) of the second *Meditation*, and a movement toward the world of instinct and modern irrationalism:

> The proximity of the body results in the estrangement or enfeeblement of the mind. In the midst of human society, which . . . seems to be so well adapted to the tragic conditions of life, Descartes discovers himself to be "bent and unsteady" and intensely aware of this tragedy. And it is then that he awakens with a feeling of spiritual sorrow and associates with the sorrow the idea of a temptation. (p. 61)

The root causes of this sorrow are "physical exile and material solitude," to which are added "moral exile and solitude" (p. 53); as Poulet generalized in his introduction, "the seventeenth

7. See my essay, "Mark Twain's Final Phase."

8. Georges Poulet, *Studies in Human Time*, pp. 50–73. Further references will appear in parentheses in the text.

century is the epoch in which the individual discovers his isolation" (p. 13). And, we may add, the United States is the country in which this general modern tendency toward individualism has been carried to an extreme, idealized, and realized as a way of life and major theme of literature.

We need go no deeper into this historical development to realize that Mark Twain was not being morbid and eccentric when he explored these issues in "No. 44." He has Forty-four say: "All things that exist were made out of thought—and out of nothing else"—thus blending rationalism with something like the traditional Creation ex nihilo. On this, August comments ironically: "It seemed to me charitable, also polite, to take him at his word and not require proof, and I said so" (333). Thus Clemens was aware of certain implications of Cartesian rationalism and also quizzically skeptical of traditional "proofs." Like Huck Finn, he had "been there before"; he was content to end this chapter with "I was alone" (334) and to end his book with Forty-four saying: "You have existed, companionless, through all the eternities" (404).

"Nothing exists but You" (404): this extreme position, this stern doctrine (which Poulet relates to "the Calvinist *Credo*: I believe, therefore I am" [p. 12]) can be seen as a remote American echo of the Cartesian *cogito*. And some of the consequences for literature can be traced back to the generation of Rabelais and Montaigne, before Descartes; and to Swift, Voltaire, and others, after him. The mind of man, that "glory, jest and riddle of the world," struggles to maintain a world view independent of merely orthodox or traditional views, sometimes by a radical criticism of, or rebellion against, them: the latest phase of this development is probably represented by that varied group of writers and thinkers loosely labeled *existential*. One of the main difficulties produced by this sort of radical assertion of freedom is a lack of stability and security; as one critic of Kafka has put it, "the quest ends in the seeker's confrontation with his own image"; and "the irony that topples" Kafka's "lesson down like a house of cards" is that "the way that is everywhere is nowhere."[9] But that is the subject for yet another book.

9. Shimon Sandbank, "Action as Self-Mirror: On Kafka's Plots," quotations from pp. 25, 26.

A Last "Image of Hannibal"

Getting back to Mark Twain: there was undoubtedly much of the fantastic and dreamlike in his career and writings, which ranged from a tiny village on the banks of the Mississippi to the courts of emperors and the yacht of a Standard Oil tycoon, from America's primitive frontier to its developing "imperialist" phase in the twentieth century. A fabulous success story, one would think; and yet, when Mark Twain wrote "My Boyhood Dreams" in Sanna, Sweden, during the months when he was trying to get on with "The Chronicle of Young Satan," he began: "The dreams of my boyhood? No, they have not been realized." Later in the same piece he applied this notion, satirically, to the career of John Hay:

> In the pride of his young ambition he had aspired to be a steamboat mate . . . I look back now, from this far distance of seventy years, and note with sorrow the stages of that dream's destruction. Hay's history is but Howells's, with differences of detail. Hay climbed high toward his ideal; when success seemed almost sure, his foot upon the very gangplank, his eye upon the capstan, misfortune came and his fall began. Down—down—down—ever down: Private Secretary to the President; Colonel in the field; Chargé d'Affaires in Paris; Chargé d'Affaires in Vienna; Poet; Editor of the *Tribune*; Biographer of Lincoln; Ambassador to England; and now at last there he lies—Secretary of State, Head of Foreign Affairs. And he has fallen like Lucifer, never to rise again. And his dream—where now is his dream? Gone down in blood and tears with the dream of the auctioneer.[10]

This is a characteristically humorous statement of the truth that experience is gained at the expense of childhood innocence, and power at the expense of freedom and carefree irresponsibility.[11]

We come back, then, to the central fact that Mark Twain was the "poet" of America's coming of age. In a variety of modes, he captured much of the public and private realities and

10. *Humorous Sketches*, pp. 678–80 (see list of short references p. xiii).

11. See Sigmund Freud, *Civilization and Its Discontents.* Note especially his comments on "the state of American civilization" (p. 67), on Christian Science (p. 72), and on Mark Twain (p. 80, note 3).

tensions of that complex process. It is foolish to rebuke him for dealing so much with experiences of adolescence, because that was his main theme, his prime subject matter; his Odysseus, someone has observed, was Huckleberry Finn. It is therefore highly appropriate, in a sense inevitable, that his last major work should be a novel of growing up, of young love, and of the search for self-knowledge.

But what a sea change there is in his metamorphosis from Hannibal, Missouri, to Eseldorf, Austria! And how beautifully right that he should have gone back, as we have seen, to the earliest facts, the deepest roots, of his knowledge of the world and human nature, to his apprenticeship to the "art" of printing, which led eventually to his rise in the "literary guild." The same man who said he gained his fullest knowledge of mankind as a steamboat pilot ("met him on the river"!), was also saying thereby that his truest insights went back to the village of his boyhood and his encounters there with work, men, women, mystery, and miracle.

The achievement of "No. 44" is that Mark Twain managed to weave so much of his dream of life, his vision of man and the universe, so skillfully into this text. His last "image of Hannibal," to use Henry Nash Smith's phrase (with additional echoes, especially in the courtship sequence, from his encounters with Elmira, New York, and Hartford, Connecticut), has been enriched and enlivened by a lifetime of experience and practice of the art of fiction. Despite some relatively minor flaws, I think it a work of sophistication and maturity; the frisky journeys and gambols of its "dream-sprites," presided over by Forty-four and spread out in space and time, are the fruits of a truly creative imagination exploring many corners of the human condition in a fresh and profound way.

No single work of fiction pretends to cover all the ground, but the master works illustrate universal truths implicit in the provincial and concrete. And when we get to know him better, I have little doubt that Mark Twain's mysterious stranger will take his place in the gallery of immortals that includes, among others, Pantagruel, Don Quixote, Gulliver, Candide, Ishmael, Huckleberry Finn, Hank Morgan, and David Wilson. Probably not as an equal—he is in some ways a queer specimen—but as a beloved, eccentric cousin, not too far removed.

Appendix A: Sources for "Cheating the Devil"

Tuckey speculated that the pointed references to "the 9th of December" derived from the political events described in "Stirring Times in Austria," the final footnote of which reads: "It is the 9th.—M.T."[1] Mark Twain certainly conceived of the events he described as devilish: "It was an odious spectacle—odious and awful. . . . pitifully real, shamefully real, hideously real" (234). We can say, with the hindsight of the next half century of European history, that he was witnessing, typologically speaking, the birth of Nazism: not only the violation of parliamentary freedoms and the subsequent establishing of martial law in Prague, but also, more particularly, "in all cases the Jew had to roast, no matter which side he was on." Tuckey writes:

> If, finding himself free from other writing commitments, he did then plunge into the composition of that first "Eseldorf" chapter, he would likely have done just what he *has* done in it: employ satiric inversion and, in mockery, celebrate this date as one marking events worthy of the highest praise.

I venture to suggest that the date of 9 December might possible be a conflation of the political events of "Stirring Times in Austria" with religious ceremonies from that time of the year. Thus, December was the month of the Roman Saturnalia, though that festival was celebrated during the week of 17–23 December. In Christian tradition, December is the season of Advent, a time of general solemnity, rather than of licence. But St. Nicholas's Day, which is sacred to children and sailors and yields the jollity and gifts of Santa Claus, is 6 December;

1. *Critics*, pp. 138–39, and *Essays*, p. 235 (see list of short references p. xiii). Further page references for "Stirring Times" inserted in the text will refer to the latter reprinting.

the Festival of Fools "fell in different places at different dates," but it was generally during the Christmas season; and Childermas, or Holy Innocents' Day, 28 December, was characterized by boy bishops and similar burlesques of ecclesiastical ritual. Also, it may not be irrelevant that, as James G. Frazer observed in a footnote: "In his youth the Bohemian reformer John Huss took part in these mummeries." Thus Twain's combination of Hussite heresy with mock ceremony may indicate that they have a common source in some biography of Huss or history of Protestantism in Europe.[2]

This episode seemed to me to contain so many traditional elements, in addition to the probable allusions to political events, that I was not surprised to learn that Mark Twain was building on history and actual folklore. William M. Gibson has sent me a copy of a letter from Chadwick Hansen (my thanks to both scholars) that contains the following sentences:

> There are many stories of demonic assistance in construction, both of buildings and of bridges (see the latter part of Book One, Chapter Eleven of Grillot de Givry's *Witchcraft, Magic and Alchemy* for some of them), and there are Devil's Bridges throughout Europe. The Devil always demands the same price—a soul—for his labor and is generally tricked out of it. It has been argued that such legends are a survival of the primitive practice of sacrificing humans or animals to ensure the success of important buildings. (In some instances sacrificial offerings were buried under the corners of buildings; our corner-stone ceremonies are probably descended from such practices.)

2. I am indebted for most of the facts in this paragraph to Sir James G. Frazer's classic *The Golden Bough*, vol. 19, *The Scapegoat*. See also the description of St. Barbara's Day, 4 December (pp. 270–71). The footnote on Huss is on p. 336. John Huss is also mentioned near the end of chapter 1 of *Joan of Arc*, which was begun in 1893.

Appendix B: "The Devil's Sunday-School"

In the working notes (436–49), we can see how many of the ideas in "Schoolhouse" were related directly to the satiric project of depicting a "converted" Devil establishing his own Sunday school. These notes are extraordinarily revealing and blend motifs used in the creation of both "Satan" and Forty-four. The theme of theory versus experience, for example, is found in an explanation of Forty-four's curiosity about the human race: though he once saw a man and child tossing in the red billows of hell, "he sees *now* it was torment, but that was only a *name* to him then, *he* has had no personal experience of pain or unhappiness, papa's crime has not descended" (437)—that is, has not been inherited by his son (or his unfallen nephew, "Satan").

There are related observations on the relationships among thought, feeling, language, and music (438–39). A problem that has bothered us, "Satan's" saying he "liked" the boys though he was without feeling, is also touched on: "He can't feel anger, ⟨like an animal, but can't hold it;⟩ can't conceive of the spirit of revenge . . . 44 can love, like dog and others" (441)—that is, instinctively.

The consequences of eating the apple are developed further with special reference to the Moral Sense. Distinctions are made among Satan's evil disposition and two other situations:

> Adam acquired the Moral Sense from the apple in a diseased form—*insanity* of mind and body; it decayed his body, filled it with disease-germs, and death resulted.
>
> The angels have the Moral Sense, but not in diseased form—just the other way, the *healthy* way, disposition to avoid evil and dislike it. They are sane. (442)

Mark Twain strikes a Whitmanesque note in relation to animals: "If you could only get rid of the Moral Sense. . . . If you and he [Adam] could be like the animals" (443).[1] Perhaps this is the essence of the angel's plan for human amelioration:

> He hopes to find a way to rid them of the Moral Sense; they can[not] get to heaven without that, still, it is worth while, because without it *this* life would be innocent and happy, and brief as it is it would be better to be happy than unhappy. He must think out a way. (437)

These ideas are similar to ones Mark Twain was formulating in his "wicked gospel," *What Is Man?*.

> Thinks if he can remove man's *vanity*, his Moral Sense may follow; his vanity in attributing merits to himself; and his fool idea that Selfishness is shameful; he didn't make it, and the wisest thing he *can do* is to raise its ideals and make it help toward making this life pleasant for all. (440)

A substantial part of these notes has to do with the satiric idea of a "Devil's Sunday-School" (447), in which Mark Twain's original notion of defending Satan and writing his "bible" for him was taking shape. Thus: "Admires Christ deeply. Likes to go to Church and Sunday-School and listen—at first. But quits, because they say such things about papa and his place" (440). "Better get up a Catechism. Yes, 44 will do it. And it is printed: 'Conscience' &c" (445). For a moment, we have a hint of the print shop in "No. 44": "Bring slathers of little red . . . cooling devils to print manuscript Bible . . . Bible—sermons—dialogues—in *Appendix*" (449).

We even have a draft of a sermon (446) and can see how Mark Twain was probably baffled by the ambiguity of his conception. Would the "Devil's Sunday-School" preach a gospel of Satan the father, himself? or of an unfallen angel, Satan's son? and would either, or both, be converted to Christianity? Probably, he consciously intended to emphasize the angel, but it was hard to keep these two possibilities separate. Thus, "he's starting an Anti-Moral Sense church," and the keynote of "*His Sermon*" is "Everything is insane—upside down."

1. Reminding me of "Song of Myself": "I think I could turn and live with animals" (section 32).

Actually, some of the themes in "No. 44" were adumbrated in the "Autobiography of a Damned Fool" (1877), which was inspired by Twain's brother Orion, who appears there as a printer's apprentice aged eighteen (*S&B*, pp. 134–64). A section of satire on Ben Franklin, for example, involves "teaching my Sunday school class the principles of infidelity" (*S&B*, p. 145) and the creation of a "Mahometan" harem.

Appendix C: Some Possible Meanings of the Name "No. 44"

Gibson estimated that notes "D-1 through D-5 were probably written before the composition of 'Schoolhouse Hill' and D-6 through D-16 after the first chapters were composed" (433). Following his lead, we find that Twain assigned the following names to his character:

> He is Admirable Chrichton. . . . Calls himself 404—gives no other name (435).
>
> He is No. 94 Prince of the vintage of a certain century—doesn't know which one—no curiosity—hasn't inquired (436).

As Gibson wrote in his explanatory note, though the name "ought to mean something," none of the explanations thus far put forward "seems wholly adequate" (472–73).

Perhaps nothing more profound than a euphonious and alliterative number was wanted. In the text itself, the name is "Quarante-quatre," but in notes probably written after "Schoolhouse" we find:

> "I am No. 45 in New Series 986,000,000. I have seen all my brothers and sisters at one time or another, and know them by Number and features. There are some billions of them." (444)

All these variations would seem to work against the suggestion put forward by Henry Nash Smith that the number *forty-four* was intended to signify twice *twenty-two*; that is, that it was an allusion, conscious or unconscious, to the Levin boys in Hannibal, who were popularly referred to as "Twenty-two." The emphasis of these variations is rather, as Gibson concluded, on the "large families" in heaven and hell, which reach astronomical numbers. In any case, in notes D-6 through D-16 (436–41), there is no deviation from the number *forty-four*, and this name did remain the permanent one.

In support of Smith's suggestion, however, is a much earlier note, written while Twain was planning for yet another Huck Finn book, about the "Levin" boys, "the first Jews I had ever seen." They made "an awful impression among us," and the boys in Hannibal asked: "Shall we crucify them?"[1] Of course, the area around Cairo, Illinois, was known in middle-western folklore as "Egypt"; and Clemens later wrote in his *Autobiography* that the Levins "carried me back to Egypt": "We called them Twenty-two—and even when the joke was old and had been worn threadbare we always followed it with the explanation, to make sure that it would be understood, 'Twice Levin—twenty-two' " (*MTA*, 2:218). Forty-four, in this context, would seem to be some sort of "double Twenty-Two" or "four times Levin."

Along religious lines, there are other possibilities worth further investigation. One derives from the fact that there are twenty-two letters in the Hebrew alphabet, and the number acquires mystical significance in certain Jewish connections (as in the *Sefer Yetzira,* "The Book of Creation"). The number recurs at various points in the Bible; there were twenty-two kings in the Davidic line; Psalm 22 begins with Jesus' last words on the cross; and so forth. Also there are twenty-two major trumps in the tarot pack of cards, which are connected with twenty-two mystic paths. No doubt the number may have other interesting associations, the very multiplicity of which makes any single attribution merely speculative—unless there is objective evidence that Clemens took that particular association seriously.

More generally, the figure of the "mysterious stranger" may have in it elements of the rich legend of "The Wandering Jew," which Mark Twain referred to frequently; in his *Autobiography,* he mentioned the popularity in the Middle West of his childhood of Eugene Sue's novel on that theme. But that is a complex question, requiring separate investigation.

1. Philip S. Foner, *Mark Twain Social Critic*, pp. 288–89.

Appendix D: Revisions of Chapter 1 for "No. 44"

Retaining chapter 1 of "Young Satan" for "No. 44" no doubt saved Mark Twain a certain amount of work; but it also kept as background for this new story (or new version of an old, uncompleted story) the entire village setting, with its "Age of Faith" by "the mental and spiritual clock," its religious hierarchy and conflicts, its evil priest and its good priest, its "sleep" and "paradise for us boys," and its "assuaging of the Devil" ceremony.

Thanks to the editorial labors of Gibson and Tuckey, we can trace in detail the stages by which some of the differences came into being. In his "Description of the Texts," Gibson tells us:

> He wrote chapter 2 first, making a note on the first manuscript page to provide a description of the setting from "Chronicle." Then he appropriated the first twenty-two pages (chapter 1) of "Chronicle," making a number of revisions on them in dark blue ink to integrate them into the new story. (489)

A facsimile of the first two pages of manuscript is provided (490); and with the help of the dark blue and the black inks of the original, Gibson distinguishes clearly for us between the revisions made when this chapter was part of "Young Satan" (Gibson's "Chronicle") and those made when it was incorporated in "No. 44." Most significantly: "The changes in title and in date were made for 'No. 44.' "

The most important change was that of the season, which was May and became "in 1490—winter." Lesser changes include specifying the name of the prince as "Rosenfeld"; sharpening the religious issue by having Frau Adler distribute "Hussite sermons, all written out" (222), instead of just "Bibles and hymn-books" (36); and eliminating the reference to Luther's famous act of throwing his inkstand at the Devil (41), which was made anachronistic now by the new date.

The lack of final revision results in a few unresolved discrepancies. Chapter 1 refers to "boys," but the age of the new protagonist-narrator, August Feldner, is sixteen; and Forty-four himself is introduced as "apparently sixteen or seventeen years old" (235); so we are dealing this time with a somewhat older young man, or "youth," as will become evident in the sequence that explores August's love life. Still, he is close enough to those boyhood days to make such references plausible.

More bothersome are the last two paragraphs of the revised chapter, in which Marget has become "Gretchen" and is made to teach the harp instead of the "spinet"—perhaps because Mark Twain had come to realize that the spinet was still a novelty in the fifteenth century and, hence, was unlikely to be used by a provincial young girl in Eseldorf. At the beginning, he may have intended to weave Gretchen and Wilhelm Meidling, somehow, into his new story; but, unlike Fathers Adolf and Peter, they are never mentioned again. When "No. 44" is published separately in a popular edition, as I think it should be some day, these two paragraphs should be eliminated.

Appendix E: Mark Twain and Printers

It was becoming an apprentice "printer's devil" at the age of 12 or 13 that launched Sam Clemens into journalism and eventually into literature, and he made good use of this experience in many of his writings. In general, the idea of "learning by doing," of apprenticeship as a basic form of education, rather than as a low rank in a feudal hierarchy, was widespread in the nineteenth century; E. M. Branch applied it excellently to Mark Twain's career in *The Literary Apprenticeship of Mark Twain* (1950), with a chapter devoted to the years 1853–1861, when Twain wandered up and down across the States as "Printer and Pilot." And Walter Blair, in his chapter on "The Duke and the Dauphin" in *Mark Twain and Huck Finn* (1960), has shown how these two "most delightful rascals in literature" (but especially the younger, "a jour printer by trade") came out of that experience and has described the rich folklore associated with the life of printers.

Jour has been properly associated with *journeyman,* the next stage in training after apprentice. But as Clemens said in a nostalgic speech, "The Old-Fashioned Printer" (delivered in 1886, soon after completion of Huckleberry Finn and in commemoration of Benjamin Franklin's birthday), the term was more precisely associated with printers who worked "by the day": "The tramping 'jour,' who flitted by in the summer and tarried a day, with his wallet stuffed with one shirt and a hatful of handbills" (*MTS,* p. 140).

That same speech, delivered when Clemens was fifty-one, began:

> The chairman's historical reminiscences of Gutenberg have caused me to fall into reminiscences, for I myself am something of an antiquity. All things change in the procession

of years, and it may be that I am among strangers. It may be that the printer of to-day is not the printer of thirty-five years ago. I was no stranger to him.

Clearly, then, printing was associated in Clemens's mind with youth, Gutenberg, and wandering strangers—"mysterious" and otherwise.

And this entire complex was an essential part of the mental preparation that went into the writing of "No. 44." As Blair, again, has shown in *Mark Twain's Hannibal, Huck and Tom* (1969), the notes headed "Villagers of 1840–43," which Mark Twain wrote in Weggis, Switzerland, included many names of printers with whom he had worked—notably Jim Wolfe and Wales McCormick, the latter being the model for "Doangivadam" (see Blair's appendix A). Even more close to home imaginatively is the fact that the very last story Mark Twain worked on before he began experimenting with the "St. Petersburg" and "Eseldorf" settings for "Young Satan" was also the last in a noteworthy series: "Tom Sawyer's Conspiracy" (the first four chapters were probably finished in Weggis, and an additional six were written at various times during 1898–1900 and 1902).[1] As Blair says: "'Tom Sawyer's Conspiracy" comes closer to completion than any other fragment in this collection," and it includes "some passages . . . not to be scorned," and "better than average satire" (p. 160).

An essential part of the "conspiracy" in this story involves the preparation and distribution of handbills that are intended by Tom Sawyer's gang to start an "insurrection" in the community. This enabled Mark Twain to weave in the figure of "old Mr. Day, the traveling jour. printer" (*HH&T*, p. 177) and technical information about the trade of printing. Most important for our purpose here is chapter 4, in which we are told that Tom "sung out to Mr. Day" in these terms:

"Tell the devil to go to hell and fetch a hatful; and quick about it."

It gave me the cold shivers to hear him. In about a minute Mr. Day says—

1. The complex dating of this manuscript is discussed at length by Blair in his appendix B (*HH&T*, pp. 375–77). Smith and Gibson stated (erroneously, it seems) that Mark Twain "had begun" this story "in Vienna during the winter of 1898–99" (*MTHL*, p. 746, note 2).

> "The devil says hell's empty sir."
> "All right, fetch a hatful of pie."
> That made my mouth water, and I was glad I came. Then the boy fetched a couple of oyster cans full of old type; it had to be old, there warn't any new in the place; and Mr. Baxter told him to fetch a stick and a rule. (*HH&T*, p. 189)

To this passage is added Mark Twain's own footnote:

> 1. *Hell,* printer's term for broken and otherwise disabled type. 2. *Printer's Devil,* apprentice. 3. *Pi,* printer's term for a mass of mixed-up type. 4. The (composing) stick and rule are used in setting the type.—Editor.

Clearly, the association between apprenticeship and "printer's devil" was fresh in his mind.

Furthermore, Tom Sawyer's first extended exercise in typesetting is a "composition" on the art of printing. Eliminating the mixed-up type and bad spelling and adding minimal punctuation, we get the following:

> The noble art of printing called by some typography the art preservative of arts was first discovered up a lane in a tower by cutting letters on birch pages [pads?] not knowing they would print and not expecting it. But they did by accident. Hence the German name for type to this day Buchstaben although made of metal ever since. Let all the nations bless the name of Gutenberg and Faust which done it. Amen.
>
> TOM SAWYER
> Printer (*HH&T*, p. 190)

This reference to a tower may account for Mark Twain's locating his print shop in a tower of the castle. And Gibson probably had Tom's linkage of Gutenberg and Faust in mind when he wrote about the "printer's devil": "The name may be associated with the belief that Faust was in league with the devil" (476).

Finally, the art of printing can be seen as one of the elements in the background of "No. 44" that help account for its "Rabelaisian" character—in the full sense of that term, as it refers to fantastic satire full of humor and a wealth of erudite learning. See my essay, "Mark Twain as American Rabelais."

Appendix F: "No. 44," Time Scheme

44		Stranger Manuscripts	
	Beginning	Chapter	Page
Absent	"It was in 1490—winter" (December?)	1	221
Present	"One cold day" at noon (January 1491?)	3	235
	"That very first night"	5	244
	"As the days went along"	5	244
	"Every few days"	5	246
	"At last"	5	247
	"These several weeks"	7	251
	Middle		
	A WEEK OF APPRENTICESHIP		
	Monday: persecutions	7	251
	"The day was finished"	7	260
	Tuesday: breakfast, etc.	8	261
	Wednesday	8	264
	Thursday	8	265
	Friday	9	266
	Saturday	9	269
	Sunday (Sabbath)	10	271
	"The day wasted away"	11	276
	ANOTHER WEEK		
	(probably February 1491)		
	Monday: Doangivadam	11	277
	Tuesday: "Next day"	13	288

	Wednesday: "The day after"	13	288
	"So things drifted along"	13	289
	Thursday(?): "At dawn"	14	292
	"About ten" (A.M.)	14	292
	"Supper"	14	298
	FEBRUARY: night and morning (?)	15	301
	"As long as I could keep awake"	15	302
	Friday (?)	16	303
Absent	Saturday (?): "The next day"	17	309
	Sunday (?): "Next day": preparations for midnight burial	17	311
	ANOTHER WEEK (?)		
Present	Monday (?): After midnight, the "corpse" is resurrected	18	312
	TIME BEGINS TO BE IMPRECISE		
	Discovery of America (October 1492) will be "next fall"	18	313
Absent	Forty-four vanishes leaving silver cup labeled "New York Yacht Club, 1903"	18	316
Present	"Day after day went by" (Forty-four and August are invisible)	19	316
	ANOTHER WEEK (?)		
Absent	"A week passed"	20	320
	Forty-four has been "home"	20	321
	ANOTHER WEEK (?)		
Present	Monday (?): Forty-four reappears	20	321
	"Come, you need an outing"	20	321
	"A wearying and troubled night"	21	323
	Tuesday (?): "Cold gray dawn"	21	323
	"A half hour of preparation"	21	326
	Forty-four invites August to break-fast" in the latter's room	22	329
Absent	"I was alone"	22	334
	"I was barely seventeen"	23	335
	"The days wore heavily by"	23	335

	"I had been missing her, a number of days"	23	336
	"Night came . . . At ten the castle was asleep"	23	337
	"Half-past eleven" (P.M.)	23	340
	Sunday (?): "At early mass the next morning"	24	344
	"That night"	25	350

End

MARCH (?)

	An "hour dragged along"	26	353
	"It was . . . midnighty"	26	353
Present	Forty-four reappears as Negro	26	354
	"It's a good night's work we've done"	26	362

TIME NOW BECOMES COMPETELY (?) RELATIVE

	Only "six minutes" of sleep	27	363
	"These few seconds"	27	363
	"In those days . . . one day"	27	364
Absent (Duplicate present)	"I think it was yesterday"	27	367
	"The psychological moment"	28	375
	With "my brother": "We talked the time away"	29	376
	Talk about "the heavens" and Saturday-Sabbath vs. "Sunday-Sabbath"	29	379
Present (Duplicate vanishes)	Forty-four returns "in the disguise of the magician"	29	380

BACK TO NORMAL TIME (?)

	"This morning"	30	381
	Newspaper clipping from "June 27, 1905"	30	383
	Roman "prophecy": Suetonius	30	384
	"A dark, sour, gloomy morning"	31	388

ECLIPSE: ASTRONOMICAL TIME

	"Ghost-Night": vernal equinox (?)	31	388

	"Hundredth Year": Analogous to a millennium (?)	31	389
	"The *gathering* darkness": eclipse: transfiguration, eternity	31	390
	"Several hours"	31	391
	"I did not stir again until ten at night"	31	391
	Midnight again: "The show is due to begin in an hour"	32	395
	"Turn backward, O Time"	32	395
	"Two or three days or a week" (but these are centuries!)	32	396
	History is confused: "Robert Bruce and Henry I and such"	32	396
	"Time drifted rearward": The sun *sets* in the east	32	399
	"Assembly of the Dead . . . from all the epochs and ages"	33	400
	"Procession": combines history and Darwinian evolution	33	403
	"Thought" in "empty space": "You have existed, companionless, through all the eternities": Metempsychosis (?)	34	404
	"The *empty* eternities": Why?	34	405
Absent	August, alone, is "appalled"	34	405

Appendix G: Mark Twain's Duplicates and the Double in Literature

The subject of the double is of central importance for nineteenth-century literature. The term had a great variety of significances: we have already noted Mark Twain's use of the German term *Doppelgänger* for the duplication of the same plot, at around the same time, by two or more authors (*MTHL*, p. 369–71). That it was more than the product of a literary fashion is suggested by the view of Jorge Luis Borges, summarized as follows:

> Borges once claimed that the basic devices of all fantastic literature are only four in number: the work within the work, the contamination of reality by dream, the voyage in time and the double. These are both his essential themes—the problematical nature of the world, of knowledge, of time, of the self—and his essential techniques of construction.[1]

To the extent that Borges is right, this confirms our sense that Mark Twain, especially in his final phase, belongs in the mainstream of fantastic (and I should add, satiric) writing. Three of these devices and themes are central in "No. 44," and the fourth, the work within the work, is used by him in "Three Thousand Years Among the Microbes" and elsewhere.

Obviously, the main thrust of the double is psychological. The basic idea may undergo many permutations: shadows and mirror reflections; portraits on canvas, in stone, or in words; identical, fraternal, and Siamese twins; the splitting of an individual into two or more persons, whether actually or by what psychologists call the "dissociation of personality"; the actual creation of a duplicate individual as in "No. 44"; and

1. Jorge Luis Borges, *Labyrinths: Selected Stories and Other Writing*, introduction, p. 18.

so on. All reflect, more or less subtly or radically, problematic aspects of the self and of human identity.[2]

We have seen that Mark Twain referred to *Strange Case of Dr. Jekyll and Mr. Hyde*, a work of great popularity in its day; and some of his ideas about "man's dual nature" might well have been derived from "Henry Jekyll's Full Statement of the Case," the concluding section of Stevenson's story. Robert Rowlette has devoted a chapter ("Mark Twain and Doubles")[3] to doubles in nineteenth-century literature generally and to "a few of the stages of Twain's development of this theme prior to 1892." A more thorough study of these materials would sharpen our awareness of what is special in Mark Twain's Duplicates: their being "fictions" that have been "pulled out" of the Originals and "materialized"; their being produced by Forty-four; their initial use as scabs in a "union" dispute, a problem of labor; their sexual liveliness, and the problems this creates; and their later use for a more subtle kind of psychological inspection; and so forth.

I know nothing quite like them in classic American literature; a remote approximation, perhaps, is in Poe's "William Wilson"—at least, in the sense that the original and his double appear there in separate bodies. But we have no explanation of the origin of Poe's double character, who is born on the same day as William Wilson and bears the same name; the characterization is elaborate and subtle, despite the brevity of the story, and it is presented as an allegory of conscience. The movement of the plot is toward a climax in which "the most absolute identity" is achieved, so that the dying double says,

2. See, among recent studies of this aspect of the subject, Robert Rogers's *A Psychoanalytic Study of the Double in Literature*. A more strictly literary treatment is by C. F. Keppler, *The Literature of the Second Self*, which includes chapters dealing with the "Second Self" as twin brother, pursuer, tempter, vision of horror, saviour, the beloved, and "in time."

3. Robert Rowlette, *Twain's "Pudd'nhead Wilson": The Development and Design*, pp. 62–82. Rowlette is concerned with the converging "themes of twinhood, training, and justice" (p. 82). Among the many writers treated by Keppler in *The Second Self* who I suspect may have influenced Clemens are Hans Christian Andersen, George du Maurier, Rudyard Kipling, and Guy de Maupassant ("The Horla")—but I shall not pursue these hypotheses here.

at the end, "thou has murdered *thyself*" (my italics); in this respect Poe's story prefigures Stevenson's idea.

As we have seen in our text, Mark Twain's Duplicates are variously presented and analyzed, depending on their changing functions in the story; the trend of their shifting mysteries is from the conventional to the strange, from the external to the more psychological. In view of Mark Twain's fondness for twins, part of the shift might be compared to the difference between identical and fraternal twins.

Finally, that Mark Twain was aware of the double theme early in his career is evident from a newspaper letter quoted by Gibson (clipping in *MTP*), which was probably written in 1868, around the time of Clemens's courtship of Olivia Langdon. "Complaining of a deadbeat 'Double' who had been writing squibs and borrowing money in his name," Gibson tells us, Mark Twain concluded:

> I am fading, still fading. Shortly, if my distress of mind continues, there may be only four of us left. (That is a joke, and it naturally takes the melancholy tint of my own feelings. I will explain it: I am Twain, which is two; my Double is Double-Twain, which is four more; four and two are six; two from six leaves four. It is very sad.)

"Thus," Gibson speculates, "in a punning non-mathematical sense, 44 might be Twain twice doubled" (473, note to 184.33 on "Quarante-quatre").

Of course, this hypothesis harmonizes well with my own speculations about autobiographical implications in "No. 44." See Appendix C.

Supplementary Notes

Almost all the following notes were written before Howard G. Baetzhold published his excellent *Mark Twain and John Bull: The British Connection* in 1970, and certainly before I had the opportunity to study carefully that exploration of "Clemens's debt to British literature," as he characterizes his own book in the foreword. There are various points at which we overlap, others where we supplement one another, and happily few where we contradict one another.

The study of influences and sources, which I think important and fascinating, is a bottomless well, of course. Since I have not tried to incorporate all the useful contributions resulting from Professor Baetzhold's industry, I am happy to recommend his book as a supplement to my own, in reference to Clemens's British "connections."

S.J.K.

Chapter 3

1. "St. Petersburg" appears only in the following summary statement:

> A number of canceled references to St. Petersburg identify the original setting. For black walnuts (which are Missouri trees) Twain later substituted chestnuts, for dollars he later substituted ducats, and for the village bank he wrote in the name of Solomon Isaacs, the moneylender. He substituted Nikolaus for Huck, Theodor for George (Tom in the notes), Father Peter for Mr. Black, Seppi for Pole, and Wilhelm Meidling for Tom Andrews "of good Kentucky stock."

> References that placed the story in the 1840's of the author's boyhood were deleted. The action includes Satan's lecture on the Moral Sense, Mr. Black's finding of the dollars, and the stir this discovery makes in the village. (5)

The working notes (415–16) include: "Human Race/Destroy Moral Sense; or/[Destroy] the Race?" When I consider Gibson's summary in conjunction with the surviving notes, I believe Mark Twain may indeed have been thinking at first of the Father of Lies himself. As the June note said, "Satan's" miracles were to be devilish.

2. It is not perfectly clear at what point Mark Twain chose the title "The Chronicle of Young Satan"; but from the indications of handwriting and ink it may well have been an integral part of the November 1897 inspiration. The first two pages of the manuscript are reproduced by Gibson on page 490 of the *Stranger Manuscripts* (see list of short references p. xiii).

There are relatively few notes relating to this phase of the writing (417–19) and they were well discussed by John S. Tuckey (*MTSatan*, pp. 20–24). He pointed out that the Austrian village was originally called "Hasenfeld" (Rabbit Field) but was very quickly changed to Eseldorf (Donkeytown)—this perhaps supplies another link to the American-Hannibal idea: Uncle Remus's Brer Rabbit? "And nominally speaking, when this change was made," Tuckey observed, "the 'Eseldorf' version as such was originated."

3. Chapter 1 is far removed from the "romantic" fairy-tale atmosphere intended in 1916 by the Paine-Duneka edition, with its soft illustrations by N. C. Wyeth. "It was 1702—May" (as against the 1916 setting: "It was in 1590—winter"), and if "Austria was far away from the world" and still in "the Middle Ages," the reader's shifting his perspective from 1590 to 1702 certainly makes a big difference.

4. Mark Twain probably chose this particular version of Protestantism not only because it could be appropriately localized in the Austro-Hungarian empire, but because John Huss and his followers were especially severe in their attacks on the corruption of the clergy. Father Adolf—who appears in the first batch of working notes as "Lueger, a drinking, spiteful, prying, overgodly, malicious priest" (417)—was also inspired

by the figure of Dr. Karl Lueger, who had been confirmed by the emperor in his position of mayor as the leader of "a clerico-anti-Semitic Tammany in Vienna" shortly before Clemens arrived in that city (*MTSatan*, pp. 18–36). The "Tammany" phrase is quoted by Tuckey from *Encyclopaedia Britannica*, 14th ed., 2:77.

5. In "Sold to Satan" (dated 1904 by Paine when he included it in *Europe and Elsewhere*), Mark Twain returned to the idea of "cheating" the Devil. This sketch takes the form of an interview with "the modern Satan" just as we see him on the stage . . . on his intellectual face the well-known and high-bred Mephistophelian smile" (*Essays*, p. 650). At one point *this* Satan says:

> " 'Do you know I have been trading with your poor pathetic race for ages, and you are the first person who has been intelligent enough to divine the large commercial value of my make up.'
>
> "I purred to myself and looked as modest as I could."

Mark Twain had been told that Satan was made of radium and immediately thought of him as a "mine."

> " 'Yes, you are the first,' he continued. 'All through the Middle Ages I used to buy Christian souls at fancy rates, building bridges and cathedrals in a single night in return, and *getting swindled out of my Christian nearly every time that I dealt with a priest*—as history will concede—but making it up on the lay square-dealer now and then, as *I* admit; but none of those people ever guessed where the real big money lay. You are the first.' " (*Essays*, p. 652, my italics)

The reference here to "history" emphasizes that this latter legend did have a historical source.

Around the time of "Schoolhouse," we have a note that (assuming that the angel is the *son* of Satan) repudiates directly this legendary episode: "Says his papa has not been cheated by monks etc.—a lot of Middle-Age lies" (436).

Chapter 4

6. This addition suggests to me that the "Group D" working notes (425–27), which Gibson placed between May 1899 and

June 1900, were actually written before "Schoolhouse." Gibson's dating here is, in any case, "probable" and is based chiefly on "an anticipation of the love rivalry episode" in chapters 4, 5, and 6 of "Young Satan" (89–111, see list of short references p. xiii).

However, there are elements of the love theme also in "Schoolhouse," where Annie Fleming appears as a variation on the "Hellfire Hotchkiss" character with whom Forty-four was to fall in love. Annie does fall in love (196–97), but there is no suggestion that her "worship" is reciprocated. That love and sex were to play a role in the "Stranger" tale, or tales, is indicated in the very first notes: "Harem, 800 women/Sandwich Islands copulation common/Christian one wife" (415).

I base my hypothesis about the early dating partly on the fact that these notes were written on the same sort of paper as "Schoolhouse"—"half-sheets of Joynson Superfine paper" (425, 489)—but chiefly on the developments in Wilhelm Meidling's character.

The italics are being used to counter emphatically an alternative proposal; and the only such surviving in the notes are the one about Meidling and one about a "Spanish barber" who "reveals that he is an Admirable Crichton" (*MTP*, 32[II], 49—written between 8 and 10 November 1898).

7. The rest of this fascinating sketch shows that Mark Twain's mind was going back to the childhood memory (which he recorded for his *Autobiography* soon after his mother's death in 1890) of Jane Lampton Clemens's compassionate suggestion that someone ought to pray for and defend the Devil.

8. Stanley Brodwin's essay, "Mark Twain's Masks of Satan: The Final Phase," touches on many of my problems and makes the necessary elementary distinctions among the three versions that constitute " 'The Mysterious Stranger' complex" (p. 217). But when he cites the passage in "Schoolhouse" about the Devil's "error," he falls back into the old habit of equating "Young Satan" and "44" (p. 221); I have emphasized the differences. And his discussion is oriented more to philosophy and theology than to imagination and literary art. I do not find "No. 44" as "artistically unfinished" (p. 224) as Brodwin makes it out to be.

9. To the examples in Smith's survey, we should add the interesting "Indiantown" sequence that was worked at spo-

radically during 1899–1902: "the region, the cotton belt on the west bank of the Mississippi river" (*WWD*, p. 153)—in the heart of Arkansas, rather than in Missouri. Its population of 1,500 is about village size, but the economy and culture are those of cotton plantations, which would imply the addition of a fairly large slave population as well. There are three substantial manuscripts: "Indiantown" (summer 1899) and "Which Was It?" (1899–1902), both in *Which Was the Dream?*; and the rather curious "A Human Bloodhound" (1899), which seems originally to have had a Hannibal–St. Petersburg setting (*HH&T*, pp. 67 ff.). In Indiantown, the transcendent figure (in Paul E. Baender's sense) is a mulatto ex-slave called Jasper (*WWD*, pp. 310 ff.).

The most curious permutation of Hannibal "as a metaphor of all human society" is in the science-fiction fantasy "Three Thousand Years among the Microbes" (*WWD*, pp. 430–553), which has a narrator-protagonist who is a cholera germ (called "Huck") and lives inside the body of a Hungarian tramp.

Chapter 5

10. John S. Tuckey has criticized the manuscript left by Mark Twain:

> But there were some almost unrelated episodes. Modes and moods were as variable: the story was satiric, comic, sentimental, farcical, didactic. Clearly, it needed integration. Paine and Duneka were not overly concerned with such matters as preserving the purity—what there was of it—of their author's text. Mark Twain's adverse representations of Father Adolf were either toned down or taken out entirely; the astrologer was introduced as a more acceptable villain. Also almost entirely deleted was a long passage in which the young Satan vied with youths of the village of Eseldorf for the regard of Lilly and Marget, using his powers to outdo his rivals. (*Critics*, p. 86, see list of short references p. xiii)

The effect, as Tuckey wrote, was that "they blunted or obscured much of the satire that was retained by omitting the specific objects of Mark Twain's attack"—a method that "tended to make Mark Twain appear bitter without sufficient grounds for bitterness." Add to this Bernard DeVeto's essay on "The Symbols of Despair" (*Critics,* pp. 92–108), which is based on a partial and often mistaken analysis of the *Stranger Manuscripts,* and we had the full-blown myth of Mark Twain's unaccountable aging pessimism, which has bemused the critics for more than a generation.

11. We also get more data about "Satan." His "country seat" in Austria or Germany (as Theodor's father thinks) is called "Himmelreich"—"The Kingdom of Heaven! What a modest name" (97). The angel admires rattlesnakes, which is a more obviously ironic development of the theme of the "higher animals" (98); and he "embroiders like an angel," which makes Theodor's father comment, "if he were my child I would see to it that he stuck to his embroidery, that I would. There's the makings of a man in him if he had the right kind of mother" (99)! I draw attention to these revelations concerning fathers because of their relative scarcity in Mark Twain's writings and autobiography. (One is struck, on the other hand, by the number of uncles in "Young Satan": "Satan's" uncle, the Devil; Theodor's uncle's farm; Father Peter is Marget's uncle; and so forth. An uncle may be thought of as a convenient substitute for a lost father.)

12. The *Stranger* and "Young Satan" texts come together at chapter 10 of each text. Both chapters begin: "Days and days went by now, and no Satan." But the first part of the "concluding" sections was drastically cut by Paine and Duneka, and therefore the parts that intervene, though both begin with "I fell asleep to pleasant music," are quite different in their total effects (midchapter 7 to the end of 9 in the *Stranger*—as against midchapter 6 to the end of chapter 9 in "Young Satan"). Both versions share the trip to China and the dialogue on a mountaintop, which culminates in an exposition of determinism; the illustrative instances of Lisa Brandt and Nikolaus Bauman and Frau Brandt (Lisa's mother) and Fischer (the weaver); the "history of the progress of the human race"; and the witch-hunt persecution of the "born lady," in which "Satan" puts his powers of prediction to spectacular use. But the cut passages put these familiar sequences—powerful even in their abridged form—in rather different contexts.

Paine and Duneka had the good sense not to touch the moving sequences growing out of Nicky's death; but they took some of the sting out of the satiric history of "civilization" by removing a paragraph about "the Holy Inquisition" and by translating the specific mention of the "awful slaughters" of Blenheim and Ramillies (1704, 1706)—almost contemporary with 1702, but not relevant to 1590—into a general statement.

A similar loss of particularity resulted from elimination of two paragraphs bringing European history up to date from 1702 (in other words, to the close of the nineteenth century), which gives greater relevance to the paragraph beginning: "Then he began to laugh in the most unfeeling way" (137). The modern Victorian world of evolutionary "progress" had *not* been excluded from the angel's derision.

13. There is a close parallel to the use of the fly in letter 6 of *Letters from the Earth,* in which "it was found that a fly had been left behind" on Noah's Ark. This fly "had not been left behind by accident. No, the hand of Providence was in it. There are no accidents" (pp. 25–26).

This is from Mark Twain's last years. From his earlier writings, we may cite the passage about Mono Lake, the "Dead Sea of California," in chapter 38 of *Roughing It* (vol. 1): "Providence leaves nothing to go by chance. All things have their uses and their part and proper place in Nature's economy: the ducks eat the flies—the flies eat the worms—the Indians eat all three—the wildcats eat the Indians—the white folks eat the wildcats—and thus all things are lovely."

14. In "Mark Twain and Socratic Dialogue" (*Mark Twain Journal* 11 [Summer 1959]:1–3), Marvin Klotz restricted the term to "a dialogue situation in which Socrates . . . demonstrates the errors in the views of his audience and forces them to admit the validity of his own views" and found that "the technique is absent from *Pudd'nhead Wilson* and *The Mysterious Stranger*" (note 6). I am using the term more loosely for a philosophic dialogue, proceeding by means of question and answer as well as by straightforward exposition involving a search for truth, in which one of the speakers is more skilled, or knows more of the truth, than the others.

William M. Gibson, in "Mark Twain's Mysterious Stranger Manuscripts: Some Questions for Textual Critics," found that in "Young Satan" there are "four Socratic dialogues . . . , in each of which Satan persuades Theodor against his will" of the truth of an argument (p. 189).

15. What I have referred to as the problem of scale (as in

Swift) and the flattening of the hierarchy of values (more characteristic of Rabelais perhaps) was a recurrent theme, associated with "bugs," and especially with the fly, in Mark Twain's writings. It is by no means a trivial idea: one thinks of Edward Taylor's "Upon a Spider Catching a Fly," of Emily Dickinson's "I heard a fly buzz when I died," and of the fly in the climactic scene of Dostoyevsky's *The Idiot,* which settles on the bed on which the body of the murdered Nastasya is lying (part 4, chapter 11). Allen Tate made this last scene central in an important essay entitled "The Hovering Fly" and subtitled "A Causerie on the Imagination and the Actual World."

16. Modern technology and science fiction have accustomed us to rapid transitions in space and time; for example, television newscasts may take us to many countries within a short time. But the crowding of months of experience into seconds is a more complex psychological phenomenon.

In "Young Satan," we go to Scotland, India, and Ceylon. The Indian episode (168–73) is well rounded and sustained, resembling the Conrad Bart episode in that an arrogant bully —here a foreign imperialist, one of the Portuguese who were "colonising" India in the early eighteenth century—is punished by "Satan." The man's terrible punishment, which includes sleepless nights (with interesting symbolic overtones) and the curious accommodation for his guiltless wife, is ingenious, to say the least.

Chapter 6

17. This never-completed, long (250 pages in print) novel occupied Mark Twain at various times between 1899 and 1903 (*WWD*, pp. 20–23, 177–429, see list of short references p. xiii). In the full story of those years, it would obviously have to get more attention than we can give it here. Working on "Which Was It?" at this stage would mean editing and revising, perhaps completing, a manuscript of over one hundred thousand words. Or perhaps the second "long book" he had in mind was his *Autobiography.*

18. There are two later references to *The Mysterious Stranger.* One occurs in an autobiographical dictation of 30 August 1906:

> There is another unfinished book, which I should probably entitle "The Refuge of the Derelicts." It is half finished, and will remain so. There is still another one, entitled "The Adventures of a Microbe During Three Thousand Years—by a Microbe." It is half finished and will remain so. There is yet another—*The Mysterious Stranger*. It is more than half finished. I would dearly like to finish it, and it causes me a real pang to reflect that it is not to be. These several tanks are full now, and those books would go gaily along and complete themselves if I would hold the pen, but I am tired of the pen. (*Mark Twain in Eruption*, pp. 198–99)

John S. Tuckey has discussed the relation of the title "Derelicts" to "The Great Dark" (*WWD*, p. 99). "The Refuge of the Derelicts" has been published in *MTFM* (pp. 157–248); and "Three Thousand Years Among the Microbes" is now available in *WWD*. As to the third item, as Tuckey has suggested, "half finished" here should not be taken as an exact estimate.

The second statement was quoted by Paine in his edition of *MTN*. While at Stormfield (1909), Paine wrote, Mark Twain pointed to a drawer containing some manuscripts and said: "There is one, *The Mysterious Stranger*, that I could finish easily, almost any time. Perhaps I shall do that one, and then some day you can get it in shape for publication" (*MTN*, p. 369). That is a precise description of the state of "No. 44" at the time. Paine's error was in linking two different creations on the basis of a superficial analysis of the manuscripts.

19. Gibson (using the prior work of Tuckey) described in careful detail the state of the surviving manuscript and typescript pages of "No. 44" and reconstructed the probable stages of the writing. (This body of editorial apparatus is found on pages 9–11, 489–92, 514–19, 559–603 of the *Manuscripts*.) The picture is complicated by changes in paper and ink and alterations in the manuscript, but the essential facts are easily summarized. There are 530 pages of manuscript (though the pagination runs higher because some pages were discarded), and there are now 185 pages of printed text (221–405), making thirty-four chapters. During the first six months of 1904 in Florence, Mark Twain wrote pages 111–432 of the manuscript, now chapters 8–25; and also the six-page fragment headed "Conclusion of the book," long notorious as the out-of-place

"conclusion" of the Paine-Duneka *Stranger* text and now in place as the final chapter of "No. 44."

Back in the States in 1905, comfortably settled in Dublin, New Hampshire, for the summer, and soon after completing an exuberant spell of writing that produced the remarkable "Three Thousand Years Among the Microbes," Mark Twain wrote on manuscript page 432: "June 30/05 Burned the rest (30,000 words) of this book this morning. Too diffusive" (518). By mid–July, he had "apparently" written through manuscript page 587 (491), to the end of chapter 32. Then "probably in 1908" (*MTSatan*, p. 71), newly settled at Redding, Connecticut, in the "Stormfield" house where he was to die, Mark Twain wrote the eight-page fragment, now chapter 33, that made "No. 44" complete.

20. This interest first crystallized with Clemens's courtship of Olivia Langdon: she had been rescued from partial paralysis by a "Doctor Newton" who, as Justin Kaplan put it, "would have been as much at home in the Mississippi Valley of Clemens' boyhood as he was in the Southern Tier in the 1860's" (*Mr. Clemens and Mark Twain: A Biography*, p. 78). Mind cure was also one of the preoccupations Clemens shared with the James family—William *and* Henry (see William James, *William James on Psychical Research*)—with the entire "Psychical Research" circle in England and elsewhere, and with his friend Howells.

Howells gave fictional expression to his ideas on the subject in various novels, including *Dr. Breen's Practice* (1881), concerning which we find Clemens writing to Howells on 3 September 1881: "Your experience in the matter of 'Dr. Breen' and the authoress of its Doppelganger [*sic*], adds a rattling strong instance to my list of cases of 'mental telegraphing' " (*MTHL*, p. 369). Mark Twain's first "Mental Telegraphy" essay appeared in the December 1891 *Harper's Magazine*, but a note by the editor tells us that the experiences described there went back to about 1874–1875.

As to Clara, see her final autobiographical book, *Awake to a Perfect Day: My Experience with Christian Science*, which opens with a reference to her father's "book against Mary Baker Eddy." Her first husband, Ossip Gabrilowitsch, died in 1936; and in 1944 Clara married Jacques Samassoud, who was a Christian Science "healer," as well as a professional musician.

21. Two tendencies came together in those late writings: an autobiographical impulse and a readiness to "let go" with respect to censored themes and techniques. Stylistic experiment, as in Mark Twain's recurring parodies and burlesques, went along with thematic explorations; and some of the deepest significances of the "Stranger" writings probably lie, as we shall see, in their relationships to the familiar Matter of Hannibal. I can only touch occasionally here on such connections in "No. 44," but the reader should be alert to the American elements in this Austrian story. Some of these pop up surrealistically, as in the chapters where Forty-four takes August into the nineteenth and early twentieth centuries.

Less obvious clues appear throughout the text, beginning with the print-shop setting, which is a reminiscence of Clemens's very first work experience in Hannibal; the character nicknamed Doangivadam, who is a takeoff on Twain's fellow printer, Wales McCormick; and so forth. In the religious vein, though the priests and ritual are naturally Catholic, there are affinities with Clemens's Protestant experiences in Hannibal, Hartford, and elsewhere. So chapter 10 begins: "It was a lovely Sunday, calm and peaceful and holy, and bright with sunshine" —and we could almost be back in Sunday school with Tom and Huck. As we shall see, Clemens found the intensely Catholic material for that chapter in a publication from Clyde, Missouri, rather than in some Austrian equivalent. The figure of Katrina may remind us of Aunty Cord, the cook and servant who inspired Clemens's first serious treatment of a Negro in fiction (Aunt Rachel, the narrator of "A True Story"). The "family room" setting parallels the boarding house in *The American Claimant*; and does not Forty-four's rejection by the print-shop community recall, mutatis mutandis, the rejection in *Pudd'nhead* of the too-bright lawyer, David Wilson, by the people of St. Petersburg? Most intimate of all, the comedy of love and the plot involving August's Duplicate (chapters 23–29) clearly parallel in many details Clemens's courtship of Olivia Langdon.

The general point behind such affinities is that the aesthetic detachment of a setting distant in time and space, as in the more familiar case of *A Connecticut Yankee in King Arthur's Court*, not only fired Mark Twain's imagination but sometimes enabled him to give fresh expression to complex aspects of his American experiences. To the "Huck Finnian" ironies we have been noting, then, we should add what might be called "Connecticut Yankee" effects: for example, the way in which we are brought back to an American point of view in chapter 10 by the idiomatic "there was not a dry eye in the house" (276). I find this sort of stylistic shift subtly humorous and roughly equivalent to the knights coming to the rescue on bicycles in the *Yankee.*

Chapter 7

22. As to the source of the title "Mysterious Stranger," the phrase was a common one and occurred in Mark Twain's writings as early as *The Innocents Abroad* (vol. 2, chapter 20, near the end), where the reference was to Jesus. Gibson assumed the title was fixed "when he began his story" (1902); but there is a possible link to a work published in 1905, which might help explain the "Mysterious Stranger's" title page's similarity in style to that of "Three Thousand Years Among the Microbes."

In *A History of American Graphic Humor, 1865–1938,* by William Murrell, there is reference to *The Mysterious Stranger and Other Cartoons* (Chicago, 1905) by John T. McCutcheon, "one of the ablest cartoonists in Chicago." McCutcheon illustrated several of George Ade's early books, and this Indiana author and his Chicago illustrator were admired by both Clemens and Howells (*MTHL,* p. 832, see list of short references p. xiii). Further, the title cartoon of McCutcheon's 1905 book had a political message that Mark Twain would probably have noticed: "A black-hatted, frock-coated Missourian," Murrell writes, "is shown having just left the Democratic column to line up with the Republicans. It appeared in the *Chicago Tribune* on the morning of November 10th, 1904, the day after election returns had told an astonished America that Theodore Roosevelt had won Missouri away from the Solid South. It was a brilliant cartoon idea, and the drawing was reproduced throughout the entire country" (pp. 148–49).

As the opening section of *Mark Twain in Eruption* makes especially clear, Roosevelt as "statesman and politician" was one of Clemens's bêtes noires. And from Paine's biography we learn that Clemens's critical attitude toward Roosevelt was evident during the winter of 1904–1905 (*MTB,* pp. 1231–32), shortly before he wrote the "Microbes" fantasy. It seems at least possible that the cartoon or book helped fix the title phrase in Mark Twain's mind.

23. There is a link, I think, between the theme of the Negro that will emerge later ("The Power of Blackness," Chapter 11) and this initial act of pity for a weary stranger. The verses I have cited from Matthew were frequently used in slave narratives, in those parts where fugitive slaves were given shelter. See, for example, the *Narrative of the Life of Frederick Douglass an American Slave, Written by Himself*, ed. Benjamin Quarles (Cambridge, Mass.: Harvard University Press, Belknap Press, 1960), p. 150. That they were very familiar to Clemens is evident from the way in which he plays with their language in a letter to Howells (28 January 1882): "I was an angered—which is just as good an expression, I take it, as an hungered" (*MTHL*, pp. 386–87).

24. The importance of this tendency in American history was demonstrated thoroughly in John Higham's classic study: *Strangers in the Land: Patterns of American Nativism, 1860–1925*. As Higham pointed out, hostility to "foreign-born minorities" was particularly strong in the 1840s, when Clemens was a boy, and also in the decade from 1886 to 1896, when he was entering into the troubled final phase that produced "No. 44."

25. See *Colonel Sellers as a Scientist* (1883), in William Dean Howells, *The Complete Plays of W. D. Howells*. See also the index of *MTHL*. For *Claimant*, see Clyde L. Grimm, "*The American Claimant*: Reclamation of a Farce."

A fresh look at *Claimant*, the first novel written after *Yankee*, is still needed, despite Grimm's excellent beginning in his essay. To our story of "Mark Twain and Printers" (Appendix E) should be added the nameless figure in *Claimant* of a printer of British origin "approaching middle age," who reads a brief paper at the Mechanics' Club and is an unsociable member of the boarding-house community (*Claimant*, chapters 11–12).

26. See note by "TRANSLATOR"—in other words, Mark Twain—for 273.20 of the *Manuscripts* (515).

27. Mark Twain was careless, however, in anachronistically using the testimony of "the Blessed Margaret Alacoque," founder of the order of the Sacred Heart of Jesus, who lived from 1647 to 1690, two centuries after the time of our narrative. She was pronounced venerable in 1824, blessed in 1864,

but not canonized till 1920. He was probably remembering the 1702 date of "Young Satan."

28. August's almost pagan response to the music of the organ ("an invention of recent date" [271]) prefigures the role that Forty-four's "heathen" music will play later in our story. The possible falsity, or at least extremity, of his response is suggested by Mark Twain's indulgence here in a set piece of rhetorical style that is almost, though not quite, parody. "You will believe that all worldly thoughts, all ungentle thoughts, were gone from that place, now; you will believe that these uplifted and yearning souls were as a garden thirsting for the fructifying dew of truth, and prepared to receive it and hold it precious and give it husbandry (271)." And so forth.

29. The figure of Wales McCormick takes us back to Hannibal; but his peculiar name links up, more generally, with the careless, wandering days of Clemens's bachelorhood. As Clemens wrote to Howells on 28 January 1882 (in an extraordinarily revealing letter that joins, incidentally, "the very devils and angels themselves"): "A life of *don't-care-a-damn* in a boarding house is what I have asked for in many a secret prayer" (*MTHL*, p. 389, my italics).

Chapter 8

30. Thereafter, despite some of the criticisms that have been leveled at the conclusion and the gap of time that existed before the final link (chapter 33) was inserted, the writing proceeded smoothly; the one major exception came on 30 June 1905, when Twain burned some thirty thousand words of manuscript with the comment: "Too diffusive" (518). By implication, we may confidently say, Clemens realized that most of the rest of "No. 44" was indeed highly concentrated (see list of short references p. xiii).

In the middle of the middle, however, the revisions and "Alterations in the Manuscript" (520 ff.) tend to be more complex. After chapter 17, some eighty-five pages of manuscript are missing; and the last sentence of chapter 19 ("But he was gone") concludes, as Gibson tells us, "a great deal of complex revision" (517–18).

31. Such "twins," of course, are a device obsessively common in Mark Twain's fictions, most notably in *The Prince and*

the Pauper, Pudd'nhead Wilson, and *Those Extraordinary Twins;* and Gibson draws attention to the presence of "this metaphor of the doppelganger"—associated later with a mirror reflection (311)—"in a passage of the holograph manuscript, later canceled, of a *Connecticut Yankee in King Arthur's Court*" (480–81).

The German noun *Doppelgänger,* usually translated as *double* or *alter ego,* points to a large body of fiction, for the most part romantic, based on this curious aspect of character. Mark Twain indicates a knowledge of the well-known variations on these themes by R. L. Stevenson, *Dr. Jekyll and Mr. Hyde* (1886); and by Adelbert von Chamisso, *Peter Schlemihl* (1814), the latter about a man without a shadow. In American literature, the most familiar and striking example is by E. A. Poe, "William Wilson" (see Appendix G). Interesting parallels to Mark Twain's duplicates may be found in F. M. Dostoyevsky's early novel, *The Double* (1846).

32. This form of lightning-flash illumination was a phenomenon much noted at the turn of the century. It was associated with mysticism and explored with great enthusiasm, historical learning, and vivid illustration by the Whitman disciple and psychiatrist, Richard M. Bucke, in *The Cosmic Consciousness: A Study in the Evolution of the Human Mind.* His citation of such an experience in a dream reported by an American businessman was given prominence when William James used it in his "Mysticism" lectures (16–17) in *The Varieties of Religious Experience: A Study in Human Nature.*

In general, "No. 44," the *Stranger Manuscripts,* and other of Mark Twain's writings are extremely rich in references to various religious, quasi-religious, and "psychic" phenomena that were current in the "Victorian" culture of Anglo-America, as well as on the European continent. This is a large subject deserving separate study, and we shall be able to note only a few obvious examples. Howard Kerr, *Mediums, and Spirit-Rappers, and Roaring Radicals: Spiritualism in American Literature, 1850–1900,* has a chapter (8) devoted to "Mark Twain and Spiritualism."

33. The latter are complicated by the paradoxical character of death in Christianity and the resulting difficulty of assimilating pagan views of tragic fate into later European drama governed by Christian views of salvation. See U. M. Ellis-Fermor,

The Frontiers of Drama, especially chapters 2 ("*Samson Agonistes* and Religious Drama") and 7 ("The Equilibrium of Tragedy"); and Herbert Weisinger, *Tragedy and the Paradox of the Fortunate Fall.*

34. A related aspect might be called the drug element (see the "alcohol," "drunkenness," and "tobacco" entries in the index of James's *Varieties of Religious Experience*). In chapter 18, there is a humorous bit (314–15) about tobacco—reminding us, in part, of the burlesque use of smoking in the *Yankee* and, in part, suggesting "a pagan religious service," though "it is only a vice, . . . but not a religious one. It originated in Mexico." Though wine is a traditional part of Jewish-Christian ritual, Mark Twain generally sees the comic possibilities of drunkenness.

35. This last fact reminds us of our guess in the last chapter that the relationship between August and Forty-four may be understood as some sort of complex allegory of Clemens–Mark Twain. If this is true, the Duplicate of August—his double or alter ego—should be added to the growing list of Mark Twain's "other selves" in "No. 44."

Chapter 9

36. As with Forty-four, but in another way, there is a puzzle about names: August has to learn from Elisabeth that he is called *Martin*; the Elisabeth-self does not know the Marget-self, whereas (especially after he has learned his second name) August shifts easily back and forth between these two identities.

August says: "Marget knew me as August Feldner, her Dream-Self knew me as Martin von Giesbach—*why*, was a matter beyond guessing" (342). I have been unable, as yet, to find sources for either of August's names.

37. Mark Twain's close reading of Shakespeare's play is evident, not only from the mock soliloquy in *Huckleberry Finn* (chapter 21), but from his attempts at producing a "Burlesque *Hamlet*" (*S&B*, pp. 49–86, see list of short references p. xiii).

Concerning "hallucinations," see William James's entire chapter 19 on "The Perception of 'Things' " and elsewhere, in *The Principles of Psychology*, vol. 2. It seems to me quite likely that some of the "wildness" in the writing of "No. 44" was influenced by quotations in James's work from the writings of people suffering from delusions, confusing dream with reality, and the like. In the chapter referred to, see the "vivid account of a fit of hasheesh-delirium . . . given me by a friend" (pp. 121–22).

Chapter 10

38. There is an interesting Freudian slip in this section. Lisbet is ready for marriage on the instant, and the wrestlings of conscience are all August's: he hesitates to have her marry "a viewless detail of the atmosphere" (his own Dream-Self). And he has decided that in the future he could get Martin-Emil locked up; meanwhile, he has little hesitation about hypnotizing Lisbet into an imaginary wedding. But even before this has taken place, August refers to "my wife's Waking-Self"; strictly speaking, he should have said: "my future wife." He is projecting a marriage for Martin and also planning to kill him and make Lisbet a widow: he would "retire" both his soul and his Duplicate; Marget would, presumably, do the same with her own Dream-Self. This is a kind of spiritual murder by anticipation. As a view of marriage in general, and as a possible allegory of the marriage of Samuel Clemens, it might provoke endless speculations.

39. This was a commonplace idea among nineteenth-century American writers, especially in the "dark" tradition of Poe, Hawthorne, and Melville. For example, in Randall Stewart, ed., *The American Notebooks by Nathaniel Hawthorne,* see "Slavery, mental," in the index; and pages lxxiii–lxxvi in the introduction.

Chapter 11

40. Besides the well-known treatment of Negro characters in his fiction (notably "A True Story," Nigger Jim, and Roxy), see some of the early chapters (especially 2–4) in Charles Neider, ed., *The Autobiography of Mark Twain.* In chapter 2 he wrote: "Color and condition interposed a subtle line which both parties were conscious of and which rendered *complete* fusion impossible" (my italics). The evidence for identification

is thus rather complex but includes Twain's falling back on the spirituals at times of deep emotional stress, his masquerading in blackface, his impersonating Negroes at a "hoe-down" or doing a "cake-walk," and, indeed, such passages in his fictions as those now being analyzed.

Perhaps, as his response to spirituals suggests, the deeper religious emotions in Clemens were associated with Negroes.

41. Here what might be called the science-fiction element (present throughout our text in other aspects and this time in that of interplanetary travel) comes to the fore with mention of "the belt of Orion" (is this name accidental, or incidental, in a chapter by Sam Clemens that begins: "I stirred my brother up"?) and "excursionists from Sirius" (376). This last may be an echo of Voltaire's *Micromégas,* long recognized as one of Mark Twain's sources (*Critics,* pp. 113 ff.): "Mr. Micromégas" is from "the land of Sirius," and so forth (see list of short references p. xiii). But the bright Dog Star has always been a favorite with stargazers and is in fact near the constellation of Orion.

Chapter 12

42. See especially "The Secret History of Eddypus, the World-Empire," in *MTFM,* pp. 315–88 (see list of short references p. xiii).

43. The eclipse, we are told, is "not a real one, but an artificial one that nobody but Simon Newcomb could tell from the original Jacobs" (388). In H. G. Wells's *The Time Machine,* section 1, we find a reference to attempts to construct a four-dimensional geometry: "Professor Simon Newcomb was expounding this to the New York Mathematical Society only a month or so ago." Simon Newcomb (1835–1909) was probably the greatest of American astronomers in the nineteenth century. In "Which Was the Dream?" the narrator's "stage name" is Edward Jacobs"; but there is a problem of identity, since he has been asleep eighteen months as the result of a mental illness (*WWD,* pp. 70–71). And the part of *Life on the Mississippi* (chapter 50) in which Clemens tells about Captain Isaiah Sellers, from whom he said he appropriated the famous pen name, "Mark Twain," is titled: *The "Original Jacobs."*

44. Time stood still, of course, when "the Lord fought for

Israel" at Gibeon (Joshua 10:1–14). The lines of verse are from "Rock Me to Sleep" (1860), an extremely sentimental poem by Elizabeth Akers Allen. The "comparatively new" methods of time travel were being "scientifically" dramatized by H. G. Wells and others. Mark Twain's treatment eschews all pretense of realism, however, and is utterly fantastic and magical.

In this connection, it is amusing to recall another instance of time reversal in fantastic fiction, approached but not really mentioned by Howard G. Baetzhold. Clemens, he tells us, had a brief meeting with "Lewis Carroll," the author of "the immortal Alice"—but C. L. Dodgson, it seems, listened more than he talked. Now, this anecdote interests me less than a possible connection between *Alice* and the climactic sequence in "No. 44" (chapters 32–33) where time is made to run backward. It is difficult to believe that Clemens wrote those chapters without recalling *Through the Looking-Glass and What Alice Found There.* In chapter 5 ("Wool and Water"), the Red Queen says, in response to Alice's finding her recent experiences "dreadfully confusing":

> "That's the effect of living backwards," the Queen said kindly: "it always makes one a little giddy at first—"
>
> "Living backwards!" Alice repeated in great astonishment. "I never heard of such a thing."
>
> "—but there's one great advantage in it, that one's memory works both ways."
>
> "I'm sure *mine* only works one way," Alice remarked. "I can't remember things before they happen."
>
> "It's a poor sort of memory that only works backwards," the Queen remarked.

This is the best brief commentary I know on certain aspects of the second half of "No. 44"; and a generation that has learned to take *Alice* seriously should certainly be capable of doing the same for "No. 44," with its intellectual and stylistic high jinks. "Life, what is it but a dream?"

45. Consider the comment by Howard Mumford Jones, in a discussion of a paper on "Mark Twain's Determinism and the Past":

> Let us take a case: Captain Stormfield dies and goes to heaven. . . . He starts off, and all of a sudden, of his own free will, his whole instinct as a captain overcomes him, and he goes

> off course and starts a race with the comet and arrives at the wrong gate of heaven, where he is not known. . . . Note that there is no indication that Captain Stormfield's sudden desire to deviate from his course is pre-determined. It is complete free will on Captain Stormfield's part. He makes a mistake, but there is no indication that the mistake was determined. He deliberately determines to change his course—and you find that again and again in the case of the imaginative artist. (See, The Hebrew University, *The Writer and the Past,* pamphlet, p. 39.)

Compare also the classic formulation of the problem of freedom, in the context of atomic materialism, by Lucretius (*De Rerum Natura,* book 2), where the "swerve" of the atoms makes possible change and creativity. This "clinamen" in Lucretius has recently been used by Harold Bloom, in *The Anxiety of Influence,* as the first of six "revisionary ratios" exhibited by poets in relation to their predecessors.

46. As early as 23 March 1878, we find Clemens wrestling with this problem in a letter to Orion:

> Now look here—I have tried, all these years, to think of some way of 'doing' hell too—and have always had to give it up. Hell, in my book, will not occupy five pages of MS I judge—it will be only covert hints, I suppose, and quickly dropped. I may end by not even referring to it.
>
> And mind you, in my opinion you will find that you can't write up hell so it will stand printing. (*MTL,* p. 323)

This was written in the context of a criticism of a manuscript on a religious theme that Orion had sent him. The same letter mentions Mark Twain's own "Journey in Heaven," which later became "Captain Stormfield's Visit to Heaven." But of central significance is the fact that the *Stranger Manuscripts* were written by an older man and were emphatically not for publication in Mark Twain's lifetime.

47. In my reading of the "Conclusion," I do not disagree with Gibson, though I emerge with different emphases. He found that it "argues the extreme Platonic view that the final and only reality resides in the individual soul"; but it seems to me unfair to reduce Platonic idealism to "solipsism," even with the qualifying adjective "extreme." Thus, when Gibson finds this version of the "extreme Platonic view" to be "a key

that . . . does fit much of the action and imagery in 'Chronicle' and nearly everything in the second half of 'No. 44' " (28), I find it difficult to follow his meaning. I agree most emphatically, however, with this sentence about chapter 34: "The sources and analogues for it in Clemens's earlier writings, his reading, and his experience, enmeshed with his creation of Satan figures and his speculations about dreams, are extraordinarily various and complex."

The discussion by Gibson of these sources and analogues (28–33) is the richest, most penetrating, we have had thus far. For him the chapter as a whole adds up to a paradox: "Mold your life nearer to the heart's desire; life is at best a dream and at worst a nightmare from which you cannot escape." Most crucial for our understanding of these pages, Gibson wrote, is the letter Clemens sent to his friend and pastor, "Joe" Twichell, on 28 July 1904, a couple of months after Livy's death, which echoes the very "language and imagery" of the "Conclusion" (30). By referring there to "the past 7 years," Mark Twain was linking the idea of nothingness to the entire period since 1897 when he was working on the "Stranger"; and the related sense of absurdity and unreality comes during "A *part* of each day—or night" (Clemens's italics)—it is *not* the whole truth. The other part, as Gibson rightly emphasizes, expresses "the long-committed artist who creates," who wields the "potent art" of Prospero-Shakespeare in *The Tempest*. Clemens's writing these ideas to the man in whom he confided most closely on religious questions surely indicates that "Clemens endowed 44 with his own questionings and grievances and griefs" (31); but I interpret the product somewhat differently than Gibson does and am happier, critically speaking, about its literary values.

Other Works Cited

(Works listed in Short References are not repeated here.)

Aler, Jan, ed. *Proceedings of the Fifth International Congress of Aesthetics: Amsterdam 1964*. The Hague: Mouton, 1968.

Allen, Charles E. "Mark Twain and Conscience." *Literature and Psychology* 7 (Spring 1957):17–21. Quoted as reprinted in *Psycholanalysis and American Fiction*, edited by Irving Malin, pp. 131–41. New York: E. P. Dutton, 1965.

Andrews, Kenneth R. *Nook Farm: Mark Twain's Hartford Circle*. Cambridge, Mass.: Harvard University Press, 1950. Paperback reprint. Seattle: University of Washington Press, 1969.

Aristotle. *The Nicomachean Ethics*. Translated by J. E. C. Welldon. London: Macmillan, 1927.

Baender, Paul E. "Mark Twain's Transcendent Figures." Ph.D. dissertation, University of California, 1956.

Baetzhold, Howard G. *Mark Twain and John Bull: The British Connection*. Bloomington: Indiana University Press, 1970.

Balz, Albert G. A. *Descartes and the Modern Mind*. New Haven, Conn.: Yale University Press, 1952.

Blair, Walter. *Mark Twain and Huckleberry Finn*. Berkeley: University of California Press, 1960.

Bloom, Harold. *The Anxiety of Influence*. New York: Oxford University Press, 1973.

Blues, Thomas. *Mark Twain and the Community*. Lexington: University of Kentucky Press, 1970.

Borges, Jorge Luis. *Labyrinths: Selected Stories and Other Writings*. Edited by D. A. Yates and J. E. Irby. Harmondsworth, Eng.: Penguin, 1970.

Bradley, A. C. *Shakespearean Tragedy*. New York: Meridian Books, 1955.

Branch, Edgar M. *The Literary Apprenticeship of Mark Twain.* Urbana: University of Illinois Press, 1950.

Brodwin, Stanley. "Mark Twain's Masks of Satan: The Final Phase." *American Literature* 45 (May 1973):206–27.

Brooks, Van Wyck. *The Ordeal of Mark Twain.* New York: E. P. Dutton, 1920. Revised 1933, with an introduction by Malcolm Cowley. New York: Meridian Books, 1955.

Bucke, Richard M. *Cosmic Consciousness: A Study in the Evolution of the Human Mind.* 4th ed. New York: E. P. Dutton, 1923 [1901].

Budd, Louis J. *Mark Twain: Social Philosopher.* Bloomington: Indiana University Press, 1962.

Clemens, Clara. *Awake to a Perfect Day: My Experience with Christian Science.* New York: Citadel Press, 1956.

Clemens, S. L. *The Autobiography of Mark Twain.* Edited by Charles Neider. New York: Harper, 1959. Paperback. New York: Washington Square Press, 1961.

———. *Letters from the Earth.* Edited by Bernard DeVoto, with a preface by H. N. Smith. New York: Harper and Row, 1962.

———. *Mark Twain's Autobiography.* With an introduction by Albert Bigelow Paine. 2 vols. New York and London: Harper, 1924.

———. *Mark Twain in Eruption.* Edited by Bernard DeVoto. New York and London: Harper, 1940.

———. *Mark Twain's Quarrel with Heaven.* Edited by Ray B. Browne. New Haven, Conn.: College and University Press, 1970.

———. *Report from Paradise.* Edited and with an introduction by Dixon Wecter. New York: Harper, 1952.

Covici, Pascal, Jr. *Mark Twain's Humor: The Image of a World.* Dallas: Southern Methodist University Press, 1962.

Cox, James M. *Mark Twain: The Fate of Humor.* Princeton, N.J.: Princeton University Press, 1966.

Dostoyevsky, F. M. *The Double: A Poem of St. Petersburg.* Translated by George Bird. Bloomington: Indiana University Press, 1958.

———. *The Idiot.* Translated by D. Magarshack. Harmondsworth, Eng.: Penguin, 1955.

Eliade, Mircea. *The Two and the One.* Translated by J. M. Cohen. New York: Harper and Row, 1969 [1955].

Eliot, T. S. *Selected Essays.* New York: Harcourt, Brace, 1950.

Ellis-Fermor, U. M. *The Frontiers of Drama.* London: Methuen, 1945.

Ellmann, Richard, and Feidelson, Charles, Jr., eds. *The Modern Tradition: Backgrounds of Modern Literature.* New York: Oxford University Press, 1965.

Ensor, Allison. *Mark Twain and the Bible.* Lexington: University of Kentucky Press, 1969.

Foner, Philip S. *Mark Twain Social Critic.* 2d ed. New York: International Publishers, 1966 [1958].

Frazer, Sir James G. *The Golden Bough.* London: Macmillan, 1963. First published in 12 vols., 1911–1915. Vol. 9, *The Scapegoat,* 1913.

Freud, Sigmund. *Civilization and Its Discontents.* Translated by Joan Riviere. New York: Doubleday, Anchor, 1958.

———. *The Interpretation of Dreams.* Translated by James Strachey. New York: Basic Books, 1955. First published 1900 as *Die Traumdeutung.*

———. *Wit and Its Relation to the Unconscious.* In *The Basic Writings of Sigmund Freud.* Edited by A. A. Brill. New York: Modern Library, 1938.

Fussell, Edwin S. "The Structural Problem of *The Mysterious Stranger.*" *Studies in Philology* 49(January 1952):95–104.

Gibson, William M. *The Art of Mark Twain.* New York: Oxford University Press, 1976.

———. "Mark Twain's Mysterious Stranger Manuscripts: Some Questions for Textual Critics." *Rocky Mountain Modern Language Association Bulletin,* December 1968, pp. 183–91.

Grimm, Clyde L. "*The American Claimant*: Reclamation of a Farce." *American Quarterly* 19(Spring 1967):86–103.

Hawthorne, Nathaniel. *The American Notebooks by Nathaniel Hawthorne.* Edited by Randall Stewart. New Haven, Conn.: Yale University Press, 1932.

The Hebrew University. *The Writer and the Past: A Joint Seminar in Jerusalem, 23–25 May 1964, at The Hebrew University.* Pamphlet. Jerusalem: Academon, 1965.

Higham, John. *Strangers in the Land: Patterns of American Nativism, 1860–1925.* Rev. ed. New Brunswick, N.J.: Rutgers University Press, 1955.

Howells, William Dean. *The Complete Plays of W. D. Howells.* Edited by Walter J. Meserve, Jr. New York: New York University Press, 1960.

James, William. *The Principles of Psychology.* 2 vols. New York: H. Holt, 1905 [1890].

———. *The Varieties of Religious Experience, A Study in Human Nature*. New York: Modern Library, n.d. [1902].

———. *William James on Psychical Research*. Edited by G. Murphy and R. O. Ballou. New York: Viking, 1960.

Johnson, Ellwood. "William James and the Art of Fiction." *Journal of Aesthetics and Art Criticism* 30(Spring 1972):285–96.

Jones, Howard Mumford. *Belief and Disbelief in American Literature*. Chicago: University of Chicago Press, 1967.

Kafka, Franz. *The Castle*. Definitive edition. London: Secker and Warburg, 1953.

Kahn, Sholom J. "Mark Twain as American Rabelais." *HSL* (*Hebrew University Studies in Literature*) 1(Spring 1973):47–75.

———. "Mark Twain's Determinism and the Past." Unpublished paper read at *The Writer and the Past*. Excerpt from discussion quoted in The Hebrew University, *The Writer and the Past: A Joint Seminar in Jerusalem, 23–25 May 1964, at The Hebrew University*, pamphlet.

———. "Mark Twain's Final Phase." *Studi Americani* 11(1965): 143–62.

———. "More Mark Twain Papers: Hannibal and Beyond." *Jahrbuch für Amerikastudien* 17(1972):277–90.

———. "New Mark Twain Materials: Fresh Perspectives." *Jahrbuch für Amerikastudien* 19(1974):375–86.

———. "The Real Mark Twain: School of Tuckey." *Jahrbuch für Amerikastudien* 14(1969):301–7.

Kaiser, Walter. *Praisers of Folly: Erasmus, Rabelais, Shakespeare*. Cambridge, Mass.: Harvard University Press, 1963.

Kaplan, Justin. *Mr. Clemens and Mark Twain: A Biography*. New York: Simon and Schuster, 1966.

Keppler, C. F. *The Literature of the Second Self*. Tucson: University of Arizona Press, 1972.

Kerr, Howard. *Mediums, and Spirit-Rappers, and Roaring Radicals: Spiritualism in American Literature, 1850–1900*. Urbana: University of Illinois Press, 1972.

Krause, S. J. *Mark Twain as Critic*. Baltimore: Johns Hopkins University Press, 1967.

Lovejoy, Arthur O. *Reflections on Human Nature*. Baltimore: Johns Hopkins University Press, 1961.

McKeithan, Daniel. *Court Trials in Mark Twain, and other essays*. The Hague: M. Nijhoff, 1958.

Maritain, Jacques. *The Dream of Descartes together with some other essays*. Translated by M. L. Andison. New York: Philosophical Library, 1944.

Murrell, William. *A History of American Graphic Humor, 1865–1938*. New York: Whitney Museum of American Art, 1938.

Nicolson, Marjorie H. *Science and Imagination*. Ithaca, N.Y.: Cornell University Press, 1956.

Parsons, Coleman O. "The Background of *The Mysterious Stranger*." *American Literature* 32(March 1960):55–74.

———. "The Devil and Samuel Clemens." *Virginia Quarterly Review* 23(Autumn 1947):582–606.

Pellowe, W. C. S. *Mark Twain Pilgrim from Hannibal*. New York: The Hobson Book Press, 1945.

Poulet, Georges. *Studies in Human Time*. Translated by Elliott Coleman. Baltimore: Johns Hopkins University Press, 1956. New York: Harper Torchbook, 1959.

Rabelais, François. *The Portable Rabelais*. Selected, translated, and edited by Samuel Putnam. New York: Viking, 1946.

Randall, John H., Jr. *The Making of the Modern Mind*. Boston: Houghton Mifflin, 1926.

Rogers, Arthur K. *A Student's History of Philosophy*. New York: Macmillan, 1921.

Rogers, Franklin R. *Mark Twain's Burlesque Patterns*. Dallas: Southern Methodist University Press, 1960.

Rogers, Robert. *A Psychoanalytic Study of the Double in Literature*. Detroit: Wayne State University Press, 1970.

Rowlette, Robert. *Twain's "Pudd'nhead Wilson": The Development and Design*. Bowling Green, Ky.: Bowling Green University Press, 1971.

Salomon, Roger B. *Mark Twain and the Image of History*. New Haven, Conn.: Yale University Press, 1961.

Sandbank, Shimon. "Action as Self-Mirror: On Kafka's Plots." *Modern Fiction Studies* 17(1971):21–29.

Scott, Arthur L. "Mark Twain as a Critic of Europe." Ph.D. dissertation, University of Michigan, 1948.

———. *Mark Twain at Large*. Chicago: H. Regnery, 1969.

Seelye, John. *The True Adventures of Huckleberry Finn*. Evanston, Ill.: Northwestern University Press, 1970.

Smith, Henry Nash. *Mark Twain: The Development of a Writer*. Cambridge, Mass.: Harvard University Press, 1962.

———. *Mark Twain's Fable of Progress: Political and Economic*

Ideas in "A Connecticut Yankee." New Brunswick, N.J.: Rutgers University Press, 1964.

———. "Mark Twain's Images of Hannibal." *The University of Texas Studies in English* 37(1958):3–23. Cited as reprinted in *Discussions of Mark Twain,* edited by Guy A. Cardwell, pp. 92–103. Boston: D. C. Heath, 1963.

Smith, Henry Nash, ed. *Mark Twain: A Collection of Critical Essays.* Englewood Cliffs, N.J.: Prentice-Hall, 1963.

Smith, Janet, ed. *Mark Twain on the Damned Human Race.* New York: Hill and Wang, 1962.

Spenser, Hazelton. *Shakespeare Improved: The Restoration Versions in Quarto and On the Stage.* Cambridge, Mass.: Harvard University Press, 1927.

Tate, Allen. "The Hovering Fly." In *The Man of Letters in the Modern World: Selected Essays, 1928–1955.* New York: Meridian Books, 1955.

Tuchman, Barbara. *Bible and Sword.* New York: New York University Press, 1956.

Tuveson, Ernest Lee. *Redeemer Nation: The Idea of America's Millennial Role.* Chicago: University of Chicago Press, 1968.

Untermeyer, Louis. *Cat O'Nine Tales.* New York: American Heritage, 1971.

Wecter, Dixon. *Sam Clemens of Hannibal.* Boston: Houghton Mifflin, 1952.

Weisinger, Herbert. *Tragedy and the Paradox of the Fortunate Fall.* London: Routledge and Kegan Paul, 1953.

Wells, H. G. *The Time Machine.* New York: Random House, 1931 [1895].

Index

G

H

I

J

K

L